COMMUNICATION AND DEMOCRACY

THE COMMUNICATION AND INFORMATION SCIENCE SERIES
Series Editor: BRENDA DERVIN, The Ohio State University

Subseries:
Progress in Communication Sciences: Brant R. Burleson
Interpersonal Communication: Donald J. Cegala
Organizational Communication: George Barnett
Mass Communication/Telecommunication Systems: Lee B. Becker
User-Based Communication/Information System Design: Michael S. Nilan
Cross-Cultural/Cross-National Communication and Social Change: Josep Rota
International Communication, Peace and Development: Majid Tehranian
Critical Cultural Studies in Communication: Leslie T. Good
Feminist Scholarship in Communication: Lana Rakow
Rhetorical Theory and Criticism: Stephen H. Browne
Communication Pedagogy and Practice: Gerald M. Phillips
Communication: The Human Context: Lee Thayer

COMMUNICATION AND DEMOCRACY

edited by

Slavko Splichal and Janet Wasko

ABLEX PUBLISHING CORPORATION
NORWOOD, NEW JERSEY

Library of Congress Cataloging-in-Publication Data

Communication and democracy / edited by Slavko Splichal and Janet
  Wasko.
    p. cm.--(Communication and information science)
    Includes bibliographical references and index.
    ISBN 0-89391-764-8
    1. Communication—Political aspects. 2. Democracy.
3. Communication and culture. I. Splichal, Slavko. II. Wasko,
Janet. III. Series.
P95.8.C558--1992
302.2--dc20   92-5310
                                                                  CIP

Ablex Publishing Corporation
355 Chestnut Street
Norwood, New Jersey 07648

Contents

v

Part I

New Visions of Communication and Democracy

1

Searching for New Paradigms: An Introduction

Slavko Splichal
Faculty of Social Sciences
University of Ljubljana

There is one surprising characteristic in the matter of democracy: All the fundamental ideas and texts on principles of democracy had appeared before the development of mass communication and the mass media in the strict sense, that is, before the end of the 19th century, and before the "information revolution," although the contemporary massive prophecy of democratic society seems to be strongly related particularly to the very recent developments of information and communication technologies. It is not surprising, then, that the 17th Conference of the International Association for Mass Communication Research to which this book is dedicated directs the spotlight onto the relationship between the communications and democracy, which implies two related considerations: democratization of society and democratization of communication. Democratic communications are the basis of any democratic culture and political system, or "general democracy"; however, a democratic environment is also necessary for democratization of communications themselves.

THE IMPORTANCE OF DEMOCRATIZATION
OF THE COMMUNICATION SPHERE

For a number of reasons, contemporary dissertations on democratization of society in general and communication sphere in particular are
mainly focused on the mass media. Although the questions of democracy cannot be restricted to mass communication, the reason for considering the mass media much more relevant for general democracy
than other forms of communication becomes quite clear when (a) contemporary society and its communication networks are compared with
the ancient and medieval societies; and (b) the general social significance of the mass media is compared with the political and economic
relevance of other forms of communication. Democracy denotes a *form
of government* that ensures to the people (a certain degree of) political
equality and involvement in decision making about public affairs. It
thus refers to all the members of a collectivity, although there is no
historical evidence anywhere that the total population would be involved, directly or indirectly, in practical decision making. As the concrete understandings of "the people" are and were restricted to a
larger or smaller part of the total population, the scope of "public affairs" to be discussed and the questions to be decided by "the people"
in a "democratic" system varies over time considerably. Nevertheless,
democracy always implies the rule by the *people* rather than a limited
number of individuals, and since mass communication is considered
the form of communication accessible, in principle, to all the people,
it is rather understandable (though not always legitimate) that precisely this form of communication is mainly discussed when the questions of democracy are at stake.

When Marx has written his famous assertion that "What I cannot
be for others, I am not for myself and cannot be for myself," he has
insisted upon the recognition of one's rights in the sphere of the press
rather than communication in general, because "the press is the most
common way (means) of individuals to communicate their mental existence" (Marx, 1974, p. 73). On the one hand, the struggle for freedom
of the press was simultaneously a struggle for general freedom and
democracy. On the other hand, nowadays there exists "a mutual dependence between government, parliament and the mass media that
none of these institutions can avoid. . . . Political institutions have increasingly become dependent on the mass media and have at the
same time increasingly made use of them" (Kepplinger, 1989, p. 182).
At the same time, this practical relationship seems to be of a high
theoretical relevance; as Carey (1985, p. 37) argues, the mass media
must become "a *site* (not a subject or discipline) on which to engage

the general question of social theory: How is it, through all sorts of change and diversity, through all sorts of conflicts and contradictions, that the miracle of social life is pulled off, that societies manage to produce and reproduce themselves?" This is certainly not a new consideration. Eighty years ago, research on modern media was defined "an enormous area of sociological work" by Weber (1976, p. 98), particularly because of "the balance of power which is created by specific newspaper publicity." Although the "publicity" considerably changed over time, it always had fundamental importance for society and its democratization.

From the ancient Greek thought onwards, the general conception of democracy was based, *inter alia*, on at least four assumptions related to the *communication sphere*, namely that:

1. Citizens are well informed.
2. Citizens are interested (as a consequence of socialization processes) in general politics.
3. Citizens have equal rights to speak and participate in decision making.
4. All decisions are submitted to public discussions.

Historically seen, the interest of citizens in collective affairs, their ability of being informed, and the power to participate in decision making and management develop in three stages (Splichal, 1984, p. 92):

1. Before the development of the liberal bourgeois public, information distribution was highly restricted and created an impression of excessive complexity of the environment, unpredictability and uncertainty within the domain of information reception, although in time both the amount of information and information capacity of individuals has been increased. Such systems were open to physical coercion in the spheres of material and mental production, while creative communication was limited by different forms of censorship. For Hobbes, censorship was one of the basic rights of sovereigns.
2. The bourgeois revolution affirmed a "system of confidence" in democratic rules (legal codes and state institutions) which decreased the degree of uncertainty for the large majority of population, although it was still based on limited access to information and communication activities. The dominant subordination to "higher," "general," or "national" interests limited individual's practical activities. Different forms of information reduction and

censorship were replaced by "mechanisms of confidence;" a direct coercion was replaced by symbolic manipulation. Information revolution per se is, however, not yet a social revolution; it is only a necessary condition for the development of radical needs that can be satisfied only by genuine revolutionizing of social relations.

3. The third stage refers to the future development when individuals and collectivities will be able tò consciously organize their relations with nature and among themselves, and not just believe in them as a force outside of, and above, themselves. The result of communication and information activities will then no longer be a mystification of social relations that require "confidence," but rather demystification of their ideologically frozen "eternal" nature.

Evidently, even in a rather simple and exclusive model of democracy developed in the small-scale, transparent, sparsely peopled society as was, for example, the ancient Greek society, where communication based on predominantly oral, interpersonal interactions was relatively easy, the fundamental assumptions of democratic communication were not materialized and the participation of citizens was restricted due to at least three factors:

1. The uneven distribution of communicative competence (e.g., oratory skills, literacy) as a consequence of differences in the individual's education, socialization, knowledge, and so on;
2. The informal (or even clandestine) communication networks (as opposed to public communication), which reduce public discussions to public legitimation of dominant opinions created by power elites;
3. The uneven access to (institutional) communication channels, which reduces the opportunities to obtain relevant information and to make information available to others.

Human communication managed to maintain its appearance of a natural human ability possessed by every member of a collectivity just because of his or her adherence to the collectivity, only as long as the development of productive forces and production relations did not expose the dependence of communication practice on material conditions of human life and its instrumental nature in social relations; it thereby revealed that human beings are as alienated from this seemingly natural ability as they are in the process of production in general. With the development of writing, the initial civilizational process of enlarging temporal and spatial horizons through communication—that is, surpassing natural existential conditions that determined human beings' relations in production as well as their relation to language as a form of *natural belonging to a collectivity*—turned for the first time into its opposite—into the growth of alienation. As Williams (1976, p. 10) pointed out, all the new means of communication, which implied a possible expansion of human powers to learn and to exchange ideas and experiences, "have been abused, for political control (as in propaganda) or for commercial profit (as in advertising)."

This struggle between the ambivalent—authoritarian and emancipatory—potentials of communication began with the transition from the oral tradition to the manuscript age based on the development of writing. With the invention of writing and, thus, the development of human ability not only to speak but also to write, a communication process can take place without the sender being present: The message can be separated, and thus *alienated*, from the sender. Even more importantly, a radical change in the relationship of an individual to "his" or "her" oral language has been introduced by alphabetical codes; the language ceased to be a natural relationship as it had been in a primitive collectivity. Learning and education became an essential part of social relations, embedded in the primal social division of labor (manual vs. mental work). Writing not only made possible the recording of communication, but also divided the previously homogeneous collectivity into those capable of the new form of communication and those being in short of it. As writing, all other kinds of communication technologies developed through centuries reveal that new forms of communication are part of human actions upon nature and other human beings, and therefore no less significant and/or contradictory as economic and political activities.

As communication reports, it also conceals; as it unites and connects, so it also separates and distorts. In this sense, the modern media of communication, although unique in their day-to-day continuous and pervasive operations that in a lifelong continuity catch public attention, are not an exception. No doubt, the growth of mass media is of vital importance for the contemporary development of social communication. But new communication technologies, complex organization of the production and distribution of messages, mass audiences, and so on, do not imply an overdetermination of activity (communication) by the means (mass media). Such an understanding of the mass media would substitute changes in the development of communication processes with the processes themselves, as if human generic communication ability and need as well as different forms of (alienated) communication had not existed before the "media revolution" and "information society."

The development of the mass press and of complex, centralized systems of electronic communication gave, in fact, the impression that massiveness and commodification were the necessary characteristics of new forms of social communication in general rather than of a specific historical form of their development. Hence, the growth of mass communication in bourgeois society was, as a form of commodity production, mainly subordinated to the laws of supply and demand. This is the dominant form of communication development in Western societies from the end of the 19th century. However, rapid technological and social changes in communications ever more falsify traditional forms of the development and understanding of mass communication as a necessarily restrictive form of (thus distorted) communication, and stimulate intellectual endeavours to reconsider both their social roots and implications.

PUBLIC COMMUNICATION AND THE RIGHT
TO COMMUNICATE

By the end of the 1960s new ideas of the possible transformation of mass communication onto public communication emerged. Genuine access to the media and a more equitable distribution of the media ownership, media time, and space to be based on the abolition of all limitations of rights (rather than on "negative" freedoms) of citizens were regarded as necessary preconditions for democratic reordering of the media and their social accountability. According to Mills (1964, p. 392), as opposed to mass communication, in public communication:

> (1) virtually as many people express opinions as receive them. (2) Public communications are so organized that there is a chance to immediately and effectively answer back any opinion expressed in public. Opinion formed by such discussion (3) readily finds an outlet in effective action, even gains—if necessary—the prevailing system of authority. And (4) authoritative institutions do not penetrate the public, which is thus more or less autonomous in its operation.

The notion of public communication primarily presupposes the abolition of the uneven distribution of social wealth, the centralized and bureaucratic management systems, the political and economic restrictions of rights and freedoms, as well as the development of new communication technology, knowledge, and critical consciousness. A number of these suppositions have not been fulfilled by any society yet. Thus, there is not yet historical evidence of the existence of public communication in the strict sense. However, it is even more important to answer the question of whether such a conception of public communication is at all feasible?

In contrast to the idea of public communication, traditional forms of mass communication attempt to limit the autonomy of recipients in the formation of opinions by a free discussion to those issues that are not critical of the politics of those in power. They represent different kinds of *distorted communication* (Mueller, 1973, p. 19), particularly those "resulting from governmental policy to structure language and communication" (*directed communication*) and/or "denoting successful attempts by private and governmental groups to structure and limit public communication in order that their interests prevail" (*constrained communication*). However, the most crude form of distortion of communication processes—*censorship*—existed long before the human "invention" of contemporary sophisticated forms of constrained and directed communication through the *mass media*, already at the beginning of the *written* history. At the time printing was invented, strict censorship was introduced by authorities with the intention that no serious problems of "offenses" against the state and authoritative institutions arose. This historical process could be perhaps best exemplified by the efforts of the Catholic Church to control the public knowledge of societies (Hardt, 1983, p. 300). At the end of the 15th century, the Church implemented a licensing system, followed by a strict censorship and the *Index Librorum Prohibitorum*, an official index of prohibited texts. The emergence of new intellectual elites, the religious reform movements, as a reaction against the abuses by the Church, and the new printing technology changed the strategy of the Church in the 17th century from an extremely restrictive control to a far more subtle and efficient strategy of strengthening its position through *propaganda* disseminated by its central institution, *Sacra Congregatio de Propaganda Fide*.

During the last two centuries, censorship was largely abolished and the former preventive systems of a direct monitoring became penal in most countries. At the same time, however, a new form of secular censorship arose: first in the forms of taxation and deposits for publishing newspapers, and later on in the form of commercialization of the communication sphere. Heine and Marx (Marx, 1974) denoted deposits as "a special type of non-freedom that was perhaps even more noxious than censorship." Historically seen, "material censorship" (deposits) acted as an equivalent and substitute of "mental censorship."

Both types of censorship have the function of lessening the flow of provoking, offensive, or upsetting issues. However, material censorship is an *abstract and general* nonfreedom while mental censorship is a *concrete and individual* nonfreedom. The former is directly subordinated to commercial interests and economic laws of capitalism, the latter to the judicial laws of the authoritarian and absolutist state or, to be more exact, to a "legalized illegality of the absolutist State," as Marx denoted it in his early writings.

The entire development of communication and the expansion of human temporal and spatial horizons to a world range gradually lessened the functionality of the repressive mental censorship and finally terminated it in all democratic societies. Simultaneously, however, material censorship and other forms of directed and constrained communication (e.g., propaganda, communication as a means of legitimation) increased and became ever more diversified. Marx believed that material censorship, in its most crude form (i.e., financial deposits for publishing newspapers), denoted the transfer of censorship from "its real sphere into the sphere of commercial speculation." In reality, this second (commercial or economic) sphere is no less real for censorship than is the first, state-dominated sphere. Yet the operation of censorship in the "new sphere" is much more obscure, less transparent, less public than was (is) the operation of the previously dominant mental censorship in absolutist states, which represents, by its very nature, a form of the *public representation of power over the people*. Only at the beginning material censorship acted in the way of mental censorship—as public repression (deposits that directly hinder or prevent the realization of entrepreneurial freedom in the communication sphere). The bourgeois revolution eliminated this contradiction which arose at the last stage of the development of the old feudal system: Material censorship started to act in the manner of the dominant (i.e., commodity) mode of production, as the mental censorship in the past (and contemporary authoritarian) systems acted in the manner of the public representation of power. However, this is not to say that mental censorship in commercial systems has been abolished. Rather, the forms of censorship have been changed.

Nowadays, mental censorship can no longer be seen in its "true" form since it no longer acts in the old way of public representation of power but rather, and ever more, as a *hidden resistance*. Besides hiding something it also hides the fact that it conceals; besides its subject ("provoking issues"), mental censorship also hides itself as an authorized intervention in communication process. It therefore operates behind one's back, outside the market, outside any visible sphere of circulation—as generally commodity production does. Material censorship, likewise, rids itself of the balast of its old reality—deposits. Both enter, in different forms of indirect censorship, into the realm of hidden persuasion.

Although commercialization of the communication sphere presupposes that all people have the right to speak freely, it forces them to speak profitably as well. Based on the liberal conception of negative freedom (freedom from political authorities), freedom of the press became ever more a freedom of owners-of-communication means, rather than of citizens. From the perspective of a genuine democratization of communications, the concept of freedom of the press has definitely proved insufficient. Since the 1960s, a number of (semi)theoretical treatises on the *right to communicate* appears attempting to define more accurately the generic human ability and need to communicate (Fisher, 1981). Four basic rights and freedoms could be defined as the cornerstones of the generic *right to communicate*:

1. The right to publish opinions in the mass media, as an extension of the traditional freedoms of thought and expression, and as a right complementary to the right to receive information;
2. The right to participate in the management of the mass media and communication organizations;
3. The right of free association and mutual interlinkage for realizing individual and common needs;
4. Equality of citizens in rights and duties of which the first requirement is that this equality is not limited by or dependent on their social status and uneven distribution of material resources.

The right to publish opinions, as the central content of the right to communicate, implies equal value for all individual opinions in society; it therefore eliminates the difference between privileged (ruling) opinions and "noncompetent" opinions. This naturally concerns only those opinions that determine the social hierarchy of *values*. All opinions must have equal significance in democratic discussion and decision making when they are based on *evaluation* and *specific interests*, not on professional knowledge or professional capability in taking technical or instrumental decisions (Splichal, 1987, p. 255). Individual opinions certainly have, due to objective circumstances, a different final probability of either being affirmed as common or even of being turned into effective action. However, the initial probability must be based on a genuine equal possibility and right to publish opinions.

To achieve an equal initial probability for all individual opinions, communications have to be organized as a *public good* and managed and controlled neither by private nor state (i.e., particularistic) interests, but rather by *society as a whole*; that is, they have to be *socialized*. This is particularly important for democratization of the mass media, where socialization has three basic aspects:

1. Social management and control of the media;
2. Providing the financial resources for mass media operation on the principles of solidarity and reciprocity of all citizens ("the people");
3. Social influence on the formulation and implementation of communication policies, programs, and so on, of the mass media.

In short, the *socialization* of communication means is considered *conditio sine qua non* for an actual—individual and social—right to communicate. It denotes a negation of the economic subordination of (mass) communication activity to the state (budgetary financing) and marketplace (commodity production). Rather, the development of communication activities should become a matter of common concern and decision making. Needless to say, social influence cannot be reduced to political influence on the management of the mass media, since the entire socialization process of the communication activity stands and falls together with the *universal democratization* of social relations.

Instead of providing only passive access to the consumption sphere, democratization implies primarily the development of conditions for *active participation*, that is, a direct and indirect incorporation of citizens into the production and exchange of messages in different forms of communication from interpersonal communication to the mass media in which the individual can realize his interests and meet his needs in collaboration with others. The actual democratization is defined by whether not only the number of active participants in the communication processes, but also the social basis of communication expands, that is, whether the new forms of communication and democracy contribute to the incorporation of, until then, excluded social categories and groups, for example, the young, women, socially, economically, or politically deprived groups, national, ethnic, linguistic, and religious minorities, and so on. In other words, democratization should dismantle "the major sources of distorted communications" which include "class privilege, gender preference, racial discrimination, age grade exclusion, and a division of labor which awards authority to a relatively few and mandates compliance to a large majority" (Young, 1982, p. 2). Within the framework of efforts to democratize the communication sphere, many different strategies have been developed elsewhere, but only with limited effects on the democratization of the total communication sphere. It would be difficult to oppose Williams's dictum (1976, p. 133) that "we have experienced the other three systems" [authoritarian, paternal, commercial], but "the democratic system, in any full sense, we can only discuss and imagine."

DEMOCRATIC COMMUNICATION BETWEEN PAST AND FUTURE

Socialization of mass communication denotes a *process of reappropriating* generic communication abilities and means by human beings in democratic societies. Socialization in general cannot be regarded as a state but as an open-ended process. The modern history of socialism clearly falsified utopians who believed that it could be accomplished by a single action, once forever and even regardless of historical circumstances. Human and social relationships are far too complex to allow radical structural changes as a consequence of a single, one-dimensional action into any sphere of human activity, and there is no reason to believe that the communication sphere could be an exception. Thus, there is little chance that merely by legal abolition of private and/or state ownership of the media or any similar action, mass communication would be democratically reordered and genuinely socialized. Also, the idea of "reappropriation" cannot be understood in the literal sense of restoration of a given form of communication practice that existed in the past.

As John Stuart Mill has already argued, for example, the ancient Greek idea of the *polis* could not be sustained in the modern society, because government by open meetings, however attractive and desirable it may be, is probably completely impracticable for any community exceeding a single small town. While Rousseau claimed—contrary to liberal traditions—that all citizens should and could be involved in the direct creation of the laws through public meetings and, similarly, Marx believed that the revolutionary though slow and contradictory transformation of society and state would gradually (in transition from socialism to communism) restore a form of direct democracy, Mill's main argument against the practicability of any form of direct democracy was essentially the same as that of Luhmann 100 years later: the necessity of reduction of complexity in social systems. According to these criticisms, Rousseau's, Marx's, and the related ideas seem to be more appropriate for democracy in a nonindustrial community than for "postindustrial" or "information" societies where traditional (until the end of the 18th century) community life was structurally and functionally destroyed, although this is firmly against Marx's "expectations" that communism and direct democracy would develop in the most economically advanced societies. Now—not only does it seem practically impossible that large populations of contemporary societies would participate in public business because of geographical and physical limits to when and where people can meet together, which would be extremely difficult to overcome in any but a very small community—the problems posed by coordination and regulation in the contemporary complex society are insuperably complex for any system of classical or direct democracy. Accordingly, the ideal of direct democracy, as for example that formulated by Rousseau, involves too many elements that complicate processes of decision making and, thus, destabilize the system (e.g., incompetence, apathy). The only alternative, then, seems to be representative democracy based on the freedom of speech, the press, and the assembly, and the right to communicate; in large-scale, complex societies it can be considered the functional equivalent of the ancient Greek democracy. In representative democracy accountability ought to be combined with professionalism and expertise, and elements of professionalism and expert knowledge also differentiate mass communication from all other, less complex forms of communication.

Contrary to the optimistic ideas and visions of democracy in the 18th and 19th centuries, conceptions of democracies developed in the last century from Weber onward are much more restricted and even pessimistic, particularly because of the growing complexity of society and plurality (division) of interests, and the sheer expansion of information needed for an effective administration and control of both the environment in general and the state in particular. As a result, the ideas of direct democracy were generally rejected as inappropriate and ineffective in both the West and (recently) the East, and new models of indirect democracy based on the competition between different interests and rival political elites and parties were developed. Direct democracy was (is) believed to be feasible only in organizations limited in the number of members and characterized by a relative equality of members, while in complex systems (well-trained) bureaucratic administration became completely indispensable. It seems that politics becomes a profession or at least has some characteristics of a profession. Generally, the role of the ordinary citizen became strongly delimited due to his or her incompetence, lack of relevant information, and general depoliticization. Although the rule by bureaucratic apparatus is not seen as inevitable, bureaucrats necessarily have a considerable power due to their expertise and information.

It is interesting to note that Marx, contrary to his early writings on freedom of the press where he strenuously pleaded for (the same kind of) press freedom that had been already established in France and England, in his later writings on (direct) political and economic democracy he underestimated the significance on the liberal idea(l)s related to the rights of free speech, expression, association, and belief, and freedom of the press. This seems to be particularly significant because the mass media can be seen not only as a cornerstone of democracy, but also as one of the most important arguments against direct democracy because they easily manipulate individual needs, desires, and choices—or at least demonstrate their manipulability. As Bertalanffy (1971, pp. 122–123) argues, human behavior falls far short of the principle of rationality; "it is the job of an influential specialty—advertisers, motivation researchers, etc.—to make choice irrational . . . Reading newspapers or listening to the radio readily shows that this applies perhaps even more to the twentieth than the seventeenth century." The media produce by and large, as Marcuse (1964) argues, false consciousness of the people and depoliticize them completely.

This, however, does not imply that the majority of people are not capable of making valid (if not rational) choices, particularly political choices, and determining their "true" interests. Although their individual capabilities—including communicative competence—along with the many inequalities in society are largely bounded by social "forces" as a result of interaction of all parts of a global society, they remain basically "bounded," as a matter of principle, by inner evolution and development of individuals resulting in new and more developed capabilities. In other words, if people's knowledge, understandings, capabilities, and actions are indeed limited and "manufactured," it does not follow that they cannot be developed, improved, and individualized in proper (ideal-democratic) circumstances to be created; among them, "proper" communication networks are inevitable. One can hardly imagine a system, either on the local or national level, in which every one would contribute to discussions and/or decision making every time a controversial issue appears. It does not follow, however, that the (political) system cannot be transformed in order to make more citizens' participation possible. On the contrary, an open information and communication system to ensure informed decisions in all public affairs can be seen as a fundamental condition for any contemporary model of general democracy which, at the same time, ought to ensure the:

1. Creation of the best circumstances for all humans to develop their nature and express their diverse qualities (. . .).

2. Protection from the arbitrary use of political authority and coercive power (. . .).
3. Involvement of citizens in the determination of the conditions of their association (. . .).
4. Expansion of economic opportunity to maximize the availability of resources (. . .). (Held, 1989, p. 270)

However, the question of how these conditions can be secured and aspirations achieved remains largely unresolved. Criticism of the theories that have been clearly falsified in practice, and systems of distorted communication already experienced, seems to be the only possible way to come closer to the working out (the idea) of a democratic communication system. This is the main intention of this book.

ABOUT THE CONTENTS OF PART I

In Part I of this volume, seven authors address the validity of "traditional" approaches to the relationship between communication and democracy from different theoretical perspectives. The seven contributions in this section attempt to identify the questions and problems that mark a dialectical break with traditional understandings of democratization processes in the communication sphere: although traditional mainstream debates identified a number of important questions which are worthy to deserve prolonged scholarly attention, the authors challenge particularly the validity of existing approaches to provide answers to these questions in the rapidly changing social and technological environment, and their concrete achievements.

Traber discusses the role of communication and communication-related human rights in historical processes, particularly from the perspectives of emerging professionalization and public responsibility. He defines three milestones in the democratization of communication: (a) French and American bourgeois revolutions, (b) 1917 revolutions in Mexico and Russia, and (c) post-colonial revolutions in developing countries.

Jakubowicz analyses some fundamental weaknesses of the "old paradigm of communication democratization" exemplified by the ideas of the MacBride Commission presented in *Many Voices, One World*, and confronts it with the recent technological and social changes in the communication sphere in order to reconceptualize the idea of democratic communication. Specifically, he identifies five conceptual and theoretical fallacies in the prevailing debate on communication democratization: fallacy of the universal need to (mass) communicate, of the mistaken level, of the autonomy of mass communication, of the mistaken historical period and the "invisible hand" that would democratize communication processes.

A similar starting position is taken by Andrén who aims at a reformulation of the liberal concept of freedom of expression to be congruent with the contemporary changes in "super-industrialized societies." In his contribution Andrén argues that the evolution of production and reproduction forces in the 20th century should shift the focus to conditions of, and obstacles to, positive freedom of expression and communicative power.

Proceeding from Williams's assertion that "no questions are more difficult than those of democracy," Sparks investigates Williams' attempts to construct a theory of democratic communication which certainly belongs to the most challenging ideas in the past decades, although they do not offer any firm guidelines of how to materialize them in social practice. Williams's critique of both paternalistic and commercial systems is highly relevant for an age dominated by state censorship and/or multinational media corporations.

Hardt discusses some major American indigenous and domesticated theoretical traditions concerning the relationship of language, communication, and culture, and the importance of communication as participation for democracy. He argues that different streams of cultural studies provide important insights into communication and new research opportunities for interdisciplinary explorations of communication and media issues.

Dervin takes a different position claiming that the "cultural stream" and "macro approach" which represent the two major streams in communication science deemphasize the procedural linkages between macro and micro levels and ignore the individual and his or her energizing behavior which constitute institutions, society, and culture. By stressing the significance of communication procedures, process rather than state, and behavior rather than person, she tries to introduce the individual in a form different from that prevailing within both macro and cultural streams, and the "administrative" approach.

Finally, Servaes discusses a number of aspects and changes in understanding of the nature of communication from a "bottom-up" perspective to outline a new research framework based on the "multiplicity paradigm" which may have important implications for the study of contemporary problems of communication and development as integral, multidimensional, and dialectic processes which differ from one collectivity to another.

REFERENCES

Bertalanffy, L. von. (1971). *General system theory*. Harmondsworth: Penguin.

Carey, J.W. (1985). Overcoming resistance to cultural studies. In M. Gurevitch & M.R. Levy (Eds.), *Mass communication review yearbook* (Vol. 5, pp. 27–40). Beverly Hills: Sage.

Fisher, D. (1981). *The right to communicate: A status report*. Paris: UNESCO.

Hardt, H. (1983). Press freedom in Western societies. In L.J. Martin & A.G. Chaudhary (Eds.), *Comparative mass media systems* (pp. 291–308). New York: Longman.

Held, D. (1989). *Models of democracy*. Oxford: Polity Press. (Original work published 1987).

Kepplinger, H.M. (1989). The changing function of the mass media: A historical perspective. *Gazette, 44*, 177–89.

Marcuse, H. (1964). *One-dimensional man*. Boston, MA: Beacon Press.

Marx, K. (1974). Die Verhandlungen des 6. Rheinischen Landtags. In *Marx-Engels-Werke* (Vol. 1, pp. 28–77). Berlin: Dietz Verlag. (Original work published 1842).

Mills, C.W. (1964). *Elita vlasti* [Power Elite]. Belgrade: Kultura.

Mueller, C. (1973). *The politics of communication*. New York: Oxford University Press.

Splichal, S. (1987). "Public Opinion" and the controversies in communication science. *Media, Culture and Society, 9*(2), 237–262.

Splichal, S. (1984). The role of information science education for social scientists and the development of information activities. *Informatologia Yugoslavica*, Separat Special No. 6, 91–98.

Weber, M. (1976). Towards a sociology of the press. *Journal of Communication, 26*(3), 96–101.

Williams, R. (1976). *Communications* (3rd ed.). Harmondsworth: Penguin.

Young, T.R. (1982). The structure of democratic communications: Interaction and information in public life. *The Red Feather Institute Paper*, No. 87.

2

Changes of Communication Needs and Rights in Social Revolutions

Michael Traber
World Association for Christian Communication
London, UK

The German communication scholar Paul Watzlawick (Watzlawick, Beavin, & Jackson, 1967, p. 53) coined the axiomatic sentence: "One cannot *not* communicate." He thus echoed Plato's early definition of the human being as the "animal which speaks" (*zoon logon echon*), which, later on, was submerged in Aristotle's definition of the human as the animal which thinks ("rational animal"). The philosophical position of Watzlawick is that human beings are both creatures and creators of language, and all other signs, symbols, and rituals. As Charles Morris (1975) explained:

> Everything which is characteristically human depends on language. The human being is in a real sense the speaking animal. Speech plays the most essential—but not the only—role in the development and preservation of the human self and its aberrations as it does in the development and maintenance of human society and its aberrations. (p. 235)

Precisely because communication is such a fundamental human need, those who control communication also control people. The English Magna Carta of 1215, for example, forbids women to testify in courts when a man has been murdered, except in the case of her own husband (Article 54). The history of communication is a long history of silencing people, culminating, perhaps, in recent years, in the transfer of "dissenters" to psychiatric wards or to solitary confinement in South African prisons. It is also a history of people's struggle to speak up and speak publicly. The MacBride Report states:

> The principle of freedom of expression is one that admits of no exceptions, and that is applicable to people all over the world by virtue of their human dignity. This freedom is one of democracy's most precious acquisitions, frequently secured through arduous struggles with political and economic powers and authorities and at the cost of heavy sacrifice, even of life itself. (International Commission for the Study of Communication Problems, 1980, pp. 18–19)

The purpose of this chapter is to show how the right to communicate grew out of the major revolutions of the last 200 years. These, and other revolutions, were rare occasions when, for whatever reasons, people's stories and people's actions and people's protests were prominent in public communication. Both these aspects, the revolutions and the people who fought for them in the streets and on the hills, are an important yet much neglected dimension of the history of the evolution of communication as a human right.

In the first section we will show the permanent imprint which the American and French Revolutions left on human rights and the right to free expression. Secondly, we discuss the contributions of the "socialist revolutions" of 1917 to the concept of the right to communicate. Both the Mexican Constitution of 1917 and the Soviet Constitution of 1918 broke new ground by invoking the cooperation of the State in implementing new rights. The "third generation" of human rights, and communication as a "solidarity right", shall subsequently be analyzed, particularly on the basis of the UNESCO proclaimed New World Information and Communication Order (NWICO). In a concluding section we reformulate the central argument about revolutions and communication rights and shall point out the many unresolved problems in this field.

COMMUNICATION RIGHTS IN THE AMERICAN AND FRENCH REVOLUTIONS

The first pair of revolutions are the best known: the American and the French. The changes wrought by the American Revolution were less than radical. Slavery was not abolished, and economic power remained largely in the same hands after the war of 1775 as before. But the Declaration of Independence in 1776 was the first successful severance from a European colonial power in modern history. New written constitutions in the various states guaranteed basic civil rights, provided for legislative predominance over the executive and extended suffrage. Above all they espoused Enlightenment ideas that were conducive to freedom: "freedom of opinion," "freedom of expression," and "freedom of the press" were considered fundamental to a democratic order. All of this, coupled with its antimonarchial character, inspired the French Revolution of 1789.

The French revolutionaries were the first to apply the principle of *liberté, egalité,* and *fraternité* to communications. The Declaration of the Rights of Man and of the Citizen adopted by the National Assembly on August 26, 1789 states, "The free communication of ideas and of opinions is one of the most precious rights of man. Any citizen may therefore speak, write and publish freely, except what is tantamount to the abuse of this liberty in the cases determined by Law" (Article 11).

A month later, on September 25, 1789, the American Congress added its famous 10 Amendments to the Federal Constitution of 1787. The First Amendment is a bold statement in defense of freedom of speech, freedom of the press, and freedom of religious worship and of association. It is clearly addressed to the law makers. Their demand was that the State should have no right to interfere with the press.

The same is true for *Les Droits de l'Homme et du Citoyen.* Its focus is individual freedom and the equality of all men. Alas, women were excluded. Equality was added at the insistence of the bourgeoisie in opposition to the aristocracy and demanded by the peasants in the face of feudal lords. But the legislators never envisaged anything like socialism. The horizon of the "Declaration of the Rights of Man and of the Citizen" was despotic government. Did the revolutionaries guess that it might soon return? Yet the Declaration, like the Marseillaise, remained a beacon of hope, even in the darkest hours of post-revolutionary France.

Both the American and the French revolutions were, in principle, movements of the middle class. Their main proponents were lawyers and artisans. Both also unleashed strong forces of nationalism, which was to become a distinctive mark of revolutions to follow. The new era of nationalism with its patriotic festivals, its flags, its hymns, its martyrs, its armies, its wars and conquests profoundly affected both the people's language and the countries' public communication. Post-revolutionary nationalism extended the public sphere more and more into private life and acted as a censor to public communication. Rules were to be worked out as to what constituted unpatriotic language and behavior.

Both the American and the French revolutions are the foundational stories of the two nations. These are stories that represent the origin and the symbolic constitution of communities and nations. They invoke the past to make sense of the present and provide a prospect for the future. The collective memories of the Americans and the French can't really deal with the negative sides of their revolutions. As Breen (1987) points out, few Americans today know that a large proportion of American colonists, perhaps the majority, were content to stay British subjects in 1776. Nor are many French children aware that the Bastille contained only seven prisoners when it was stormed, one of whom had been put there for safekeeping by his own family. Nor, for that matter, are many Soviet children aware that the "Storming" of the Winter Palace in 1917 was a rather peaceful affair. No blood was shed.

Though women played a major role in the French Revolution, few people know that they were excluded from the Declaration of the Rights of Man of 1789 nor are they fully conscious of the atrocities committed by the Committee for Public Safety in the years of the Great Terror, 1793–1794. When the French government decided to limit its 200th anniversary celebrations in 1989 to the year 1789 and nothing beyond, it acted precisely according to the popular myth of its foundational story.

COMMUNICATION AND THE "SOCIALIST REVOLUTIONS" OF 1917

A second phase in the evolvement of human rights occurred in the wake of the upheavals of the 19th and early 20th centuries. The labor conditions created by the industrial revolution and the plight of the landless peasants were, among other factors, the cause of the Mexican revolution of 1910–1917 and of the Russian revolution of 1917. The leaders of both aimed at overthrowing a government. But they had in addition a vision of radically new social orders. Both these revolutions are usually referred to as socialist.

They ushered in the second generation of human rights. These rights were to be realized in cooperation with the State rather than without it. The national government should take an active role in promoting the social, economic, and cultural well-being of its citizens. It was made jointly responsible for decent working conditions, social security, education, and so on.

Mexico's Constitution of 1917 guarantees freedom of expression. Article 6 states (quoted in Article 19 Report. 1989, p. 93):

The expression of ideas shall not be subject to any judicial or administrative investigation, unless it offends good morals, infringes the rights
of others, incites to crime, or disturbs the public order; the right to information shall be guaranteed by the State.

Article 7, first paragraph, reads:

Freedom to write and to publish writings on any subject is inviolable.
No law or authority may establish censorship, require bonds from
authors or printers, or restrict the freedom of printing, which shall be
limited only by the respect due to private life, morals and public peace.
Under no circumstances may a printing press be sequestrated as the
instrument of the offence. (quoted in Article 19 Report, 1989, p. 93)

The operative sentence in Article 6 is that "the right to information
shall be guaranteed by the State." The first communist Constitution
was to be even more precise about the role of the State. The day after
a Soviet government was proclaimed in the wake of the October Revolution of 1917, Lenin signed the Decree of the Press (Pisarek, 1989, p.
97), which stated:

[A]s soon as the new system gets firmly established, all administrative
influence on the press will cease, and it will fully enjoy freedom within
the limits of legal accountability under the broadest and most progressive relevant legislation.

The Soviet Constitution of 1918 abolishes all dependence of the press
on capital and turns over to the working people and the poorest peasantry "all technical and material means for the publication of newspapers, pamphlets, books," and so on (*Encyclopedia Britannica*, Vol.
8, 1980, p. 1184). Likewise, in order to ensure complete freedom of
assembly to the working class and peasantry, the Constitution offers
"all premises convenient for public gatherings together with lighting,
heating and furniture."

The Lenin Constitution thus committed the State to take positive
measures "for the purpose of securing freedom of expression to the
toiling masses." But with the law being regarded as an instrument of
the State, it was up to the Soviet leadership to implement these radical constitutional provisions.

The story of the Russian Revolution, like all foundational stories,
is subject to fairly uniform interpretation. Cooper and Navone (1981,
p. 248) write: "There can be no community life, no consensus, and
thus no common action without participation in the *common understanding* of the meaning of a common story, and without a common

commitment to that story's value." But, as Soviet history shows, the interpretation of their revolution and the freedoms promised by Lenin have changed from time to time. It also shows that the official consensus about the Soviet Union's foundational story has been challenged by counter-stories. They are an explicit endeavor to put the record straight, to counteract false interpretations of foundational stories or of the community story and to demask unauthentic and pseudo-stories. They want to generate dialogue and, indeed, controversy in order to renegotiate the true meaning of stories. Counter-stories are also a rebellion against the power of the established story of their tellers. Rumor is another form of counter-story. Rumor-mongering usually arises in situations when information is withheld and/or when information is no longer believed or trusted. People then start speculating as to what is really happening. Rumor-mongering is, as it were, the people's revenge for the lack, or distortion, of public information.

The Russian Revolution has one great advantage. It has its classic texts or "scripture." But as we know from Judaism, Christianity, or Islam, such "scriptures" are also interpreted differently by different people at different times. Socialism has its towering symbolic figures: Marx, Engels, and Lenin, something the French Revolution lacked.

The leaders of the Mexican Revolution have also become symbols of what it stood for. Francisco I. Madero is called the "Apostle of Democracy." Another hero is Emilio Zapata, whose main concern was land reform. His triumph came when his peasant army occupied Mexico City in 1917. The interpretation of the story of the Mexican Revolution suffered a similar fate as in the Soviet Union. It became institutionalized in a political party, the Partido Revolucionario Institucional (Institutional Revolutionary Party), which has not lost a single election since 1929.

COMMUNICATION AS A "SOLIDARITY RIGHT"

The third generation of human rights is still evolving. It has its origin in the anticolonial revolutions of the years after the Second World War. These rights emphasize national self-determination and nondiscrimination. They are also bound up with the spirit of internationalism that emerged after 1945 and the United Nations system that enshrines it. The adoption of the Universal Declaration of Human Rights on December 10, 1948 was of special significance. It has been described as "a revolutionary development, perhaps the most important development in the history of law in the twentieth century" (Humphrey, 1988, p. 5). Yet in spite of its Article 19 it did not formulate communication as a fundamental human right. Nevertheless, the Universal Declaration of Human Rights and, in 1960, the UN's Declaration on the Granting of Independence to colonial countries and peoples had a far-reaching impact on the process of decolonization.

The third generation of human rights pertain primarily to certain planetary concerns, such as peace, development, ecological balance, and communication. Their horizon is the family of nations, and their rights are, in principle, "solidarity rights," thus carrying the notion of fraternity to its logical, global conclusion (see Marks, 1981).

All of these third-generation rights have an individual and collective dimension. They mean, in the final analysis, that the State and all social organizations have a duty to place common human interests before national and individual interest. Secondly, they imply that they can only be implemented through international cooperation.

As yet there is no definition of the right to communicate (see Fisher & Harms, 1983; Trudel, Boucher, Piotte, & Brisson, 1981). But the majority of thinkers want it to stress the equality of all partners in the communication process. It should embrace a multiway flow of information, including a passive as well as an active right to communicate, while promoting the highest possible degree of feedback, participation, and access.

According to different political traditions and socioeconomic circumstances, some will emphasize the international, others the national, connotation of this right. It will differ depending on whether one places society or the human being at the center of the communication process; whether it means providing communication resources or protecting individuals and communities from the redundancy of information and entertainment; whether there is a primary necessity to satisfy the basic need of all people to have information or to safeguard them against the abuses and manipulation of the mass media; or whether the universal right to communicate can also mean the right to be silent.

The right to communicate, as a fundamental human right, clearly anticipates a communication model that is democratic rather than authoritarian. As Servaes (1988, p. 17) has pointed out, it aims at a redistribution of communication power; its "point of departure is not an elitist position, but development from the grassroots." It further stipulates another role for the State than the one described in the second generation of human rights. The State is only one of several players, because the right to communicate embraces individual rights, institutional rights, or "people's rights" which were the main conflict at UNESCO in the 1980s (see Roach, 1988, pp. 19–20). The policy makers of the Reagan administration consistently refused to accept that there are such rights, including solidarity rights, and the demand for a free and balanced flow of information among nations. John R. Bolten, Assistant Secretary for International Organisation Affairs, took exception to a UNESCO document titled "Communication and Solidarity" and to a sentence that speaks about "improving the flow of information between developing and industrialized countries with a view to correcting the existing imbalance" (Bolten, 1989, pp. 2, 3).

Roach (1988, p. 21) comes to the conclusion that the U.S. government's rejection of the notion of "people's rights" "is but one aspect of a larger picture: the inherent rejection of the decolonisation process of the Third World."

This short sketch on the three generations of human rights and the emergence of communication as a *fundamental* human right may clarify some of the issues in the debate on the New World Information and Communication Order (NWICO). It is against the background of historical developments that the following paragraphs of the MacBride Report should be read:

> Communication . . . is a matter of human rights. . . . It is increasingly interpreted as the right to communicate, going beyond the right to receive communication or to be given information. Communication is thus seen as a two-way process, in which the partners—individual and collective—carry on a democratic and balanced dialogue. The idea of dialogue, in contrast to monologue, is at the heart of much contemporary thinking, which is leading towards a process of developing a new area of social rights.
>
> The right to communicate is an extension of the continuing advance towards liberty and democracy. In every age, man has fought to be free from dominating powers—political, economic, social, religious—that tried to curtail communication. Only through fervent, unflagging efforts did peoples achieve freedom of speech, of the press, of information. Today, the struggle still goes on for extending human rights in order to make the world of communications more democratic than it is today. But the present stage of the struggle introduces new aspects of the basic concept of freedom. The demands for a two-way flow, for free exchange, for access and participation, make a qualitatively new addition to the freedom successfully attained in the past. Indeed, the idea of the right to communicate lifts the whole debate on "free flow" to a higher level, and gives promise to bringing it out of the deadlock to which it was confined for the last thirty years.
>
> The call for democratization of communication has many connotations, many more than are usually considered. It obviously includes providing more and varied means to more people, but democratization cannot be simply reduced to its quantitative aspects, to additional facilities.

It means broader access to existing media by the general public; but access is only a part of the democratization process.

It also means broader possibilities for nations, political forces, cultural communities, economic entites, and social groups to interchange information on a more equal footing, without dominance over the weaker partners and without discrimination against any one. In other words, it implies a change of outlook. (International Commission for the Study of Communication Problems, 1980, pp. 172–173)

The stories told about the NWICO fall into two almost contradictory categories, and they have been documented on both sides. Preston, Herman, and Schiller (1989) give the most recent account of the backlash of the U.S. media treatment of the NWICO and the USA's withdrawal from UNESCO. Stevenson (1988) provides a summary of the arguments against the NWICO. So there is no need to expound on the various positions, except to add that "NWICO has become a people's movement" in many parts of the Third World:

We may forget that NWICO is a *movement* which involves, not just governmental policy makers, but many other socio-political and cultural actors which have important roles in developing the communication patterns and media of a nation and are motivated by the NWICO ideal.

One of the problems in presenting a Third World perspective and evaluating progress toward the implementation of a new order of communication in the developing countries is precisely that the NWICO is a symbol. Like all symbols its inspirational power lies in its ability to bring together in a unified and inter-related paradigm of objectives and actions a response to virtually all of the major questions and problems of communication development.

The national independence movements which have given rise to the NWICO movement have made an important contribution to the new perception of communication. They shattered the notion that the North Atlantic nations are the privileged source of culture and progress. As students of communication, we must be deeply indebted to Mahatma Gandhi, Julius Nyerere and Paulo Freire. (White, 1988, p. 25)

If any evidence for NWICO being a movement is needed, one could cite the example of the international communication Congress of the World Association for Christian Communication which took place in Manila in October 1989. The approximately 450 participants from over 80 different nations, most from the Third World, endorsed a Declaration which reads in part:

The Search for new principles of communication for the 1990's is grounded in the historical experience of the last 15 years. The imbalance in the state of public communication was analysed in detail by an international commission 10 years ago. It produced the MacBride Report under the title *Many Voices, One World: Towards a new more just and more efficient world information and communication order* (NWICO).

The Congress participants, committed to a vision of democratic communication, are anxious to enter into a new phase of dialogue with related organisations and all people of goodwill to achieve a common understanding of communication in the service of free, just and peaceful communities at the local and international levels. The growth of technology, the increase in the monopolisation of the media and the vulgarisation of content, make this task all the more urgent. The principles of communication envisaged should be based on the power of the people, going beyond the formal processes of party politics and seeking new ways of participation which increase the freedom of all people to communicate. (The Manila Declaration, 1990, p. 21)

CONCLUSION

No attempt was made in the preceding sections to define revolution. But it is obvious that revolution in our interpretation means a great deal more than the overthrow of a government by popular upheaval. The juxtaposition of revolution and communication reveals, perhaps better than any other factor, the human-rights dimension of all genuine revolutions.

We have argued that communication, both public and interpersonal, is a *fundamental* human right, and as such the basis and precondition for other human rights, because communication is intimately bound up with what it means to be human. The freedom to speak and to publicize and to create works of communication (cultural goods) is not only an essential component of human dignity and cultural identity, but is also necessary for the progress in other rights, such as food, clothing, shelter, education, health care, and work. It is obvious that all revolutions were concerned with these issues. But the core issue was, and still is, the right to be fully and truly human both as an individual and as a member of a community and a society. It would seem that the human being is better able to cope with physical degradation or material poverty than with the systematic suppression and control of the means and possibilities of communication.

Secondly, we have argued that revolutions happen when the "people's stories" and actions become the dominant political discourse at a certain time. Revolutionary fervor is, in fact, embedded in and spurred on by such stories and actions. Once the people feel that they are no longer in a position to make their voices heard, the potential for change crumbles. When the "counter-stories" are suppressed, the revolution dies.

This leads us to the third and central argument: Historically, revolutions provided the primary motor for the process of democratization. The "bourgeois revolutions" of the 19th century demanded democratic rights for the individual within the newly emergent nation states. The "socialist revolutions" of the early 20th century aimed at the fundamental restructuring of society on the basis of people's power. And the "anti-colonial revolutions" following the Second World War encompassed political self-determination of peoples, equality among races and cultures, and equal status of nations on an international level.

It is one of the principal insights of the International Commission for the Study of Communication Problems, chaired by Sean MacBride, to have analyzed communication as a human right on the international level and to have boldly tied this to the democratization of communication. Thus the right to communicate should not only exist within a nation but equally *between* nations. How the latter should be ordered and conceptualized was the primary subject of debate on the New World Information and Communication Order.

However, many questions remain. The first is the problem of the nation-state, with its concomitant phenomenon of patriotism. Nationalism and patriotism have profoundly affected public communication both within and between nations. What roles can they play, or should they play, on the different levels of a new and democratic communication order? How can national sovereignty be maintained *together* with the international solidarity rights of the third generation of human rights? Policy research on this question has hardly started.

Another unresolved problem is that of ethnicity and cultural identity. The reassertion of these cultural and "people's" rights within and sometimes even between nation-states presents one of the most formidable communication challenges today. It is one of the basic issues in most parts of the Third World and in many countries of Europe. It is not good enough to treat ethnicity and cultural identity under the rubric of "minority groups" who, presumably, have minority rights—as the MacBride Report tends to do (International Commission for the Study of Communication Problems, 1980, p. 309). Each ethnic and cultural group must be seen to make a unique contribution to public communication and its new national and international order.

Finally, the problem of communication technology and power. In this respect, the world of communication has changed radically since the MacBride Report first appeared. The gap between the technology-rich and the technology-poor has widened. Deregulation has increased monopolization of media ownership and trivialization of media content, particularly in the electronic media. What is lacking in research is not the analysis of these trends but policy proposals in the search for alternatives. The active right to communicate, not only interpersonally but over distances and with "dispersed communities," calls for radical rethinking of technological alternatives, of which video technology is only one. The NWICO movement, or the democratization process, particularly in the Third World, calls for such alternatives and the policies to go with them.

The hypothesis in need of further investigation is this: All genuine revolutions are fundamentally communication revolutions, or they are none at all. A revolution is the very opposite of dictatorship of whatever kind—aristocratic, oligarchical, monopolistic, or proletarian, or a mixture of these. When communication is suppressed or if it requires self-censorship, the revolution as an extension of human rights has ended. That is the real counterrevolution.

REFERENCES

Article 19 Report. (1989). *In the Shadow of Buendia*. The Mass Media and Censorship in Mexico, London, Article 19.

Bolten, J.R. (1989). *The United States and UNESCO 1989*. Statement before the Subcommit'₊e on International Operations of the House Foreign Affairs Committee, Washington, DC, September 19, 1989, U.S. Department of State, Bureau of Public Affairs.

Breen, M. (1987). Definitions and functions of myths in mass media. In *Media Development*, 34(2), 8–10.

Encyclopaedia Britannica. (1980). Macropaedia (Vol. 8). Chicago, IL.

Fisher, D., & Harms, L.S. (Ed.). (1983). *The right to communicate: A new human right*. Dublin: Boole Press.

Humphrey, J.P. (1988). The greatest achievement of the United Nation forty years on. *Media Development*, 35(4), 4–5.

International Commission for the Study of Communication Problems. (1980). London/New York/Paris: UNESCO (MacBride Report).

Manila Declaration on Communication and Community. (1990). In *Media Development*, Post-Congress Issue, 37(2), 21–22.

Marks, S.P. (1981). Emerging human rights: A new generation for the 1980s? *Rutgers Law Review*, 33(2), 435–452.

Morris, C. (1975). Sprechen und menschliches Handeln. In H.-G. Gadamer & P. Vogler, (Eds.), *Neue Anthropologie* (Bd.7, pp. 235–251). Stuttgart. (Translation by M. Traber).

Navone, J., & Cooper, T. (1981). *Tellers of the word*. New York: Le Jacq Publishing.

Pisarek, W. (1989). European Socialist Countries. In K. Nordenstreng, & H. Topuz, *Journalist: Status, rights, responsibilities* (pp. 97–135). Prague: International Organisation of Journalists.

Preston, W., Herman, E.S., & Schiller, H.I. (1989). *Hope and folly. The United States and UNESCO, 1945–1984*. Minneapolis: University of Minnesota Press.

Roach, C. (1988). U.S. arguments on the right to communicate and people's rights. *Media Development, 35*(4), 18–21.

Servaes, J. (1988). The right to communicate is a basic human right. *Media Development, 35*(4), 15–17.

Stevenson, R.L. (1988). *Communication, development and the Third World. The global politics of information*. New York: Longman.

Trudel, P., Boucher, J., Piotte, R., & Brisson, J-M. (1981). *Le Droit à l'Information: Emergence, Reconnaissance, Mise en Oeuvre*. Montreal: Les Presses de l'Université de Montréal.

Watzlawick, P., Beavin, J.H., & Jackson, D.D. (1967). *Menschliche Kommunikation. Formen, Störungen, Paradoxien*. Bern: Peter Lang.

White, R. (1988). NWICO has become a people's movement. *Media Development, 35*(1), 20–25.

3

Stuck in a Groove:
Why the 1960s Approach
to Communication
Democratization Will
No Longer Do*

Karol Jakubowicz
Polish Radio and Television
Warsaw, Poland

INTRODUCTION

The MacBride Commission has defined the democratization of communication as:

> the process whereby: (a) the individual becomes an active partner and not a mere object of communication; (b) the variety of messages exchanged increases; and (c) the extent and quality of social representation or participation in communication is augmented. (MacBride et al., 1980, p. 166)

It is a measure of the conceptual confusion prevailing in the whole communication democratization debate that when confronted with

---

* This chapter draws and elaborates on some ideas first formulated in my earlier work: *The New Information and Communication Technologies and Democratization of Communication*, a paper presented at the IAMCR conference in Barcelona, and "To Democratise Communication, First Democratise Society," *Media Development*, No. 4, 1988.

such a definition, one is immediately forced to ask: *What* communication? Interpersonal, group, institutional, public, mass, international, or some other? Given that the mass media and, in particular, the old model of centralized and monopolistic broadcasting, were in the democratization movement's first line of attack, this definition raises more questions than it answers, for example:

- How does an individual become an "active partner" in broadcasting, or of the broadcast media, and what in practical terms would that involve?
- How does an individual join in the social "exchange" of messages conducted by means of the broadcast media?
- If the extent and quality of social representation or participation in the operation of a broadcast medium are augmented, what, in fact, is democratized? Social communication or just the medium itself?

After some two decades of an intense international debate on the democratization of communication, we must conclude that:

- It has so far been unable to produce a generally accepted definition of, or a blueprint for, democratic communication, mass or otherwise.
- Due to the deregulation of broadcasting and the "innovatory onslaught" of the new technologies, the old frame of reference within which the issue has been approached is fast losing its validity.

We propose to analyze here some of the weaknesses of the "old paradigm of communication democratization" and to attempt to show how the changes unfolding in the field of communications affect the problematic. The analysis will concern chiefly developed Western countries. One reason is that that is where the 1960s communication democratization was born and they—and especially their old model of broadcasting—provide the frame of reference for its concepts and strategies, and therefore also for our discussion. As we will see, one of the problems with "old paradigm of communication democratization research" is that it has not made the transition required by the new frame of reference created by processes of change in mass communication. Secondly, we will concern ourselves with developed Western countries because they are the ones to have claimed for a long time that their media are democratic, or at least free from politically motivated legal and administrative constraints.

HISTORICAL BACKGROUND

The predominant socioinstitutional model of broadcasting has until recently been that of a *monocentric* (or, as in the United States, *polycentric*) *system of uniformizing communication*[1]—so called because, all their democratic rhetoric aside, most mainstream, national broadcasting systems have sought to "define" or "construct" reality (cf. Hall, 1983; Vreg, 1985; Connell, 1980; Thomas, 1986; Signorielli, 1986) so as to "propagate and re-present the dominant class ideology" (Fiske & Hartley, 1984, p. 89) and in so doing draw their audience into the mainstream culture, values, and ideology. This allocutory, "repressive" (Enzensberger, 1972) model favored unequal and asymmetrical communication relationships (being a reflection of social relations in general).

One area of efforts to develop concepts of democratic broadcasting (the following can only be a brief and very selective overview of these efforts) concerned the communication rights and needs of individuals and groups. Already in 1932, Brecht argued in his *Theory of Radio* that it must be changed from a means of distribution to one of communication, "allowing the listener not only to hear, but to speak."[2] In later formulations, this found an echo in "the right to receive" and "the right to transmit" as "the basis of any democratic culture" (Williams, 1968, p. 120); in "each receiver a potential transmitter" (Enzensberger, 1972); and in "the right to communicate is . . . a fundamental human right' (Fisher & Harms, 1983, p. 19) later supplemented by the view that "a right to communicate includes a right to *telecommunicate*" (Harms, 1985, p. 160).

As the idea of the right to transmit (or communicate) gained acceptance, and as new research showed communication to be a process of

---

[1] Some broadcasting systems covered by this term involve elaborate structures of social participation in running and overseeing stations or networks, based on the principles of majoritarian or even consensual democracy (Downs, 1987). However, their other features make them inherently undemocratic.

[2] Brecht can be said to be following in the footsteps of Lenin who in 1904 wrote: "Let us do away with the old bourgeois attitude: ours is not to write [for the press], ours is but to read what others write." The movement of worker and peasant correspondents initiated by Lenin still in prerevolutionary times can be seen in part as an early forerunner of ideas about feedback, social access and participation, deprofessionalization, and demonopolization of the media.

exchange rather than an act of one-way transmission of content (Wiio, 1981; Rogers, 1982), the nature of social communication was redefined in a way consistent with the spirit of interactive, participatory communication (Beltran, n.d.). A new normative press theory, the democratic-participant media theory (McQuail, 1987) emerged as a sum of new ideas on the social nature of communication.

Coupled with this was an interest in how to reform existing broadcasting systems (Branscomb & Savage, 1978; "Broadcasting Policy and Media Reform," 1980) and in the kind of broadcasting policy and media structures needed to ensure feedback (*Broadcasters and their Audiences*, 1974), access (Berrigan, 1977), or "participatory programming" (Groombridge, 1972). Indeed, some forms of broadcast media democratization serving precisely these goals[3] had been introduced already in the 1930s.

A special dimension of this strand of the debate has been the study of local and community broadcasting in terms of its democratization potential (Beaud, 1980; Downing, 1984; Barlow, 1988; Jankowski, 1988). Another has concerned the impact of the new technologies on prospects for communication democratization.

A third area of debate has dealt with the general social context. Especially representatives of critical theory have been "democratization of communication [as forming] part of a broader process of distribution of social power and influence in society" (White, 1984, p. 5) and have studied macrostructural determinants affecting the operation of broadcasting.

And yet, the old paradigm of communication democratization research has yielded a surprisingly meager harvest, though other authors have tried to conceptualize involvement, access, participation, social management of the media, and so on (these efforts are reviewed in Jankowski, 1988, pp. 11–22), Jouet's (1977) early typology of the three levels and degrees of media democratization still stands, despite the ambiguity of some of her terms (e.g., "self-management;" see below).

More work has been done on criteria for judging pluralism and diversity in mass communication (Blumler, 1985; Hoffman-Riem, 1987), with Jacklin (1978) and McQuail and van Cuilenburg (1983) perhaps coming closest to defining them.

---

[3] For example, the French PTT Minister decreed in 1933 that each community having a state-owned station would hold an annual meeting (open to all license-fee payers) to elect representatives to a community council of management that would be responsible for the station's programming (Emery, 1969, p. 242). In Belgium organizations representing major groups within the audience were given regular access to programming in 1930 (Emery, 1969, pp. 125–126).

Though efforts to define democratic communication have not been spectacularly successful (various definitions or attempts to formulate them are reviewed in Sreberny-Mohammadi, n.d.), there is broad agreement that it should remove the distinction, built into many communication patterns, between the sender and the receiver (Harms, 1978; Sreberny-Mohammadi, n.d., p. 15; Wiio, 1981; Banks & Robinson, 1988). What is lacking, however, is any practical idea on how to achieve this in the sphere of mass communication, let alone telecommunication.

Critical research sees communication democratization as part and parcel of a process of structural social change which alone can create conditions for it (White, 1984). Scholars from socialist countries, too, have argued for a comprehensive approach to this issue (cf. Szecskö, 1986; Jakubowicz, 1987), in that democratization of social communication should go hand in hand with the democratization of society in general. It can precede general democratization and contribute to its progress, but is not secure and cannot last without it (Jakubowicz, 1988).

THE OLD PARADIGM: PLAGUED BY FALLACIES

The debate on communication democratization has been inconclusive in part because it lacks conceptual or theoretical clarity and coherence. Indeed, it is plagued by a number of major fallacies which prevent some of its aspects from gaining a firm purchase on the reality of social communication. These fallacies are discussed below.

Fallacy of the Universal Need to (Mass)communicate

The general population has historically played a passive role in shaping broadcasting systems.[4] The only time when a sizable part of it stirred itself to take an active stand on the matter came in the late 1960s and early 1970s when the counterculture and the New Left sought (as part of their general program of social reform) to democra-

---

[4] This could be explained by early fascination with broadcasting, a lack of criteria by which to judge their performance in social terms; "a mass media mentality" (D'Arcy, 1983), that is, acceptance of the social pattern of broadcasting that relegated the audience to the "passive receiver" role; preoccupation with other issues (World War II, postwar reconstruction, in more recent times—economic depression and its consequences, etc.). All of these may account for a predominantly escapist motivation for broadcast media use (Frissen, 1988).

tize mass communication. That relatively small, socially unrepresentative movement of idealistic, educated, and articulate youth dissenters seemed to proceed on the assumption that its communication needs and capabilities were universally shared.[5] Many communication scholars have, in effect, accepted this assumption and have still not extricated their thinking from it.

It has been demonstrated time and again that the mass of the population fails to take advantage of opportunities for access to programming, whether offered by establishment media or alternative ones, specially dedicated to this goal ("European Experiments in Cable Television," 1977; Cavalli-Sforza, 1978; Beaud, 1980; Browne, 1984, 1988; Jankowski & Mol, 1988). Ordinarily, the urge to (mass) communicate simply is not there. Moreover, Enzensberger (1972, p. 108) could not have been more wrong when he said that "potentially, the new media do away with all educational privileges and thereby with the cultural monopoly of the bourgeois intelligentsia." In fact, if anyone takes advantage of communication opportunities offered by the media, it is usually precisely the intelligentsia, bourgeois or otherwise,[6] that has the communication competence others lack.

In any case, many commentators doubt whether the practical realization of *every individual*'s right to be heard, even assuming that it is possible to achieve, would amount to democratic communication. Baudrillard (1986, p. 129) actually sees it as meaningless from this point of view: If communication is to be an exchange, then what is required is breaking the monopoly of speech:

> [O]ne cannot break the monopoly of speech if one's goal is simply to distribute it to everyone. Speech must be able to exchange, give and repay itself . . . It cannot simply be interrupted, congealed, stockpiled, and redistributed in some corner of the social process.

---

[5] Cf. Simon Partridge's (1982, p. 2) call for "a voice for everyone," and his confident assertion that people badly served by existing radio systems (including women, trade unionists, the minorities, the blind, the housebound) "given half a chance, might also become, broadcasters in their own right."

[6] As Mattelart and Piemme (1980, p. 326) note, "In a society where cultural segregation is structurally linked to the operation of the mode of production . . . the different strata of society, and, even more, the different social classes are not equidistant from all types of technology, each ready to use all of them as and when necessary." Cf. Berrigan's (1977) list of groups pressing the demand for "social," "creative," "political," and "educational" access to the media, and including also entrepreneurs and "futurists." Nigg and Wade (1980) mention photographers, filmmakers, artists, community workers, researchers, school teachers, and so on, as pioneering community communication.

Szecskö (1986, p. 73) sees it as not only meaningless but, in fact, counterproductive:

If everybody speaks at the same time—as suggested by the naive models of access and participation or by the "microsociety" approach—probably nobody listens. Absolute communication turns into its opposite: into a state of noncommunication. This is just where the fallacy of trying to model the system of social communication on the liberal "marketplace" concept shows its shortcomings most drastically . . . communication . . . is not a mere information-exchange: it is sharing a common meaning.

Thus, the entire edifice of communication democratization as the concept is understood by some scholars is shown to be without foundation; a struggle fought on behalf of those who have little interest in its outcome.

Fallacy of the Mistaken Level

We owe this phrase to Rafael Roncagliolo (1988), who notes that the flow of messages is carried out on at least three different levels (the individual and the group, the national, and the international) and that on each of these levels democratization of communication must be seen in a different light.

Also, Szecskö (1986) points out that from a sociological point of view the concept of communication encompasses different levels: interpersonal communicative interactions, the written word, mass communications, and global communications. Szecskö believes that one can properly speak of democratizing communication only with regard to mass communications, but this seems too narrow an interpretation of the concept.

It is perhaps best to distinguish social communication processes by the levels of social organization at which they take place, for example, societywide, intergroup, and interpersonal communication. Each of these levels involves different types of communication relationships and offers quite different prospects for democratization.

It is by not isolating these different levels in their analysis that some authors forfeit any realistic chance of formulating concepts of democratic communication appropriate and practicable at each level. Hence the common tendency of equating democratization of the *mass media* with democratization of *communication*, which is a major fallacy in its own right.

One "fallacy of the mistaken level" is to demand that systems of societywide (i.e., mass) communication make provision for the assumed and nonexistent universal need of all or most individuals to become active mass communicators. Not only is this impossible to achieve; there is serious doubt as to whether it is really needed and, in fact, whether its attainment would make for democratic communication.

If communication is seen as an exchange, and if its democratization is understood, in general terms, as creating conditions for all actors to participate in such an exchange freely, without hindrance of any kind, then we face a real dilemma if we also agree with Baudrillard (1986, pp. 123–129) that:

> The mass media are anti-mediatory and intransitive. They fabricate non-communication—this is what characterizes them . . . *they are what prevents response*, making all processes of exchange impossible (except in the various forms of response simulation, themselves integrated in the transmission process, thus leaving the unilateral nature of the communication intact). . . . This is why the only revolution in this domain . . . lies in restoring this possibility of response. But such a simple possibility presupposes an upheaval in the entire existing structure of the media.

The MacBride Commission argues: "Since democracy implies the voicing of divergent opinions, even an inventive model of democratic control over a system speaking with a single voice can have nothing in common with real democratization" (MacBride et al., 1980, p. 168). True, but what Baudrillard is saying is that even if such a system (e.g., built on the principle of internal pluralism) did speak with many voices, it would still be practicing undemocratic communication, because there would still be no possibility of response—or, perhaps, direct and immediate response and feedback between participants in communication, which Baudrillard seems to consider a necessary component of democratic communication.

There seems to be no other way out of this dilemma than to develop *different* conceptualizations of democratic communication *for each of these levels*. Free, equal, and unhindered exchange between "send-ceivers" (i.e., participants who alternate in roles of senders and receivers) is a goal that can be aspired to at the level of interpersonal communication. Let us add that given the enormous variety of social, cultural, psychological, and other factors which affect interpersonal communication, attainment of this goal is about as easy as achieving full equality among people.

In the case of mass communication at the intergroup or society-wide level, the criterion of democratic communication must be different. Democratic control and operation of the media themselves are a necessary but insufficient condition here. The decisive thing is that each segment of society should be in a position to introduce ideas, symbols, information, and elements of culture into social circulation in such a way as to be able to reach all other segments of society (cf. White, 1984). In short, as the MacBride Report also makes clear, societywide communication cannot be regarded as democratic if any segment of society is prevented from either adding its own messages to the social pool of information or from receiving the messages of another segment. Thus, even if there cannot be immediate response and direct debate, over a period of time every point of view can be expressed and made known to everyone else—and, if necessary, responded to. That in turn presupposes the existence of not only democratic media, but also of democratic arrangements in society in general.

Fallacy of the Autonomy of Mass Communication

Stuart Hall (1989, p. 48) argues that "there is no way the study of communication systems could proceed without understanding . . . how they are linked to particular positions and structures of power and how they are crosscut by the field and operation of power."[7] Yet, some scholars still seek to devise methods of democratizing the media without reference to that context.

When radio first emerged, the assumption of its great powers of persuasion prompted the power elite to assume control over it—first in order to neutralize it politically, later to use it with a view to reproducing the social order. The counterculture and the New Left of the late 1960s and early 1970s sought to create an *open, polycentric system of pluralistic, participatory mass communication*. That would have made broadcasting an agent of destabilization in the political system, so only a limited process of change—from government- or state-run systems to some variety of public service broadcasting systems—in fact took place in some Western European countries.

Then, in the 1980s, came deregulation. Vincent Mosco (1988, pp.

---

[7] In fact, Banks and Robinson (1988) believe that precisely because of the ubiquitous and necessary presence of power in society, democratization of communication is ultimately impossible to achieve.

120–121) believes that in the United States deregulation was a response to a situation in which "nondominant groups were beginning to achieve success in applying pressure on the regulatory apparatus to implement public interest values more forcefully. . . . Deregulation is one way the state re-forms itself to eliminate an arena of potential class conflict." So just as political considerations originally prompted the choice of institutional structures for broadcasting that were somewhat untypical for capitalist societies at the time, so now political considerations have promoted a change in this respect. Capitalism has at long last caught up with broadcasting. West European business elites evidently no longer need the state to safeguard their interests in and through broadcasting and seek to assume direct, hands-on control. This can hardly improve prospects for democratization of society-wide mass communication.

Fallacy of the Mistaken Historical Period

The explosion of alternative media and alternative communication in the 1960s and 1970s arose out of a coincidence of *political turmoil* in industrially advanced societies with the increasing availability of small-scale media technologies. This serves to bring out the fact that opportunities to engage in mass communication are rarely sought for their own sake, but chiefly as a means of championing a cause, projecting an identity, defending interests, and pursuing other goals. They are usually sought not by individuals, but by groups, movements, and organizations as a means to an end, as yet another means of achieving their objectives.

Thus, fast social change, conflicts, and social upheavals, with their attendant disintegration of social patterns and value systems, dissent, a sense of injustice and being discriminated against, the flare-up of discontent over a particular issue—all these have the effect of radicalizing and politicizing groups and individuals, and encouraging them to use communication as part of their struggle. At the same time, differences in communicative competence give an edge to better-educated, middle-class activists who are usually to be found actually managing and operating alternative media, and teaching others how to use them (Jankowski, Voos, & Brouwer, 1988).

Once relative stability returns, the situation changes. Accordingly, with most of their once enthusiastic, voluntary supporters now occupying themselves with other matters, "free radio" which exploded in

France in the early 1980s and alternative radio and television which mushroomed in Italy in the late 1970s have largely been taken over by commercial interests. What is left is an "alternative public sphere" (Downing, 1988), either as a long-term phenomenon, existing on the fringes of the establishment media, or springing up around a specific issue.

Thus, the "fallacy of the mistaken historical period" consists in assuming that attitudes to communication and communication needs characteristic of times of strife and dissent are also prevalent at other times—and proceeding from there to build concepts of, and strategies supposed to lead to, democratization of social communication. These are less supported by needs and desires actually felt by most people in this respect than might be assumed by a supporter of the cause.

Fallacy of the "Invisible Hand"

Briefly, this is the fallacy underlying the hope, voiced for example by those who engage in what has been called "discourse of the new technologies," that increased choice, diversity, and democratic communication will emerge automatically, as it were, given enough new technologies to go round. It is the product of what Szecskö calls "the fallacy of trying to model the system of social communication on the liberal 'market-place' concept," coupled perhaps with technological determinism. A well-known exponent of this approach is Ithiel de Sola Pool (1983, p. 39) who regards the new technologies as "technologies of freedom" which "allow for more knowledge, easier access and freer speech than ever enjoyed before" and will "overwhelm all attempts to control them."

In proposing a democratic system of mass communication, Raymond Williams (1968, p. 120) said that it was "firmly against authoritarian control of what can be said, and against paternal control of what ought be said. But also it is against commercial control of what can profitably be said, because this also can be a tyranny." In short, under all the other systems free and democratic communication is either out of the question or can be negated fully in keeping with the logic of the system. That is why he believed in the need for a deliberate policy of safeguarding the right to transmit, and for a publicly controlled and socially accountable institutional infrastructure serving the practical exercise of this right. No "invisible hand" can make that happen.

LAYING THE FOUNDATION FOR A NEW PARADIGM

Democratic Communication:
A Tentative Reconceptualization

Since democratic mass communication may be seen to be a contradiction in terms, let us try to solve this dilemma by approaching the matter in terms not of kinds of communication processes, but of "communicative democracy" achievable at each of the levels distinguished above.

Direct communicative democracy, creating opportunities for everyone to be a "sendceiver" engaged in participatory horizontal communication, incorporating immediate response and feedback, is feasible only in face-to-face communication, or in mediated communication conducted by means of interactive new media (Rogers, 1986), that is, at the level of interpersonal, intragroup, and—in some cases—of intergroup communication.

Representative communicative democracy obtains when all segments of society do, or can—without hindrance—own or control their own media (a case of open[8] external pluralism) or have adequate access to them (e.g., open internal pluralism, exemplified by the Dutch broadcasting system) for the purposes of communicating to their own members and to society at large. Few of their members need to be active mass communicators in their own right. Still, the group's views, ideas, culture, and world outlook do enter social circulation at a level appropriate to the group's size and scale of operation (i.e., through the intermediary of national or regional, local, or community media), can be known to the community at large and can potentially influence its views, policies, or outlook.

Under ordinary circumstances most people would seem to be content to accept representative communicative democracy in the sphere of mass communication, as long as it is a diversified system corresponding to the differentiation of society, including broad participation in the formulation of communication policies, in the organization and management of the media and direct accountability of the media to society and the groups they represent. In representative democracy,

---

[8] "Open pluralism" denotes a situation in which legal or other conditions exist for *every* social group to own, control, or have adequate access to the media. This system was introduced in the Netherlands in 1967 (van der Haak, 1977). Previous to that, the Dutch system was one of "closed pluralism," with only five broadcasting organizations sharing all air time.

Figure 3.1. Types of Communicative Democracy

	Level of Communication		
	Society-wide	Intergroup	Interpersonal
Goal	Democratize social communication and society	Defend and project group interests and identity	Self-realization, equality, freedom
Type of democracy	Representative	Representative/ participatory representative	Direct
Kinds of media	Mass, new	All media, face-to-face communication	Face-to-face communication interactive media
Roles offered to participants	Receivers, media co-managers, communication facilitators	Receivers, media co-managers, communication facilitators, communicators	"Sendceivers"
Obstacles	Social relations and structure, sociopolitical system	Group structure, differences of communication competence, dominance of establishment media	Socioeconomic, cultural psychological factors affecting interrelationships

decision-making processes should take place in conditions of equality, autonomy, and adequate representation. If these conditions are met in the way media are organized and run, and in social communication itself, then representative communicative democracy has a chance of satisfying most of the expectations of a democratic-minded society.

This, incidentally, is why we find Jouet's term "self-management" ambiguous. She defines it as a situation in which "the public exercises the power of decision-making within communication enterprises" (Jouet, 1977, p. 5). In fact the term really means self-management (i.e., autonomy) of the media (or any other entity) run by their staffs, without outside interference, and is so used both with regard to the media themselves (cf. Downing, 1984) and in the sociology of organizations in general. A certain degree of self-management is, of course, a welcome sign of internal democracy. However, full self-management is exactly the reverse of what Jouet understands by it, that is, a situation in which the public has *no* power of decision making within communication enterprises. Even if we accept that the term refers here to the self-management of society in general, of which media self-management is a part, the contradiction is not removed. Therefore, the term should perhaps be changed to "socialization of the media," which denotes a situation in which society as such genuinely owns and controls the media which in turn genuinely operate in the social interest.

The autonomous, "alternative," "free," or community stations dealt with by Downing (1984) or in other studies can be said to combine aspects of both the direct and representative communicative democracy. If the groups or movements they speak for are structured and organized in a truly democratic way, all or most of their members are able to influence the operation of their media and participate in the determination of their goals; in short, they can, with some exaggeration, be called *media comanagers*. Moreover, a fairly large number of them is involved in the running and operation of those media, contributing time, effort, and money to ensure their functioning and survival; in short, they become *communication facilitators*, without necessarily becoming communicators themselves. Accordingly, we have to do here with something we might call *representative participatory communicative democracy*.

The main aspects of this tentative conceptualization of different kinds of communicative democracy are summed up in Figure 3.1.

The Changing Context of Communication Democratization

As far as mass communication is concerned, the democratization battle has been fought mainly in the sphere of broadcasting and can, to all intents and purposes, be summed up as follows:

- its objective has, in most cases, been the dismantling of a legally protected broadcasting monopoly exercised by centralized broadcasting systems, and obtaining the passage of new laws, democratizing existing radio and television organizations and creating conditions for the free establishment of other ones;
- thus, the fight has been fought in the political and administrative domain;
- the "enemy" has been the state;
- the "battlefield" has been coextensive with the nation-state.

It is obvious that in Western European countries these conditions no longer prevail.

There, the early 1980s saw the beginning of the processes of *commercialization* and *internationalization* in mass communication, caused in part by (a) the political and ideological reorientation of developed Western countries towards *laissez-faire* capitalism, (b) the development of a transnational economy and globalization of economic processes, and (c) by the emergence of new technologies, including satellite television, which promote the internationalization of broadcasting by their very nature. If unchecked, this process may in an extreme situation result in the emergence of *a global oligopolistic system of uniformizing communication*, serving the purpose of "world-system legitimation" (Mosco, 1982).

Thus, a great deal has changed in the field of broadcasting:

- its ecology is different due to deregulation, growth of the number of channels, also at regional, local, and community levels, and the spread of the new media;
- new actors (transnational corporations at one extreme and local and community media organizations at the other) have appeared;
- deregulation has removed many of the old legal and institutional barriers to becoming an active mass communicator;
- the new media have removed many of the old technical and financial barriers to engaging in mass communication, though they have not eased the problem of doing so on a regular basis in a commercial environment;
- commoditization of information and communication is redefining their social role and uses (Mosco & Wasko, 1988).

And so, many of the old obstacles to democratization have disappeared. The "enemy" is much more amorphous and it is much more difficult to pin the blame for the lack of democratic communication on any specific policy, set of rules, or administrative or institutional structures. In the place of the old obstacles, three major new ones have arisen.

The first one has to do with the logic of the commercial system, where, as Williams (1968, p. 119) has put it, "anything can be said, provided that you can afford to say it and that you can say it profitably." What this means, of course, is that many groups cannot afford to finance and operate the media necessary to introduce messages into social circulation. Equally important is the fact that, as has been amply documented, the profit orientation of the commercial media significantly reduces the range of content being communicated. This militates against pluralistic communication, makes it hard for content representing or catering to minorities to reach the general public and for new ideas to break through. Mass communication oriented to mass audiences becomes "safe" and predictable.

The second one ties in with the gradual emergence of an international public sphere in response to the transnationalization of economic activity and concentration of power in a few major countries. Accordingly, if by communicative democracy we understand in part the ability of every group or social force to seek to affect policy making on matters of importance to them by means of reaching the policy makers with information and opinions on those matters, then this now increasingly involves introducing those messages into international circulation.[9]

And finally, there is the gradual disappearance of the national public sphere. As Habermas has noted (1983), the system of legitimation applied in Western countries is based on the principle of formal democracy and is designed to ensure the loyalty of the masses but to prevent, or minimize, their political participation. The public service broadcasting system, oriented to serving the public sphere of the nation-state, and to involving members of the audience in society as political citizens, is dysfunctional from this point of view. Hence "broadcasting is being increasingly seen as an internationally tradeable service, as an 'industry.' Viewers are being redefined as 'consumers' " (Dyson, Humphreys, Negrine & Simon, 1983, p. 306).

The general public, aware of its lack of access to, and any control of, mechanisms of power, displays little interest in following events in the political sphere (cf. Sparks, 1988, for evidence of this trend as shown by press readership patterns in Britain) and has allowed the tension-reduction function of media use to come to the fore. Therefore: "Our research indicates that the public's perception of 'television' remains little changed from that of the previous generation. To most of the public, television is still a one-way medium with little or no role outside of entertainment" (Negrine & Goodfriend, 1988, p. 319). Practically the entire literature on the subject confirms this finding.

The result is a curious paradox. The active communication capabilities of individuals and groups are now much greater than ever before. The alternative public sphere continues to exist and seems well estab-

---

[9] This is understood perfectly well by organizers of demonstrations the world over. They usually prepare a few signs and banners in English, so that crews from agencies like VISNEWS can more easily pick them out and film them. In that way, their slogans and demands will be made known to television audiences all over the world without the need for translation (and possible distortion) of their meaning.

lished also in the field of information technology and telecommunications (Downing, n.d.). The volume of communication activity has grown exponentially and so has the number of active senders of messages that reach large numbers of receivers. Yet it would be hard to argue that social communication is becoming democratized. After all, the frantic communication activity mainly serves the pursuit of commercial goals and objectives. Is this what the struggle for democratic communication was all about?

Therefore, future thinking about communicative democracy, especially at the societywide level, should perhaps seek to pursue five goals:

1. Tightening up definitions of the *formal* prerequisites for democratization of communication in terms of the ability actively to engage in mass communication, including the requisite communication, including the requisite communication competence and the ownership, control of, or access to mass media and the new technologies in order to introduce messages into social circulation;

2. Developing policies and institutional structures enabling social groups and forces to be active mass communicators. True, it is now much easier to engage in mass communication. However, the need to survive in a commercial environment, with audiences quite indifferent to "issue broadcasting" and preferring entertainment even in community stations that presumably deal with matters close to home (Petersen, Prehn, & Svendsen, 1988), has led to the commercialization of many erstwhile alternative and socially motivated stations. Accordingly, such policies and structures are needed now as much as they have ever been;

3. Developing a fuller conceptualization and a practical program for the socialization of the media, as part of a general program of democratization. Some inspiration for it might be drawn from the way the Yugoslav system has been designed to embody this principle, as well as from the debate on the socialization of the means of production conducted in the field of political economy and political theory;

4. Developing or elaborating possible *substantive* criteria of communicative democracy. In adopting this term we emphasize the notion of democracy (whereas in "democratic communication" the stress is mainly on the process of communication itself, and only secondarily on what makes it democratic). This suggests that

those criteria might have to do with the essence of democracy, that is, the democratic governance of whatever entity is relevant in the particular case. One of the policy objectives in the democratization of communication has been that of permitting "all sectors of the population to contribute to the pool of information that provides the basis for local or national decision-making and the basis for the allocation of resources in society" (White, 1984, p. 4). After all, the pressure for communication democratization sprang from the growing awareness of various local communities, groups, social movements, minorities, or segments of society from beyond the mainstream of the crucial importance of access to the media at a time when more and more of the affairs of public life are played out in media content. This is why they regard unequal access to, or inadequate presentation in, media content as a gravely prejudicial form of *injustice*. Thus, if the need for substantive criteria is accepted, we might distinguish between *formal communicative democracy* and *full communicative democracy*. In the latter case, not only do conditions exist for social groups and forces to engage in mass communication, but also communicative democracy is an integral element of political democracy and an essential part of the process of democratic governance. If, for whatever reason, this is not happening, we cannot speak of the existence of a full communicative democracy, nor indeed of genuine democracy as such. This again serves to underscore the need for general democracy as a prerequisite for communicative democracy;

5. With the emergence of an international public sphere, there seems to be a need to return to something like the NWICO debate which was oriented, after all, to democratizing international communication. It has been terminated by the fiat of some major Western countries. Now it seems to be slowly gathering momentum once again (ironically — in the West itself). It is prompted by rising concerns on the part of Western European countries that feel threatened by emerging patterns of international communication in much the same way as do developing nations. From our point of view, pride of place should go to a debate on mechanisms needed to enable societies or their segments to reach world public opinion or centers of international power with messages that might influence policies or actions on matters of importance to those societies or parts of their population.

REFERENCES

Banks, J., & Robinson, D.C. (1988). *The Impossibility of Democratic Communication.* Paper presented at the IAMCR Conference, Barcelona, Spain.

Barlow, W. (1988). Community radio in the U.S.: The struggle for a democratic medium. *Media, Culture and Society, 1*, 81–105.

Baudrillard, J. (1986). Requiem for the media. In J.G. Hanhardt (Ed.), *Video culture. A critical investigation* (pp. 124–143). New York: Peregrine Smith Books.

Beaud, P. (1980). *Community Media? Local radio and television and audiovisual animation experiments in Europe.* Strasbourg: Council of Europe.

Beltran, L.R. (n.d.). *L'adieu a Aristotle: La communication horizontale.* Paris: UNESCO.

Berrigan, F.J. (Ed.). (1977). *Access: Some Western models of community media.* Paris: UNESCO.

Blumler, J.G. (1985). The social character of media gratifications. In K.E. Rosengren, L.A. Wenner, & P. Palmgreen (Eds.), *Media gratifications research. Current perspectives* (pp. 41–60). Beverly Hills, CA: Sage Publications.

Branscomb, A.W., & Savage, M. (1978). The broadcast reform movement: At a crossroads. *Journal of Communication, 4*, 24–34.

Broadcasters and their Audiences. (1974). Vol. 1. Torino: Edizioni Radiotelevisione Italiana.

Broadcasting Policy and Media Reform. (1980). *Communication Research Trends, 1*(3).

Browne, D.R. (1984). Alternatives for local and regional radio: Three Nordic solutions. *Journal of Communication, 2*, 36–55.

Browne, D.R. (1988). What's local about local radio? *RTV Theory and Practice 3*, 122–144.

Cavalli-Sforza, F. (1978). *Remarks on citizen participation in the making of communication through local media centre.* Strasbourg: Council of Europe.

Connell, I. (1980). Television news and the social contract. In S. Hall, D. Hobson, A. Lowe, & P. Willis (Eds.), *Culture, media language* (pp. 138–158). London, Melbourne, Sydney, Auckland, Johannesburg: Hutchinson.

D'Arcy, J. (1983). An ascending progression. In D. Fisher & L.S. Harms (Eds.), *The right to communicate: A new human right.* Dublin: Poole Press.

Downing, J. (1984). *Radical media. The political experience of alternative communication.* South End Press.

Downing, J. (1988). The alternative public realm: The organization of the 1980s anti-nuclear press in West Germany and Britain. *Media Culture and Society, 2*, 163–182.

Downing, J. (n.d.). *Alternative telecommunications: PeaceNet and public data access.* Mimeo.

Downs, A. (1987). The evolution of democracy: How its axioms and institution-al forms have been adapted to changing social forces. *Daedalus*, *3*, 119–147.

Dyson, K., Humphreys, P., Negrine, R., & Simon, J-P. (1982). *Broadcasting and new media policies in Western Europe*. London: Routledge.

Emery, W.B. (1969). *National and international systems of broadcasting. Their history, operation and control*. East Lansing: Michigan State University Press.

Enzensberger, H.M. (1972). Constituents of a theory of the media. In D. McQuail (Ed.), *Sociology of mass communications* (pp. 99–116). Harmondsworth: Penguin Books.

European experiments in cable television: Local radio and video: Lessons to be learned and prospects for the future. (1977). Strasbourg: Council of Europe.

Fisher, D., & Harms, L.S. (Eds.). (1983). *The right to communicate: A new human right*. Dublin: Boole Press.

Fiske, J., & Hartley, J. (1984). *Reading television*. London and New York: Methuen.

Frissen, V. (1988). *Towards a conceptualization of heavy viewing*. Paper presented at the 16th IAMCR Conference, Barcelona, Spain.

Groombridge, B. (1972). *Television and the people. A program for democratic participation*. Harmondsworth: Penguin Books.

Habermas, J. (1983). *Teoria i praktvka*. Warszawa: PIW.

Hall, S. (1983). Culture, the media and the "ideological effect." In J. Curran, M. Gurevitch, & J. Woolacott (Eds.), *Mass communication and society* (pp. 315–348). London: Edward Arnold.

Hall, S. (1989). Ideology and communication theory. In B. Dervin, L. Grossberg, B.J. O'Keefe, & E. Wartella (Eds.), *Rethinking communication* (Vol. 1, pp. 40–52). Beverly Hills, CA: Sage Publications.

Harms, L.S. (1978). *The right to communicate and its achievement within a New World Communication Order*. Paper presented at the IAMCR Conference, Warsaw.

Harms, L.S. (1985). The Right to Communicate: What a Small World. *The Third Channel*, *2*, 158–172.

Hoffman-Riem, W. (1987). National identity and cultural values: Broadcasting safeguards. *Journal of Broadcasting and Electronic Media*, *3*, 57–72.

Jacklin, P. (1978). Representative diversity. *Journal of Communication*, *2*, 85–88.

Jakab, Z. (1989). On the institutional infrastructure of "glasnost": Centralisation and concentration of the Hungarian press. *European Journal of Communication*, *3*, 255–266.

Jakubowicz, K. (1987). Democratizing communication in Eastern Europe. *InterMedia*, *3*, 34–39.

Jakubowicz, K. (1988). To democratise communication, first democratise society. *Media Development*, *4*, 10–12.

Jakubowicz, K. (1989). *A delicate balancing act: Co-opting dissident public spheres and journalists in Poland.* Paper presented at a seminar "Journalism and the Public Sphere in the New Media Age," Dubrovnik.

Jankowski, N.W. (1988). *Community television in Amsterdam.* Amsterdam: University of Amsterdam.

Jankowski, N.W., & Mol, A.-M. (1988). Democratization of Communication and Local Radio in the Netherlands. *RTV Theory and Practice, 3,* 97–121.

Jankowski, N.W., Voos, K., & Brouwer, W. (1988). *Media in their own hands: Training citizen groups in video production techniques.* Paper presented at the IAMCR Conference, Barcelona, Spain.

Jouet, J. (1977). *Community Media and Development: Problems of Adaptation.* Working paper of the UNESCO Meeting on Self-management, Access and Participation in Communication, Belgrade.

MacBride, S. et al. (1980). *Many voices, one world.* London, New York, Paris: Kogan Page, Unipub, UNESCO.

Mattelart, A., & Piemme, J.-M. (1980). New means of communication: New questions for the Left. *Media, Culture and Society, 2,* 321–338.

McQuail, D., & van Cuilenburg, J.J. (1983). Diversity as a media policy goal: A strategy for evaluative research and a Netherlands case study. *Gazette, 3,* 145–162.

McQuail, D. (1987). *Mass communication theory. An Introduction.* Beverly Hills: Sage Publications.

Mosco, V. (1982). *Pushbutton fantasies. Critical perspectives on videotex and information technology.* Norwood, NJ: Ablex.

Mosco, V. (1983). Towards a theory of the state and telecommunications policy. *Journal of Communication, 1,* 107–124.

Mosco, V. & Wasko, J. (Eds.). (1988). *The political economy of information.* Madison: The University of Wisconsin Press.

Negrine, R., & Goodfriend, A. (1988). Public perceptions of the new media: A survey of British attitudes. *Media, Culture and Society, 3,* 303–321.

Nigg, H., & Wade, G. (1980). *Community media.* Zürich: Regenbogen-Verlag.

Partridge, S. (1982). *Not the BBC/IBA: The case for community radio.* London: Comedia.

Petersen, V.G., Prehn, O., & Svendsen, E. N. (1988). *Community radio and TV in Denmark. Breaking a monopoly or introducing new media?* Paper presented at the IAMCR conference, Barcelona, Spain.

Pool, I. de Sola. (1983). Guiding the technologies of freedom. *InterMedia, 6,* 32–39.

Rogers, E.M. (1982). Future directions in mass communication research: Towards network analysis and convergence models. In *New structures of international communication? The role of research* (pp. 122–136). Leicester: IAMCR.

Rogers, E.M. (1986). *Communication technology. The new media in society.* New York: The Free Press.

Roncagliolo, R. (1988). *Democratization of communications. An outline*. Paper presented at the IAMCR conference, Barcelona, Spain.

Signorielli, N. (1986). Selective television watching: A limited possibility. *Journal of Communication, 3,* 64–76.

Sparks, C. (1988). The popular press and political democracy. *Media, Culture and Society, 2,* 209–224.

Sreberny-Mohammadi, A. (n.d.). *Communication and democracy: Directions in research*. Leicester: IAMCR.

Szecskö, T. (1986). Theses on the democratization of communication. In *Communication and innovation: Notes from Hungary* (pp. 77–81). Budapest: Mass Communications Research Centre.

Thomas, S. (1986). Mass media and the social order. In G. Gumpert & R. Cathcart (Eds.), *Inter/media. Interpersonal communication in a media world* (pp. 611–623). New York: Oxford University Press.

Van der Haak, K. (1977). *Broadcasting in the Netherlands*. London: Routledge & Kegan Paul.

Vreg, F. (1985). Political communication and the construction of social reality. *Informatologia Yugoslavica, 1–2,* 39–45.

White, R.A. (1984). *The need for new strategies of research on the democratization of communication*. Paper presented at the ICA Conference, San Francisco, CA.

Wiio, O.A. (1977). Open and closed mass media systems and problems of international communication policy. *Studies of Broadcasting, 13,* 67–90.

Wiio, O.A. (1981). *Information and communication: A conceptual analysis*. Helsinki: University of Helsinki.

Williams, R. (1968). *Communications*. Hammondsworth: Penguin Books.

4

A Concept of Freedom of Expression for Superindustrialized Societies

Gunnar Andrén
Unit of Media and Cultural Theory
University of Stockholm

INTRODUCTION

The evolution of the forces of production and reproduction[1] during the last century comprises tendencies that will, or ought to, affect our notions about freedom of expression.

An (or the) essential aspect of contemporary history is the unprecedented rise in human productivity and the consequent transformations of individual and societal practices and patterns of behavior. In northern Europe, for instance, the effectivity of the productive forces has increased more than 15 times during the 20th century (see Maddison, 1982). This means, among other things, that nonmaterial needs, wants, and interests are coming more to the fore. When basic material needs are, or can be, satisfied, it is to an increasing extent possible for the citizens to turn their attention towards cultural enti-

---

[1] The productive forces consist of those means and powers that are used to produce things of various kinds, and the term "forces of reproduction" is used here to denote those means and powers that are used in bringing up, educating, breeding, entertaining, encouraging, etc. the persons who constitute that part of the productive forces that contains the labor power. It is clear that the mass media and cultural entities form an increasingly important part of the forces of reproduction.

ties and to be involved in the process of culture.[2] And studies of the time budgets of the citizenries of contemporary superindustrial societies indicate that the use of mass-mediated messages today is the dominant activity (see, e.g., Gahlin, 1983); so we can assume that mass communication is a main factor in the development and reproduction of the mental faculties and dispositions (beliefs, attitudes, volitions, etc.) of the human labor power.

A society is "superindustrialized" when not only the production of material goods and evils is carried out by industrial means, but also the reproduction of the citizenry and the labor force (household work, care, nursing, medical treatment, education, and other forms of establishing or preserving more or less functional beliefs and attitudes). A preliminary analysis of the concept of "industrialized activity" says that it refers to processes where (a) the sequence of actions are systematically broken down into discrete units; (b) the decomposition of the sequences of actions referred to in (a) involves an extensive division of labor; and (c) the individual units of the sequences of actions are to an increasing extent effected by nonhuman powers (machines, robots, electricity, etc.). It is then evident that, in our times, processes of culture and of reproduction are to an increasing extent performed by industrial means.

My employment of the term "superindustrial society" is, of course, a polemic against the current misnomer "postindustrial society." Another label widely used to refer to superindustrialized societies is the phrase "information society." This is, however, an apologetic and more or less misleading epithet. The standard meaning of information implies that you are informed when you have adequate answers to your questions, and it is certainly presumptuous to maintain that the mass media, databases, and so on, of contemporary superindustrialized societies to a satisfactory extent contain adequate answers to the various questions we might pose.

Of the various rights treated in political discourses and debates, and discussed within the social sciences and philosophy, freedom of the mind and of expressing the results of mental activities and endeavors belong to the rights that concern the process of culture, and as the import of culture is increasing, ethical and political concepts of this kind also become more salient. But the development of the forces of production and reproduction does not only entail a growing signifi-

---

[2] The term "cultural entity" is here used to refer to bearers of meaning that are public in a society, and the "process of culture" is accordingly the sequences of events where such entities are produced, transmitted, and recepted.

cance of freedom of expression and kindred constructs, it may also be the case that it renders traditional notions of spiritual freedom less productive. The object of this chapter is, then, to formulate a concept of freedom of expression that is adequate in relation to the conditions of contemporary superindustrialized societies, and to identify some of the factors that restrict and reduce this kind of freedom.

NEGATIVE AND POSITIVE FREEDOM

"Freedom" is a dear term, so it is only natural that it has been used, and misused, in many ways; there are several more or less divergent concepts and kinds of freedom, which may be classified along different lines. However, the different notions of freedom are as a rule internally related to the concept of power. Power can be considered as the kernel of freedom; the basic meaning of "freedom" is that a person is free if he or she can do what he or she[3] wants to do.[4] This elemental definition is the foundation of the subsequent discussion on freedom of expression, and it will be referred to several times, so let us put it as a formula:

$F1$ A person, is *free* = $_{df}$ he can do what he wants to do.

$F1$ implies the following definition of "freedom of expression":

$FE1$ A person enjoys *freedom of expression* = $_{df}$ she may make known whatever she wants to make known.

"Power" is a paradigmatic example of a continuous variable, and consequently the same is true of "freedom." Let us first consider that concept of freedom that seems to be least demanding.

The power of a person is determined by internal as well as external factors. If you are imprisoned, you probably cannot do what you want to do, but the same is also true when, for instance, you are frightened by internalized conventions and therefore do not dare to follow your wants or desires, or when you are weakened by a disease. No one

---

[3] Instead of using circumstantial phrases like "he or she" and "her or his" I will in the sequel alternate between feminine and masculine nouns.

[4] John Locke, who was a founding father of liberalism, the political tradition wherein freedom is the cardinal value, wrote that liberty consists of "a power to act or to forbear acting, and in that only" (Locke, 1689/1964, p. 170).

would deny that you are impoverished by the chains, the conventions, or the malady, but according to the minimal conception of freedom, it is *only* external and societal elements like the chains that impair your freedom. This notion of equating freedom with freedom from societal preventions and restrictions plays a prominent role in Western individualism and liberalism, and it implies that the definition of freedom just contains one negative clause:[5]

> *F2*   A person, P, is *free* = $_{df}$ P's actions are not constrained by another person or by any societal authority or institution.

This gives us the following definition of "freedom of expression":

> *FE2* A person, P, enjoys *freedom of expression* = $_{df}$ P's efforts to make known his opinions or attitudes are not constrained by another person or by any societal authority or institution.

We can directly see that F2 and FE2 are more inclusive than F1 and FE1: When someone is free or enjoys freedom of expression according to *F1* or *FE1*, she also enjoys the kinds of freedom defined by *F2* or *FE2*, but the reverse does not hold. Thus F2 and FE2 do not cover the basic intuitions captured by *F1* and *FE1*. F2 and FE2 do not give us an adequate picture of the ideal of freedom.

The concept defined by *F2* is called negative freedom (cf. Berlin, 1958), since it refers to a freedom *from* something; it is not a notion that directly or by itself mentions the possession of certain capacities or faculties. One reason why individualists and liberals can be content with a negative notion of freedom is, we may conjecture, that they cherish an optimistic assumption which says that if an individual is not constrained by external forces and bonds, he will have the powers to further his interests and to promote his ends in satisfactory ways.

Others—and in this camp we will find collectivists of different kinds, conservatives as well as socialists—argue that freedom in the

---

[5] In the canonical text of contemporary liberalism, *On Liberty*, J.S. Mill presupposes a definition of this kind. In the introduction to the book he delineates the subject of the treatise as "the nature and limit of the power which can be legitimately exercised by society over the individual" (Mill, 1962, p. 126).

negative sense does not necessarily lead to that kind of freedom which is an obvious societal goal (i.e., the power of the citizens to further their goals or interests). This line of thought implies that the definiens of *F2* states a necessary but not sufficient condition for freedom. A set of conditions for freedom that, according to intuitions of the positive kind, could be considered as jointly sufficient, says that a free agent has certain definite opinions, attitudes, and desires that can rightly be said to be her own and that she has the capacities or resources to act, or to forbear from acting, in accordance with these opinions, attitudes, or desires. Thus I propose the following definition:

F3   A person, P, is *free* = df   (i) P has consciously developed evaluations, norms and wants of his own;

(ii) P knows how his evaluations, norms, and wants could be satisfied;

(iii) P has the capacities and opportunities to act in accordance with the knowledge referred to in (ii) in order to satisfy his evaluations, norms, and wants.

F3 suggests a definition of "freedom of expression" that implies that a person enjoys this kind of freedom when she has definite opinions and wants that she is also able and has the opportunity to express.

FE3   A person, p, enjoys *freedom of expression* = df   (i) P has consciously developed opinions and wants of his own;

(ii) P knows how to express his own opinions and wants in an adequate way;

(iii) P has access to media where he may express his opinions and wants.

In many contexts the problem is not whether a given person is free in a general sense, but if she is free to perform or forbear from a certain action, and by being relativized to particular actions *F3* and *FE3* are naturally expounded in the following ways:

F4   A person, P, is *free* to do action A = df   (i) it is physically possible for P to do A;

(ii) P knows that A is a possible alternative for him;

(iii) P has consciously developed evaluations, norms, and wants of his own that pertain to A;

(iv) P knows how his evaluations, norms, and wants
pertaining to A could be
satisfied;

(v) P has the mental capacities and material re-
sources neccessary for attempts to do A or to forbear
from doing A;

(vi) if P chooses to do A,
nothing will prevent him
from trying to do A.

FE4 A person, P, is *free to express* her opinions and attitudes on a
certain issue, I = $_{df}$ (i) it is physically pos-
sible for P to express her opinions and attitudes on I (this means i.e., that there are
one or several media where she may express
her opinions and attitudes on I);

(ii) P knows that the expressing of her opinions
and attitudes on I is a possible alternative;

(iii) P has consciously developed evaluations,
norms, and wants that pertain to the option
of expressing her opinions and attitudes on
I in a mass medium;

(iv) P knows how her evaluations, norms, and
wants that pertain to the expressing of her
opinions and attitudes on I in a mass medium could be satisfied;

(v) P has the mental capacities and material
resources which are necessary for attempts
to express her opinions and attitudes on I in
a mass medium;

(vi) if P chooses to express her opinions and attitudes on I in a mass medium, nothing will
prevent her from trying to do so.

FE3 and *FE4* are explications of that elemental and original notion
of freedom of expression, *FE1*, which expresses an attractive and increasingly important societal goal. However, freedom of expression is
not so interesting in itself. Even though it may, in some cases, for
therapeutic reasons be satisfying just to express one's beliefs and attitudes, the point of expressing oneself is, in general, to communicate
with others and to influence them in specific ways. Thus the idea of

freedom of expression should be incorporated within a more general concept that has to do with the citizen's "power to communicate," a concept that could be built upon *FE3* in the following way:

> *CP A person has communicative power* to the extent that he (i) has consciously developed opinions and attitudes of his own; (ii) he knows how to express his opinions and attitudes in adequate ways; (iii) he has access to media where he can express his opinions and attitudes; (iv) by (iii) he can reach a large and/or influential audience or a particular audience which he wants to influence; (v) by (iv) he will, in fact, influence the opinions, attitudes, or behaviors of other citizens in accordance with his intentions.[6]

THE NEED FOR FREEDOM OF EXPRESSION

Human beings must move around in order to collect and acquire what they require. And we are societal beings who must cooperate with others in order to make a living. Thus information, knowledge, and communication are basic needs for all humans, and the definitions above delineate important human requirements. If they are not satisfied, we cannot further our goals and interests adequately and consequently we may not fare well.

The three different notions of negative freedom, positive freedom, and power to communicate form an order of needs and of corresponding rights. Negative freedom is a prerequisite for positive freedom, which in turn is a condition for communicative power. So if we look at the issue of freedom of expression from a historical point of view, it is natural that we will find that it was freedom of expression in the negative sense that was first taken up in political arguments and struggles. In all times censorship has been a powerful instrument in the hands of different kinds of rulers and tyrants, by which it has been possible for them to obstruct, more or less effectively, opposition and societal evolution. One of the main objects of oppositional movements has accordingly been to have censorship modified or abandoned.

John Milton is usually regarded as the founder of the claim for freedom of expression. He wrote several defenses of the revolt against Charles I, and his writings are a blend of puritanism and Christian

---

[6] This definition can be seen as one possible explication of the notion of the citizen's "communication potential," discussed in Thunberg, Nowak, Rosengren, and Sigurd (1982).

humanism, as is well evidenced by what he says is *Areopagitica* (1644) on the nature and power of the printed word:

> For Books are not absolutely dead things, but do contain a potencie of life in them to be as active as that soule was whose progency they are; nay they do preserve as a violl the purest efficace and extraction of that living intellect that bred them. I know they are as lively, and as vigorously productive, as those fabulous Dragons teeth; and being sown up and down, may chance to spring up armed men. And yet on the other hand unless wariness be us'd, as good almost kill a Man as kill a good Book; who kills a Man kills a reasonable creature, God's Image; but hee who destroys a good Booke, kills reason it 'selfe, kills the Image of God, as it were in the eye. (p. 492)

Milton's claim for freedom of expression has been considered a response to the cultural evolution that was a result of the invention of the technology of printing. He belonged to the rising bourgeoisie that demanded the setting up of rights for the use of the new technical means for communicating their ideas and interests. The bourgeoisie's striving for power or freedom was in many countries entirely successful, and today negative freedom of expression belongs to the defining characteristics of liberal democracies of the Western kind.

The victory of the bourgeoisie has many facets. It was not only the case that its members won negative freedom of expression; they also acquired a position from which it was possible for them to satisfy the conditions of the definition of positive freedom of expression (*FE3*). They developed an ideology and a Weltanschauung of their own (cf. condition (i) of *FE3*). They established an educational system that reproduced the beliefs and attitudes contained in the ideational systems referred to in the preceding sentence and taught young and aspiring citizens how to express such opinions in attractive and opportune fashions (cf. condition (ii) of *FE3*). And last but not least they developed[7] a system for mass or industrial communication which is to a large extent controlled or dominated by institutions or economic interests allied to the bourgoisie (cf. condition (iii) of *FE3*).

The political evolution sometimes referred to as the bourgeois revolution has meant that at the same time as almost the entire citizenry has been granted negative freedom of expression, only a segment of it enjoys positive freedom of expression to a satisfactory extent. This is

---

[7] The phrases "they developed" and "they established" are not very felicitous in this context, as they indicate that individual persons first formulate precise plans and then consciously act in order to realize them. These are convenient but certainly simplistic, individualistic and misleading ways of describing complex societal processes.

due to a variety of factors, economic as well as cultural, which are related to the different clauses that constitute the definiens of *FE3*. But here I confine the discussion to two factors inherent in the system of mass communication itself. One of these concerns the inner or mental aspect of power and freedom to communicate, while the other point regards the outer and economic aspect of cultural freedom and power.

OBSTACLES TO CULTURAL POWER AND FREEDOM

The first condition in the general definitions of positive freedom and of freedom of expression (*F3* and *FE3*) says that a free person has consciously developed opinions and attitudes of her own, that she is an autonomous agent. Autonomy has much to do with ego-strength and self-assuredness, and these are certainly phenomena that can be reinforced or weakened in social processes like those of mass communications and culture.

To be a free and autonomous person, and to be a person who enjoys freedom of expression in the positive sense, is to be an individual who has something he himself wants to do or to express, and this implies that freedom of expression, as it is defined by *FE3* and *FE4*, can only be enjoyed by an individual who has certain definite beliefs and attitudes that are integrated in his personality. We can also assume that the richer an individual's personality is, the more likely it is that she will turn out to be a person who enjoys positive freedom of expression to a satisfactory extent.

For a person to develop, entertain, and express definite beliefs and attitudes of his own, and not just reproduce those that he meets in his social environment or considers opportune, is an active undertaking that presupposes more or less considerable funds of autonomy, maturity, and in certain cases even courage. These are virtues that tend to be weakened by insecurity and depreciations. For instance, if a person continuously receives messages to the effect that she belongs to a group whose members are insignificant or of less import or inferior worth, this is likely to undermine her powers to act and argue in accordance with her own interests, beliefs, and attitudes. And a repudiation of this kind is precisely what is communicated to a majority of the citizens by means of patterns in the contents of the mass media.

Our attentiveness is limited; it is a scarce resource. Accordingly we tend to pay attention to what we consider significant or important. Thus a simple but productive method of enveloping societal valuations concerning the import of persons belonging to different classes or groups is to observe how often and for how long they speak, are depicted or otherwise occur in radio and television programs, newspapers, magazines, books, and so on. The contents of these mass media form an ideational or cultural environment that fosters certain beliefs, attitudes, and other dispositions in the citizenry. And it is well evidenced in a multitude of studies that majority groups like ordinary wage earners and women are highly underrepresented in the cultural environment (see, e.g., Signorielli, 1984).

Repudiations of large strata of the population by means of patterns of underrepresentation in the cultural environment is for several reasons relevant in the present context. First, it seems reasonable to assume that these patterns cultivate ego weakness and heteronomy among those groups subjected to this form of cultural disparagement. Their members are ignored and it becomes less likely that they will meet model characters who may function as positive objects of identification, and accordingly these patterns of underrepresentation to some extent obstruct the satisfaction of the first condition of freedom of expression (in the general sense defined by *FE3*) and of communicative power. Second, repudiative patterns of culture make it natural for large strata of the population to take it for granted that it is not for them to express their opinions and attitudes. The alternative of doing so does not readily come to mind, and thus the second condition of *FE4* is, to a varying extent, not realized.

So far patterns of underrepresentation, and the valuations inherent in them, have been taken as factors that reduce the freedom of expression and communicative power of ordinary citizens, but they can of course also be considered as indicators of other obstacles to their freedom of expression. The fact that manual workers constitute around 57 percent of the population in Sweden but are responsible for only 7 percent of the speech acts in Swedish television[8] strongly suggests that their freedom of expression (in the positive sense) and communicative power are somehow restricted.

The inequalities pertaining to people's possibilities and propensities to proclaim their views and positions in public media are, of course, based upon other inequalities. Some of these are, like the one already taken up, of a mental or cultural kind—they have to do with education, attitudes, wants, personal tastes, manners and customs,

---

[8] These figures apply to 1982. The data on Swedish television have kindly been forwarded to us by Hans Strand at the Center for Mass Communication Research at the University of Stockholm, and they derive from his ongoing project on linguistic communication and interaction on television.

and so on, while others are of a more material or economic kind. It can be conjectured that, in many instances, economic circumstances determine, to a considerable extent, a person's cultural capital and his propensities for different kinds of values and activities, but we can also assume that cultural patterns and circumstances in many cases tend to cement and act as justifying reasons for established material conditions and inequalities.

Thus we may assume that there exist causal interactions and interdependencies between the economic and cultural systems of a society. These interactions occur at different levels. In the preceding paragraph we saw that they exist on personal and political levels—the cultural inclinations and practices of an individual are to a certain extent determined by her position in the economic system, and economic inequalities may be motivated or rationalized by reference to cultural differences. But interactions between the cultural and the economic fields of a society can also occur at the systemic level. And the most pronounced examples of the interrelationship between the economic and cultural systems are advertising and related phenomena like sponsoring.

In Western societies the main financing of mass communications and hence of culture in the wide sociological meaning of the term comes from advertising. And accordingly advertising influences the mass media in several ways—the principal fact here being, of course, that the advertisements form a large segment of the content of the mass media and hence make up a considerable sector of the cultural environment, but advertising certainly also influences the mass media in other indirect ways (cf. Curran, 1981; Lappalainen, 1988). This interaction between the economic and cultural fields via advertising is relevant in this context, as it affects the amount and distribution of freedom of expression (as defined by *FE3* and *FE4*) and of communicative powers within the citizenry.

Advertising can be seen as a predemocratic form of communication, and to the extent that it influences the entire cultural system the same holds for that sphere as well. In a way advertising reminds us of an early stage in that evolution of polity that has led to contemporary democracy of the parliamentary or representative form. Before there existed a common and equal right to vote and to be elected to the political assemblies, it was only possible for those who belonged to a certain sex and who had enough property to cast their votes or to be elected. The political powers of the citizens were directly related to the amount of capital and property in their possession. In much the same way as political power has been an aspect of economic power, the cultural power to communicate and to influence the content of mass media via advertising is today an aspect of financial power. Furthermore it may be conjectured that advertising not only influences the editorial contents of the mass media but also the audience's way of receiving and interpreting mass media contents. The editorial contents must compete with the advertisements for the receivers' attention. And it is one thing to receive texts and pictures that occur alongside with, and are partly financed by, messages whose form and content is determined by their object to persuade the receivers to buy various commodities and services, and quite another thing to receive texts and pictures that are not framed and financed in that way. It can be assumed that the fact that the cultural system is mingled with obviously biased and nonobjective messages will, in different ways, affect the citizens' attitudes towards the contents of culture—the standards used when assessing their tenability may be loosened, the media may appear as less reliable, and so on. And the ideas, images, and meaning patterns of advertising form a considerable part of that ideational horizon or background, which guides or determines our interpretations of and reactions to messages of other kinds.

Thus advertising influences the citizens' communicative freedom and powers in different ways. It increases or decreases their possibilities to act as senders, but it also affects the responses of the audiences to noncommercial messages and, in that way, it may restrict the senders' possibilities to influence the audience in accordance with their intentions.[9]

REFERENCES

Berlin, I. (1958). *Two concepts of liberty*. Oxford: Clarendon Press.

Curran, J. (1981). The impact of advertising on the British mass media. *Media, Culture and Society*, 3(1), 43–69.

Gahlin, A. (1983). *Dagliga aktiviteter*. Stockholm: Sveriges Radio.

Lappalainen, T. (1988). Cultural functionalism: The function of the press for economic power relations. *European Journal of Communication*, 3(4), p. 375–396.

Locke, J. (1964). *An essay concerning human understanding*. (Abridged and edited with an introduction by A.D. Woozley.) London: Fontana/Collins. (Original work published 1689).

Maddison, A. (1982). *Phases of capitalist development*. Oxford: Oxford University Press.

---

[9] Slavko Splichal read an earlier version of this chapter and made several useful comments.

Mill, J.S. (1962). *On liberty*. (John Stuart Mill: Utilitarianism, On Liberty, Essay on Bentham together with selected writings of Jeremy Bentham and John Austin. Edited with an introduction by Mary Warnock.) London: Collins (The Fontana Library). (Original work published 1859).

Milton, J. (1959). *Areopagitica*. (Complete Prose Works of John Milton, volume II.) New Haven: Yale University Press. (Original work published 1644).

Signorielli, N. (1984). The demography of the television world. In G. Melishek, K.E. Rosengren & J. Stappers (Eds.), *Cultural indicators* (pp. 137–157). Wien: Akademie der Wissenschaften.

Thunberg, A.-M., Nowak, K., Rosengren, K.E., & Sigurd, B. (1982). *Communication and Equality*. Stockholm: Almqvist & Wiksell.

5

Raymond Williams and the Theory of Democratic Communication

Colin Sparks
PCL School of Communication
London

INTRODUCTION

"No questions are more difficult than those of democracy" (Williams, 1976, p. 86), said Raymond Williams in his *Vocabulary of Culture and Society*. His work undoubtedly forms one of the most systematic and impressive attempts to construct a theory of democratic communication which has ever been produced in the English language. In both his critique of the existing systems of communication—in particular, "mass communication"—and in his proposals for the development of alternative forms of communication, Williams was concerned to establish democracy as a central and guiding principle. This effort led him to confront some of the major theoretical problems facing the idea of democratic communication in the modern age. Williams demonstrated how the dominant theories of mass communication contained anti-democratic propositions as part of their fundamental definitions. He provided a rationale for the equal right of all forms of human communication and an account of the historical development that had led to the privileging of some forms over others. Finally, he put forward concrete proposals as to how democratic communication might be made into a human reality. This chapter explores these features of Williams's work in some detail before asking how far they fit the demands of contemporary reality.

In the manner that was characteristic of much of his work, Williams traced the evolution of the various meanings of "democracy" from its doubtful origins in Antiquity through its evolution as a term with negative connotations, to its current status as the term which is claimed by almost all political tendencies as their own peculiar property. In particular, he identified two important shifts in the term that had radically changed its substantive content. The first of these occurred in what became the U.S., between the Rhode Island Constitution of 1641—in which the exercise of sovereign power was the immediate collective prerogative of "the body of freemen"—and Hamilton, in 1777, for whom this power was vested in individuals selected by the people to act on their behalf (Williams, 1976, p. 84). The second, and more general, shift of sense was the way in which, from around the middle of the last century onwards, the dominant discourse surrounding the term shifted from a negative to a positive valuation (Williams, 1976, p. 83).

These two parameters of current usage had, in Williams' view, led the term to a state of extraordinary confusion:

> To the positive opposed senses of the socialist and liberal traditions we have to add, in a century which unlike any other finds nearly all political movements claiming to stand for democracy or real democracy, innumerable conscious distortions: reduction of the concepts of election, representation, and mandate to deliberate formalities or merely manipulated forms; reduction of the concept of popular power, or government in the popular interest, to nominal slogans covering the rule of a bureaucracy or an oligarchy. It would sometimes be easier to believe in democracy, or to stand for it, if the C19 change had not happened and it were still an unfavourable or factional term. (Williams, 1976, p. 86)

Nevertheless, Williams did, throughout his life, remain someone who persistently and publicly refused the distortions and who believed in and stood for democracy. The struggle for democracy was, of course, part of his general political commitment, and it served to mark him off sharply from both sets of ideologues of the Cold War, of whose particular and partial definitions he was indiscriminately scathing [1]. However, this democratic determination was not merely a compartmentalized aspect of his life as a political thinker, separate from his scholarly work. On the contrary, in this chapter we see how that commitment to democracy was a central part of his theory of culture and communication. Neither the general project in which he was engaged, nor the particular inflections of his arguments within the field, can be considered apart from his democratic concerns[2].

"THERE ARE IN FACT NO MASSES"

The critique of the notion of "mass communication" was central to Williams' overall project of establishing a theory of democratic communication for three reasons. In the first place, as he observed, the term "mass" is another of those common-sense words that carries with it a long and tortuous history. In particular, it signaled one of the ways of thinking about the social structure of modern societies that tended to dehumanize the industrial working class created by the de-

---

[1] As a socialist thinker, Williams was naturally scathing of the extent to which capitalism was able to satisfy democratic criteria: "The aspiration to control the general directions of our economic life is an essential element of democratic growth, but is still very far from being realized. . . . It is difficult to feel that we are really governing ourselves if in so central a part of our lives as our work most of us have no share in the decisions that immediately affect us," he wrote in *The Long Revolution* (Williams, 1961a, pp. 305–306). He was, however, almost equally critical of the Russian model, writing in *May Day Manifesto 1968* that "the remaking of Soviet society remains urgent, and in expressing our opposition to its disciplinary and manipulative features we are also expressing support for, and confidence in, the growing volume of democratic criticism within that society" (Williams, 1968a, p. 142). More generally, his mature position was that: "socialist democracy must be the direct exercise of popular power. It can have no other meaning. In the sense that it is also historically the oldest meaning of democracy, it is reasonable to speak of it in very early periods of socialist or even pre-socialist struggle, as well as in the perspective of an emerging socialist system of the future. The key emphasis must fall on the direct exercise of popular power. . . . The conventional opposition between democracy and socialism, democracy and Marxism, is now extremely damaging to the left. It is precisely in showing, against it, that socialist democracy is not only qualitatively different from capitalist democracy, but is quite clearly more democratic, that the whole future of the left will lie" (Williams, 1979a, p. 426).

[2] We cannot, in the space of one brief chapter, summarize the whole of Williams's complex and changing thought. There is a developing body of material which outlines Williams's overall intellectual project, of which the most recent, and most immediately approachable, is A. O'Connor's *Raymond Williams* (1989a). This contains a fair summary of the main points of his development, and also contains a very valuable bibliography of works by and on Williams.

velopment of modern capitalist industry and housed in the modern city. To use categories like "mass communication," "mass civilization," and "mass democracy" was, whether one willed it or not, to take a position in a complex set of discriminations in which one counterposed the cultural life and values of one group of people against that of the majority of the inhabitants of a modern society. For Williams, "masses" was a term used to describe the unknown other, and its limitations could easily be understood if one asked the question: "Who are the masses?" The answer was obvious: "The masses are always the others, whom we don't know, and can't know. . . . To other people we are also masses. Masses are other people. . . . There are in fact no masses: there are only ways of seeing people as masses" (Williams, 1963, p. 289).

Secondly, and deriving more or less directly from this critique, Williams identified a particular problem in the field of "mass communication." This tended to define the canonical objects of study as those produced for the mass by other people. The popular newspaper, the cinema film, broadcast radio, and television are the central concerns of the field of the study of mass communication. Williams was not concerned to deny the obvious facts that these phenomena existed or that they were an important part of contemporary reality that deserved serious study, but to ask whether the dominant conceptual framework for thinking about them, and the vocabulary and assumptions habitually employed in their discussions, were either adequate or appropriate to illuminate their true role. The usual terms suppose a central and elite group of producers who generate material consumed by others, geographically and socially remote from the originators. In that, they reproduce, not merely in their vocabulary but in the underlying theory of the place and nature of communication in society, the negative and antidemocratic associations of the term "mass" itself. Against this conception, Williams argued that the new institutions of communications were not a product of working people themselves, but produced for them by others, usually for profit. The actual radical newspapers and other cultural artifacts produced by working people for themselves were invariably very significantly different from commercial "mass culture" (Williams, 1963, p. 296). What he called the "structures of feeling" informing the works of different classes, even when articulated in an identical medium like television, would tend to be radically different (O'Connor, 1989b, p. 172).

Built into the practice of mass communication, and thus to ways of thinking about it, was, Williams argued, the idea of communication as manipulation. Certainly, what he termed the technologies of multiple transmission were and are important social realities and important sites of investigation, but they were "at worst neutral" (Williams, 1963, p. 290). They could be put to uses that tended to produce and reproduce relations of domination or they could be put to uses which tended toward equality and emancipation: The proper focus of concern was over the ends to which they were put rather than their technical properties (Williams, 1974, *passim*; 1983, pp. 128–152).

Central to this conception of the major media of communication as sites of social practices was the notion of intention, which Williams found to be quite absent from the classic definitions of the study of mass communication. He contrasted the strengths of the interpretative traditions of the "cultural sciences" with the dominant definition of "mass communication," to the detriment of the latter:

> Cultural science, when it emerged as a method in early classical sociology, was concerned with the necessary differentiation of its procedures from those of the natural sciences. In its central concept of "understanding," and in its sensitivity to the problems of judgement of value and of the participation and involvement of the investigator, it was radically different from the assumptions and methods of the "sociology of mass communications" which is now orthodox and which at times even claims the authority of just this classical sociology. The change can be seen in one simple way, in the formula which was established by Lasswell as the methodological principle of studies of communication: the question "who says what, how, to whom, with what effect?" For what this question has excluded is *intention*, and therefore all real social and cultural process. (Williams, 1974, p. 119)

The innocent term "mass," functioning here in what appears to be a merely descriptive sense to distinguish certain technologies of distribution, is in fact part of a strategy whereby critical enquiry about the concrete social content of particular forms of communication is abstracted from the problems under consideration and the categories of an allegedly neutral science are derived directly from common sense. The examples Williams cites of this are indeed familiar and central ones from the sociology of mass communication: studies of the effects on the audience of representations of violence on TV and studies of the effects of TV on political behavior (Williams, 1974, pp. 122–126). It is difficult not to agree with his overall conclusion that whatever partial illuminations such studies may have produced they are conducted within a view of communication that rests upon a largely unproblematized and unexamined set of social relations (Carey, 1977).

This tendency to abstract the nature of communication from the actual social relations in which it is lived points to Williams' third major criticism of the tradition of "mass communication." In the process of abstraction, the real history and proportions of the development of communication tends to be lost sight of: The mass media, in their developed modern forms, become the central and exclusive model and site of investigation. This limitation was most sharply exposed by Williams in his alternative account of the development of the press. The dominant tendency of "press history" is to see the modern newspaper as the end result of a teleological project embodied in the first products of Gutenberg's press. There is, undeniably, an important sense in which the daily newspaper has a history, a continuity, and a development that can, in Britain at least, be traced back for around 200 years. However, even these continuities tend to be overestimated: The nature and place of *The Times* in the life of its rather small number of readers in 1789 was rather different from that which it occupies at the present. What is more, the concentration upon this type of publication not only gives us an unrealistic conception of the history of the daily newspaper but it obscures other forms of publication that have played at least as important a part in the overall development of the press. Williams' most detailed account of this alternative history stressed that the popular Sunday press had, from the first quarter of the 19th century both reached the largest number of readers and consistently pioneered the forms and types of journalism that were to come to dominate the daily press (Williams, 1961a, pp. 173–313). The sources of the characteristic content of the modern popular press were to be found in the older, preindustrial forms of popular culture rather than in the supposed relative degeneracy of the new working class. The decisive passage, for Williams, was the mechanism by which these popular forms, which had been an integral part of an emergent radical culture, were isolated and transformed in the process of the establishment of modern capitalist society. To isolate the development of the press from other contemporary forms of cultural activity and social life leads to a misunderstanding of that history. The early radical newspaper, which was produced by and for people with quite different interests and situations, is seen simply as the precursor of the modern commercial "popular press" (Williams, 1978, p. 41).

For all of these reasons, it was, for Williams, impossible to construct any theory of democratic communication with a starting point in the conception of "mass" in its modern form. As he put it, sharply but distinctively: "In most of its uses masses is a cant word" (Williams, 1976, p. 163). Communication, and communications, were at the very center of Williams' intellectual project, but throughout his long engagement with the problems they posed he was never willing to reduce them to "mass communication." Quite apart from the problems of usage that we have detailed above, there was an additional difficulty: Many of the forms of communication with which Williams was centrally concerned, and that formed the substance of a number of his most detailed investigations, were not "mass communication" at all. On the contrary, Williams was at least as interested in what we can allow the names of "art and literature" as he was in television or the press, and it is to his position on these that we must now turn.

"CULTURE IS ORDINARY"

Raymond Williams began his academic career as an undergraduate student of English Literature at Cambridge and ended it as Professor of Drama at the same university. These biographical facts in themselves go some way to explaining why, for Williams, the field of communication was wider and more complex than that of the mass media alone. It is, however, important to recall that the particular inflection of English Literature that Williams encountered in October 1939 was that associated with F.R. Leavis, which was, along with Marxism, one of the "two serious influences" he claimed to have retained respect for despite later disagreements (Williams, 1958, p. 7). There is no doubt that this form of literary analysis influenced Williams very deeply indeed and can be seen, for example, in both his conception of the tradition with which he was dealing in *Culture and Society 1780–1950* and in his handling of particular figures within it (Williams, 1979a, pp. 123–126). There is no space here to explore in detail the nature of Leavis' thought, but we must briefly indicate the major ways in which it was important in defining the nature of Williams' project. For Leavis literature was primarily and essentially an articulation of experience, and that literature was best which embodied the richest and fullest "life." The mass media were important because in modern society they were among the major mechanisms whereby something other than the best was widely disseminated[3].

The problem with Leavis' account of cultural life was that while it rested in theory on an "anthropological" account of culture as a social process, it tended in practice to rest very heavily upon a series of restrictive "aesthetic," or "literary-moral" judgments of particular artifacts. Programmatically, Leavis was committed to the proposition that: "A culture expressing itself in a tradition of literature and art. . . . can be in a healthy state only if this tradition is in a living relation with a real culture, shared by the people at large" (Leavis, 1932, p. 169). However, he could also begin one of his major critical works with the flat statement that: "The great English novelists are Jane Austen, George Eliot, Henry James, and Joseph Conrad" and go on to argue it is necessary to concentrate on these few really great writers (Leavis, 1967, pp. 1–3). Leavis in practice operated with a thoroughly antidemocratic theory of communication. One of the uses to which this theory was put was to attempt to develop, both as a body of ideas and an educational practice, the habits of discrimination that could arm the reader against the pernicious influences of the mass media: They were one of the key agencies by means of which the conditions for a living culture were being daily eroded (Masterman, 1985, pp. 38–70).

Williams' reaction to this was to attempt to democratize the project by returning to the emphasis on the relationship, indeed identity, between the whole of cultural life and the society in and through which it was articulated. This was the reason for his stress upon the "anthropological" definition of culture which was so marked in the "Conclusion" of *Culture and Society 1780–1959* and in *The Long Revolution* (Hall, 1980, pp. 18–19). His famous claim that "a culture is not only a body of intellectual and imaginative work; it is also and essentially a whole way of life" was in its immediate terms a formulation to which Leavis could have acceded (Williams, 1963, p. 312). It went be-

---

[3] Assessments of Leavis and his journal, *Scrutiny*, abound and differ. The major critical work, F. Mulhearn's *The Moment of Scrutiny* (Mulhearn, 1979), is, to this writer's mind, excessively sympathetic but is certainly right in arguing that "*Scrutiny* had opened up an educational space within which the cultural institutions of bourgeois-democratic capitalism could be subjected to critical analysis—a space which was to be utilized to remarkable effect, most notably by Raymond Williams and the Centre for Contemporary Cultural Studies founded by Richard Hoggart at Birmingham University" (Mulhearn, 1979, p. 329).

yond him to the extent that it was also embedded in a theory of how far any understanding of the contours of a "body of intellectual and imaginative work" was the product of a particular historical situation. Every self-evident "tradition" in cultural analysis—for example, the one in the English novel cited from Leavis above, was essentially a "selective tradition" in which: "In a society as a whole . . . the cultural tradition can be seen as a continual selection and re-selection of ancestors" (Williams, 1961a, p. 52).

However, Williams was also centrally concerned with the fact that within "society as a whole" there were differential social positions: Different classes have different access to education, to leisure, and to the means of cultural consumption: "It is impossible to discuss communication or culture in our society without in the end coming to discuss power" (Williams, 1961b, p. 19). The emphasis upon "the best" and "the greatest" in culture was in itself often an emphasis upon a class position rather than upon a truth about culture. There was little or no evidence that "minority culture" was better than "mass culture," and the former was too often compromised by its own exclusivity (Williams, 1962, p. 73).

Cultures other than those of elite and privileged minority groups could not be judged with the methods and by the standards developed for minority culture. On the contrary, other cultures would have a radically different structure and be organized and articulated in quite different ways. In particular, the cultural life of the modern working class was primarily not embodied in "proletarian" novels or poems or paintings. Williams claimed that the working class had not "produced a culture in the narrower sense" but "collective democratic institutions": "working class culture, in the stage through which it has been passing, is primarily social. . .rather than individual" (Williams, 1963, p. 314). For Williams, particular cultural artifacts and the particular institutional forms in which cultural production and reproduction took place were articulations of whole ways of life and thus embodied ways of thinking and feeling about the world, or what he called a "structure of feeling." This was primarily a communicative reality and thus the study of human communication was central, not only to the study of culture, but to the study of society: "What we call society is not only a network of political and economic arrangements, but also a process of learning and communication" (Williams, 1962, p. 13). But to assert this centrality, and to proclaim the democratic essence of communication is one thing: To provide a theoretical account is another. Williams did indeed attempt such a task, and it to that which we must now turn.

"COMMUNICATION IS THE CRUX OF ART"

Art and communication are normally considered, in British culture at least, as terms inhabiting rather different planes. "Art" is usually thought of in terms of a special creative kind of human activity while "communication" is conceived of as the transmission of the known and established. In order to justify a democratic theory of culture, Williams found it necessary to try to elaborate a theory of art as communicative. Only on this basis would it be possible to justify the notion that the whole of human life and activity needed to be given the same detailed and close attention as the products of one minor and privileged grouping. His argument, resting upon the work of a biologist, J.Z. Young, was that it was a universal feature of the human mind that it needs to learn how to perceive the world. While for the animal world this was a fixed acquisition of a relatively static set of rules of perception, in the case of human beings, learning and relearning were processes which extended over time and were always changing. In this sense, all human beings are creative in that they continually make and remake the world for themselves and for each other. The very fact that this process of learning is a social process meant for Williams that it was also a process of communication, universal in human society and without which humanity is unthinkable.

As human beings develop they constantly encounter new experiences, which they can only think about within the forms of communication. The arts, then, are "certain intense forms of general communication" which differ in degree but not in kind from the normal human activities of experiencing, communicating, and remaking the world (Williams, 1961, p. 25). This general feature of art might in one time and place involve the communication of the known and settled features of a society and in another might be concerned with the new and the innovative, but in both cases "art comes to us as part of our actual growth, not entering a 'special area' of the mind, but acting on and interacting with our whole personal and social organisation" (Williams, 1961, p. 33). If art, since the collapse of widespread religious belief the most reified and abstracted of human activities, shares with the humblest of human labors it very essential nature, then the same must be true of all other specialized types of thinking and feeling. This is, of course, a radical argument for human equality: as Williams put it not an equality of achievement but an "equality of being" (Williams, 1963, p. 305).

Any set of social relations that crippled this equality of being, and that arrogated the rights of communication in one area or another to a particular group or class, was a mechanism for crippling human creative power. Historically, the modern systems of "mass communication" have played precisely the role of restricting and controlling access to the right to communication, and we now examine Williams' own typology of such systems.

"COMMUNICATION IS THE RECORD OF HUMAN GROWTH"

The development of the modern world was, according to Williams, characterized by a "long revolution." This involved the obvious transformations of the industrial revolution, the expansion of democratic control over social life, and the wider dissemination of modern communications, but it was at bottom concerned with the development of human potential (Williams, 1961, p. 121). In the process of this development various systems of "mass communication" had been evolved, all of which, Williams argued, were inadequate by the standard of the maximization of human potential.

In his most direct and systematic attempt to provide an account of the shortcomings of existing systems of communication, Williams was motivated at least in part by a desire to provide the groundwork for a future reform of the media as part of social reconstruction, and consequently his analysis of the present is accompanied by a model of a new, democratic system of communication (Williams, 1979a, pp. 369–370). The starting point of his analysis is a familiar enough one: He identifies the "Authoritarian" system in which "communications are seen as part of the total machine through which a minority governs a society" (Williams, 1962, p. 91). Unlike some other theorists, however, he did not identify this as a product of an older form of political organization—for example, the absolute state—but argued that it was a form that persisted in modern society because of the fact that it is an appropriate form of organization for those groups whose goal it is to maintain their own minority power. More radically innovative was his second category, of "paternal" systems, which he defined as "an authoritarian system with a conscience" (Williams, 1962, p. 90). Many, if not most, modern communication systems contain a strong dash of this way of organizing communications in that they have as an aim the "improvement" of the majority of the population. The BBC was a good example (Williams, 1961b, p. 25). Such systems tend to be rather less restrictive than the purely authoritarian. He contrasted the BBC with the press in Franco's Spain and "a good deal of the East European press" to illustrate that there are different degrees of control (Williams, 1979b, pp. 20–21).

Obviously, these two types of communication would fail on every aspect of Williams's idea of a democratic communication system. The third type he identified, the commercial, represented for him a form of organization that had historically been much closer to the criteria of democracy than the other two. In this system "men have the right to offer for sale any kind of work" and "in its early stages, and in some of its later stages, such a system is certainly a means to freedom by comparison with either of the former systems" (Williams, 1962, p. 91). On the other hand, Williams, unlike the crude ideologists of free enterprise, was concerned to examine not merely the claims of the commercial system to provide a greater diversity of views and opinions but also the actual record of its delivery of such human goods. As he put it:

> Whenever I take part in a discussion of communication, nowadays, I feel myself on a kind of time machine, hearing arguments which would have been just as articulate—perhaps more articulate—in about 1780. People learned these rules very thoroughly: that state control is a bad thing; that we should let the market decide. Scratch any Englishman on this subject, and that is what he will say. Why do I not say the system has reached perfection? Well, it would be a feat of abstraction indeed to reach that conclusion, and then to look around at the examples. But what is it in the thing itself, in this way of organising, that makes it in the end a bad system, the bad system we now have? It is a bad system in this way, that although it establishes the freedom to publish and the freedom to read, as against control by authoritarian or paternal systems, in the end it imposes a new control. Because it is bound by the law of the market, it is not now what is allowed to be said, but what can profitably be said. (Williams, 1961b, p. 26)

The logic of mass communication under the laws of the market was, Williams argued, very similar to the logic governing any other industry: There was a tendency to centralize and concentrate control in the hands of fewer and fewer owners and the survivors were bound, in order to remain survivors, to ask of all communications whether or not they would produce an adequate rate of return on the greater and greater sums invested in their production and distribution.

In contrast, Williams recognized that his account of the alternative, democratic system of communication would necessarily be abstract. Although some aspects of local communication attracted him, he was unable to find any concrete embodiments of fully developed systems in the modern world (Williams, 1963, p. 300). The starting point of his theoretical account of the nature of a democratic communication system was that such a system would have both to guarantee the right of all citizens to speak and the right of all citizens to hear whatever they wished:

> There are two related considerations: the right to transmit and the right to receive. It must be the basis of any democratic culture, first, that these are basic rights; second, that they can never be tampered with by minorities; third, that if they are ever in any way limited, by some majority decision of the society, this can happen only after open and adequate public discussion, to which all are free to contribute and which will remain open to challenge and review.

> On the right to transmit, the basic principle of democracy is that since all are full members of the society, all have the right to speak as they wish or find. This is not only an individual right, but a social need, since democracy depends on the active participation of all its members. The right to receive is complementary to this: it is the means of participation and of common discussion. (Williams, 1962, p. 93)

With such a definition, it is clear that Williams could not accept the limitations imposed upon the right to communicate by any of three preceding systems, although the organizational form he selected, communication as "public service," obviously draws heavily on the experience of the paternal model. Since he recognized the dangers inherent in such an arrangement, and in particular the risk of the monopolization of communication by one faction, he proposed that the production of material should be separated from its distribution and that a plurality of different producing centers established. This compromise, he believed, would combine the freedom from commercial constraints needed to allow room for production of the innovative, the unpopular, and the minority works, and at the same time avoid the monolithic and elitist practices that characterized the actual practice of state systems.

Public ownership, Williams argued, was unavoidable in a modern society in which the scale of the effort needed to produce and distribute the central kinds of media was such that it was quite beyond the resources, human or financial, of any individual or private group. The subordination of producers to bureaucrats was one of the major shortcomings of existing public service institutions like the BBC. To avoid these pressures, the institutions should be governed not by the state but by the professional producers. At the same time: "Any public ownership of the means of communication should include, as an integral part of its system, the creation of independent production companies"

(Williams, 1962, p. 125). This duality of ownership would, he believed, ensure both a plurality of voices and freedom from arbitrary restriction. At the same time, it would be necessary to institutionalize education in understanding the media and their workings throughout the society in order to equip people with an understanding of the ways in which media messages were produced and how they could be understood. The result of these arrangements would be that:

> We can conceive of a cultural organisation in which there could be genuine freedom and variety, protected alike from the bureaucrat and the speculator. Actual work would be in the hands of those who in any case have to do it, and the society as a whole would take on the responsibility of maintaining this freedom, since freedom of individual contribution is in fact a general interest. At the same time, we would have broken out of the social situation in which it is taken for granted that the arts and learning are minority interests, and that the ordinary use of general communication is to get power or profit from the combination of people's needs and their inexperience. We would be using our means of communication for their most general human purposes. (Williams, 1962, p. 129)

In his outline of the ways in which the structures of modern media could be transformed to give a voice to the voiceless, Williams brought together the most disparate aspects of his cultural theory and political thought. The democratic communication system was for him the mechanism by which a common culture could be constructed.

SOME CRITICAL CONCLUSIONS

It will not, I think, be doubted that Williams provides one of the most systematic and coherent theories of democratic communication available to us. Nor will it be seriously disputed that his ides have been immensely productive and stimulating in the study of the media and of cultural life in general. The contemporary relevance of many of the ideas he first advanced more than 30 years ago is also beyond dispute. If anything, recognition of the need for serious discussion of *democratic* communication has increased. As modern commercial communication systems have developed on a world scale, and the shortcomings of state-directed systems have been more and more openly acknowledged even by their erstwhile enthusiasts, discussion of the conditions for democratic communication have gained a new lease of life. Williams' critique both of authoritarian systems in which an elite prescribes what may be said and of commercial systems in which the market prescribes what it is profitable to say has an obvious relevance for an age dominated by both state censorship and the multinational media corporation. It is, however, legitimate to ask whether his theoretical construction can be accepted as a whole or in part: It is certainly impressive, but is it quite as solid as it appears at first glance? Obviously, the answer one gives to this question will depend upon the intellectual position of the writer and, since the present author is a Marxist of positively antediluvian orthodoxy, some of the criticisms I would make are perhaps already obvious.

One of the ways of considering this question is to examine the evolution of Williams's positive program for communications, outlined most clearly in his eponymous book. At the time of publication, his argument was widely criticized from both right and left, with the latter tending to stress the evasion of the problem of the nature and role of the state that the book undoubtedly has. To the extent that the book was an attempt to influence thinking inside the British Labour Party this is a wholly understandable evasion, but Williams, in the second edition of the book, answered some of his critics by a theorization of his position. He criticized the standard socialist stress upon the role of the state and the need to transform institutions as "negative" and posed against them:

> The changes I propose are in terms of growth: that we can find ways to intervene in this continuing process, by a realisation and assertion of our own shared needs, and that in the shock of this intervention there is a good chance of the changes of substance which I do not believe can come in any other way. (Williams, 1968b, p. 13)

At one level, this is a simple restatement of the general theoretical position of the British Labour Party. The "long revolution" itself can be seen as a more general attempt to theorize social change as essentially continuous in nature. However, the same edition of *Communications* contains a "Postscript," dated May 1967, that concludes: "We shall have to leave the Labour Government to its dinners and its friends, and make the change for ourselves, in quite different ways" (Williams, 1968b, p. 185). The coupling of this explicit assertion of a "reformist" political strategy with an equally explicit rejection of the only viable vehicle for a reformist strategy in Britain seems to represent a deeper ambiguity in Williams' work. As he got older, Williams defied the laws of political life and moved sharply to the left. In the third edition of *Communications*, he withdrew the Preface and explained why he had done so in a new Postscript. However, it seems wrong to make the claim that is frequently heard to the effect that "Williams became a revolutionary socialist."

It is certainly true that after 1968 Williams was prepared to call himself a "Marxist," presumably for the first time since he drifted out of the Communist Party in the 1940s, but one can question whether that shift was anything more than, an admittedly very brave, act of political identification. The essay in which he "came out," an obituary tribute to Lucien Goldmann, was given the covering title "From Leavis to Goldman" by its editor and it can indeed be read as a meditation upon the relationship between those two possible ways of thinking about culture. Despite his generous acknowledgement of his debt to Goldman and Lukacs, Williams in the end does not make the journey suggested. One key point is where he contrasts his own idea of the "structure of feeling" with Lukacs' and Goldmann's idea of "maximum potential consciousness." The very different vocabulary, "feeling" rather than "consciousness," points clearly to the distinction, that is articulated in terms drawn more or less unchanged from *The Long Revolution* (Williams, 1971, p. 14). There remained, even during Williams' "Marxist" phase, an extremely heavy reliance on immediate "experience" as the touchstone of valuation. Since we have argued that this is one of the central elements in his overall theory of democratic communication, this is hardly surprising. Williams' move to the left in his later life did not alter the fundamental framework of his thought or resolve its problems. Williams was never entirely clear as to the vehicle and mechanisms by which the transformation of society and of communication for which he so persistently argued could be achieved (Birchall, 1988).

From the point of view of our current concerns, the ambiguity over the nature and role of the state is a severe limitation on a theory of democratic communication. As we have seen, Williams was careful to construct a theory of communication that distanced itself from the more direct forms of state control that characterize authoritarian systems of communication. There are, however, two distinctions Williams did not make and that seem important in terms of current debates. In the first place, although Williams distinguished between different general forms of cultural life in terms of the "dominant," "residual," and "emergent" content they could have, he did not examine the differences between a *system of communication* that is dominant and one that is emergent (Williams, 1977, pp. 121–127). The problems and possibilities of emergent systems of communication are quite different to those of dominant systems, and their chances of approximating to democratic communication seem to me very much greater. If we accept, as Williams did, that the existing media system is the product of a deeply undemocratic social order, then it seems logical to look for democratic communication in those emergent forms, however marginal and struggling they may be at any given time, rather than to propose schemes for tinkering with the existing order.

Secondly, and in the longer view, Williams does not seem to have distinguished sufficiently clearly between social ownership of the mass media and state ownership. Since the state is, by definition, an instrument of repression, it is unthinkable that there could be any fully developed democratic communication system with state ownership. That is why even relatively liberal types of media organisations like the BBC are unacceptable even as partial models for a democratic communication system. A system of democratic communication is only possible in a democratic society that has no need of a state machine.

In the last analysis, Williams's theory of democratic communication is a valuable but incomplete insight in to some of the elements that such a system would have, but it is of rather less use as a guide to how we might reach such a desirable end.

REFERENCES

Birchall, I.H. (1988). Raymond Williams: Centrist tragedy? *International Socialism*, 2(39), 139–61.

Carey, J. (1977). Mass communication research and cultural studies: An American view. In J. Curran, M. Gurevitch, & J. Woollacott (Eds.), *Mass communication and society* (pp. 409–425). London: Arnold.

Hall, S. (1980). Cultural studies and the centre: Some problematics and problems. In S. Hall, D. Hobson, A. Lowe, & P. Willis (Eds.), *Culture, media, language* (pp. 15–47) . London: Hutchinson.

Leavis, F.R. (1967). *The great tradition*. London: Penguin.

Leavis, F.R. (1968). Under which king, Bezonian? In F.R. Leavis (Ed.), *A selection from scrutiny: Volume one* (pp. 166–174). Cambridge: Cambridge University Press.

Masterman, L. (1985). *Teaching the media*. London: Comedia.

Mulhearn, F. (1979). *The moment of scrutiny*. London: New Left Books.

O'Connor, A. (1989a). *Raymond Williams*. Oxford: Basil Blackwell.

O'Connor, A. (1989b). *Raymond Williams on television*. London: Routledge.

Williams, R. (1989). *Resources of hope*. London: Verso.

Williams, R. (1983). *Towards 2000*. London: Penguin.

Williams, R. (1979a). *Politics and letters*. London: New Left Books.

Williams, R. (1979b). The growth and role of the mass media. In C. Gardner (Ed.), *Media, politics, culture: A socialist view* (pp. 14–24). London: Macmillan.

Williams, R. (1978). The press and popular culture: An historical perspective. In G. Boyce, J. Curran, & P. Wingate (Eds.), *Newspaper history: From the 17th century to the present day* (pp. 41–50). London: Constable.

Williams, R. (1977). *Marxism and literature*. Oxford: Oxford University Press.

Williams, R. (1976). *Keywords: A vocabulary of culture and society*. London: Fontana.

Williams, R. (1974). *Television: Technology and cultural form*. London: Fontana.

Williams, R. (1971, May–June). Literature and sociology: In memory of Lucien Goldmann. *New Left Review, 67*, 3–18.

Williams, R. (1968a). *The Mayday manifesto*. London: Penguin.

Williams, R. (1968b). *Communications* (2nd ed.). London: Penguin.

Williams, R. (1963). *Culture and society 1780–1950*. London: Penguin.

Williams, R. (1962). *Communications* (1st ed.). London: Penguin.

Williams, R. (1961a). *The long revolution*. London: Chatto and Windus.

Williams, R. (1961b). Communication and community. In *Resources of hope*. London: Verso.

Williams, R. (1958). Culture is ordinary. In *Resources of hope*. London: Verso.

6

Alternative Visions of Democracy: Theories of Culture and Communication in the United States*

Hanno Hardt
School of Journalism and Mass Communication
University of Iowa

Throughout the recent history of the field, repeated demands for more theoretical considerations and the call for new theories to help explain communication and media phenomena in modern society have met with a variety of responses. Central to these discussions has been the notion of culture as a context for communication and media research, both within the established boundaries of a traditional sociology of mass communication and as a central concern of a Marxist challenge to the American idealism of classical communication and media studies.

The quest for a theoretical grounding of the search for specific answers to a myriad of social and political problems has resulted in renewed efforts to glean answers from the philosophical traditions of American pragmatism and its reformist demands. It has also resulted in a discovery of contemporary European Marxist thought as a poten-

---
* A shorter version of this contribution, entitled "Between Pragmatism and Marxism," appeared in *Critical Studies in Mass Communication*, December 1989, pp. 421–426. Reprinted here by permission.

tial and alternative source of theoretical insights about the nature of communication and media practices. Subsequently, considerations of culture have become a common concern of non-Marxist and Marxist scholarship.

Theories about the relationship of language, communication, and culture typically extend into inquiries about the social (and political) nature of democracy—that is, the relationship between communication in society and the emergence of a democratic way of life. Modern social theorists from Dewey to Habermas, for instance, maintain that the potential of democracy rests in the ability of society to ensure participation through communication. Dewey spoke of the significance of democracy as a social idea based in communication, saying, "it is primarily a mode of associated living, of conjoint communicated experience" (1954, p. 87), while Habermas has suggested the need for creating conditions of undistorted communication that form the foundation of democratic practice, "only in an emancipated society, whose members' autonomy and responsibility had been realized, would communication have developed into the non-authoritarian and universally practiced dialogue from which . . . our idea of true consensus (is) always implicitly derived" (1971, p. 314). In either case, communication constitutes a major concern in visions of democracy; in fact, definitions or understandings of communication in society provide a major difference between liberal-pluralist and Marxist versions of democracy.

The idea of culture as the context for the creation of meaning includes notions of culture as a communication system (Leach, 1965), joining earlier views of communication as participation and its importance for democracy (Dewey, 1966) or suggestions of communication as cultural environments (McLuhan, 1964). Marxist understandings of communication have focused on questions of competence (Habermas, 1979) and the political economy of communication within capitalist structures (Schiller, 1969) or were subsumed within a cultural notion of life processes (Williams, 1961).

However, the variety of theoretical positions in pragmatist and Marxist writings, ranging from a narrow definition of communication as exercising influence over others to the view of communication as a cultural environment, is also grounded in varying understandings of "culture" as a potential theoretical turning point.

For instance, where culture as an American social scientific concern is less associated with the study of how people live together through communication (culture as a way of life) or with an analysis of specific intellectual or artistic activities (the demise of high culture and the rise of popular culture), but more with the study of real or potential effects on individuals or groups or the power to manipulate or transform society, it offers equally narrow explanations of behavioral changes. In fact, the expressed interest in the study of human behavior reduces the notion of culture to reflect such a preoccupation of communication and media research with its search for effects. Geertz, for instance, observes that the "dominant concept of culture in American social science identified culture with learned behavior" (1973, p. 249).

On the other hand, culture as an anthropological project in American scholarship typically insisted upon coherence and totality since the writings of Malinowski (1944), Benedict (1961), or Douglas (1966) and, therefore, resembled the notion of social totality in Marxist theory. In fact, Archer (1988, p. 3) suggests that the "myth of cultural integration" which exhibited an aesthetic rather than an analytical orientation and which insisted on finding a coherence in culture "surfaced intact in Functionalist thought" and "received monumental reinforcement by its adoption into Western humanistic Marxism" sharing the idea of coherence with the Parsonian normative system. The difference, however, lies in the dialectical, historically determined nature of totality, reflecting the dynamics of its parts and complexes.

Culture as a central Marxist concern (since the emergence of Western Marxism with Lukàcs and Gramcsi) is context and subject of contemporary critiques of capitalist societies. Marcuse (1968, p. 94) provides a useful definition of culture in Marxist thought. He suggests in *Negations* that there is a "concept of culture that can serve as an important instrument of social research because it expresses the implication of the mind in the historical process of society. It signifies the totality of social life in a given situation, in so far as both the areas of ideational reproduction (culture, in the narrower sense, the 'spiritual world') and of material reproduction ('civilization') form a historically distinguishable and comprehensible unity." His formulation stresses the importance of culture as a point of departure (and return) for a critical analysis of bourgeois society, but it fails to recognize the need to overcome the preoccupation with the demise of high culture and to address issues related to modes of production within an existing material culture.

Although some advocates of a critical approach to media and communication may labor under the impression that a shared critique of society justifies a merging or obfuscation of their specific positions, critical positions remain imbedded in competing ideologies.

Traditionally, communication and media scholars have engaged in a theoretical discourse through their respective research agendas rather than through outright theoretical propositions. Subsequently, throughout the decades there have been few theoretical contributions to the periodical literature of the field. Instead, theory was revealed by doing, and a review of contemporary mass communication research in the United States will demonstrate the firm commitment to a liberal-pluralist interpretation of the media and their relationship to society; such research emphasizes control (over minds or organizations) at the expense of raising questions about participants (audiences and newsworkers, for instance) and their culture (or their social or economic positions) vis-á-vis media ownership.

Along similar lines, American press historians continue to exhibit their fundamental belief in the political and economic system by concentrating their work on issues of ownership, freedom of trade, and the adoption of media technologies as signs of progress and safeguards for democracy. Their accumulation of facts strengthens a prevailing idea of media and their history, while there are no considerations of the historical consequence of capitalism and their effects upon any theory of communication, media, or society (Hardt, 1989b). In fact, "readers of press histories rarely get a sense of culture, that is of the social, political or economic concerns of the community of newsworkers and their readers, for instance, or the nature of an American culture and the diversity of cultures within the boundaries of the nation, and of the economic realities of industrialization as historical conditions of change" (Hardt, 1989a). Instead, history is presented in a top-down fashion as a series of "interlocking technological inevitabilities about media institutions and their political or economic relationships to each other, it is the creation of authors, whose philosophical positions reflect a belief in progress as the engine of democracy and technology as a means of seeing the future" (Hardt, 1989a).

Similarly, the study of newsworkers and their activities continues to occupy the literature of mass communication in ways that reinforce the ahistorical nature of social scientific research. The historical rule of newsworkers vis-á-vis media management and the creation of conditions of permanent change with the introduction of media technologies under ownership control, the issue of professionalization and the curtailment of its freedom of expression, as well as the antilabor attitudes of media owners may offer explanations for the contemporary status and working habits of newsworkers, the production of content matter, and the understanding of audiences as consumers.

Generally, in efforts to define culture or cultural patterns (in the analyses of media as popular culture), the idea of communication has emerged as fundamental to the process of life, or as an instrument of social control (in the tradition of effects studies), implicitly suggesting that communication *is* culture.

Since the development of communication and media research in the United States, analyses of communication have typically grown out of studies of individual and group behavior or group processes, ranging from an interest in an individual's creation of knowledge, conduct, and self-control (Mead, 1969), to the role of media in the process of constructing and sharing social realities. In these contexts communication as an essential way of understanding the other (as well as the self) emerges as an ordering mechanism and constitutes a process of control.

For instance, in discussing the "social foundations and functions of thought and communication," Mead argues for a principle of "communication involving participation in the other" as "basic to human organization." The result is a "taking the role of the other" which involves control of the self, self-criticism, and, in the final analysis, social control (1969, pp. 253–254). In addition, he confirms the organizing principle of social communication by suggesting that the "development of communication is not simply a matter of abstract ideas, but a process of putting one's self in the place of the other person's attitude, communicating through significant symbols," serving as an "organizing process in the community" (1969, p. 327). By extending this process to include the media, Mead sees journalism as a mechanism through which individuals "can enter into the attitude and experience of other persons" (1969, p. 257). Consequently, media begin to play a significant role in the formation and maintenance of democracy when they become facilitators of community structure and control.

Another major strand of theoretical considerations concerning culture and communication was introduced with Dewey's insistence upon the importance of inquiry as a mode of conduct and of advancing the idea of knowledge as the basis of a self-correcting process that involves participation. Since communication is necessary for the shared process of inquiry, it becomes the condition under which common attitudes and experiences will lead to the realization of mutual goals. Under these circumstances Dewey's understanding of democracy is informed by the spirit of community and the potential of communication. Such a vision allows for the diversity of ideas, but also suggests the importance of social control in the interest of the common good. He proceeds, in the scientific spirit of his times, to join the notion of democracy with the appeal of science to individuals by suggesting that "freedom of inquiry, toleration of diverse views, freedom of communication, the distribution of what is found out to every individual as the ultimate intellectual consumer, are involved in the democratic as in the scientific method" (1963, p. 102). Rorty, a contemporary exponent of the pragmatist tradition, also stresses the importance of inquiry, conversation, and the need to see knowledge as "coping with reality" and the "social sciences as continuous with literature—as interpreting other people to us, and thus enlarging and deepening our sense of community." As a result, "the lines between novels, newspaper articles and sociological research get blurred" (1982, pp. 202–203).

When communication and media practices have been deemed viable objects of social scientific investigation, they have received attention primarily as instruments of social control and ordering of society while "conversations" remained "objective," or "scientific," and certainly focused on the separated and separating nature of the inquiry.

For example, Robert Park's work on the immigrant press (1922) was less an attempt to reconstruct the cultural diversity of this genre, or to document the contribution of immigrants to the formation of an American culture, but rather an exercise designed to deal with the (social and political) problems of assimilation and integration in American society, particularly after the antiwar and prolabor activities of radical, ethnic groups before and after the First World War. Similarly, histories of the American press since the latter part of the 19th century consistently offer overwhelming evidence of the strength and homogeneity of English-language newspapers.

The problem of media history is precisely its lack of commitment to a form of historical inquiry that acknowledges the importance of cultural diversity and the need to question the "truth" of observations about American media and society that are based upon previous, unchallenged cycles of inquiry that continue to affect the production and status of contemporary social knowledge. In either case, the contributions of these sociologists and historians are examples of media research aiding the preservation of a dominant cultural and political perspective and shaping an understanding of reality.

The contributions of social scientific inquiry into the role of communication and the place of the media in modern society have consistently ignored the importance of history and concentrated upon identifying real or potential sources of social problems. Generally speaking, they have dealt with specific social or political conditions of the media as they might effect the structure of the democratic system. Even critical approaches to questions of media and society have remained firmly committed to visions of pluralism and the potential of capitalism, despite the recent introduction of Marxist perspectives like the cultural critiques of the Frankfurt School and British Cultural Studies (Hardt, 1989c). It seems, instead, that an overwhelming number of studies have served to reinforce existing notions of society without questioning premises or conditions of existence that could significantly alter an understanding of democracy. Lazarsfeld, for instance, whose own work reflects the need to yield to industry demands for this type of social research, admitted the problems of "administrative" research and pleaded for a "critical" approach as early as 1941, at least acknowledging the problems of social inquiry in a capitalist society. One must hasten to add, however, that his own work was hardly effected by his observations about the nature of research. Indeed, "his remarks about critical research represented the repositioning of traditional social science research within the practice of what C. Wright Mills has called abstracted empiricism. . . . The notion of critical research . . . became a point of legitimation in the development of mass communication studies. It asserted the neutral, independent position of mass communication research in the study of society and established mass communication research as a recognized field of study, and therefore, as an administrative unit within American universities. The field also represented a relevant and important methodological specialization as a branch of sociology, with the result that in the following years the priorities of method frequently became the determinants of social research and the source of research agendas" (Hardt, 1990, p. 253).

Over 60 years ago, Lippmann (1922) suggested that people were unable to grasp the complexity of the modern world, and contemporary sociological findings provide increasing evidence of the failure to educate and prepare individuals for assuming their respective roles in society. Peters has stated that "Lippmann's vision of democracy rested on the capacity of the ordinary citizen to participate knowledgeably in public-governmental-affairs. In his theoretical framework, democracy rose or fell with the intelligence of the masses" (1989, p. 212). Yet, the understanding of communication (and participation, sharing of experience, community, or democracy) continues to be embedded in a view of a world in which individuals are capable and willing to participate as "ultimate intellectual consumers" in society, presumably understanding and directing the democratic process.

The legacy of such visions of culture and society, as they emerged from theoretical and practical considerations of America's major source of intellectual activities—pragmatism and the reform movement—is also the major challenge in the years to come. For communication and media scholars who adhere to the visions of a pluralist society and believe in the pursuit of Dewey's ideal democracy, for instance, it is time to engage in a type of inquiry about the political, economic, and cultural premises for participation, community, or communication that goes beyond reasserting the importance of these concepts. Instead, it must address the need for a critique of existing (historical) knowledge, that avoids reducing the new to what is already known.

In addition, the more recent works by Bloom (1987) and Jacobi (1987) or Hirsch (1987) suggest most urgently that lingering ideas of the relationship between democracy and communication may have to be revised, since communicative competencies and the need to articulate social or political positions and to develop options are severely restricted for many individuals. The decline of education not only intensifies the problems of intellectuals in American society, but indicates the need to redefine notions of freedom and participation and to reassess the conditions for democratic practice. These developments are a serious challenge for the study of culture and the role of communication and media in the social and political struggle.

Specifically, the vested interests of classical sociology have emphasized questions of individualism, rationality, freedom, and control of the marketplace, while a pragmatist tradition of culture has formulated ideas of community and advanced a pluralist notion of democracy that help confirm a shared belief in the path of progress. As basic elements in any approach to the study of (American) society, these ideas have kept their appeal and offer contemporary guidelines for the development of cultural theories or models of communication and society.

The scholarship of James Carey is particularly relevant at this point; his recent collection of essays in *Communication as Culture* (1989) provides substantive proof not only of his position as a cultural theorist, but also of his widespread appeal. He works in the tradition of American pragmatism and furnishes the link between past theories and a contemporary revival of pragmatist thought. He represents a cultural tradition in communication scholarship that has survived as a fringe element in the field of American mass communication research. Carey (1989, p. 110) pleads for a cultural studies approach which builds on the contributions of Dewey, Park, Rorty, and others by arguing for diversity, rejecting the narrow preoccupation with media (and their effects), and by reminding his readers that "it is through communication, through the integrated relations of symbols and social structure, that societies . . . are created, maintained, and transformed."

The problems with Carey's suggestion lie in the social scientific culture he addresses and in the nature of pragmatism; for example, the ideological power and the (political) effects of a social science establishment in communication and media research (and its industry support) and the premises of a social theory which pits a belief in the ability of individuals to share in Dewey's dream of a democratic society, against the economic and political realities of capitalism. In other words, a cultural studies perspective (in Carey's sense) must take into account the fact that, although Dewey recognized the potential of communication in the realm of mediating between technocratic strategies and value orientations of participant groupings, his reliance upon the power of common sense ignored structural changes in society and the determination of culture by social and economic forces that redefined the public sphere, including the relationship between science and democracy. The result has been the emergence of what Milliband (1969, pp. 47–48) has called "elite pluralism," and the cooperation among various elites to form a dominant economic class that operates and controls the media as well as communication and media research in its attempt to forge alliances and maintain class solidarity.

The prevailing mass communication research and media history reflect a strong belief in the benefits of technology and the structure of the economic support system. They also reveal a proximity to the progressive ideas and pragmatic considerations of the dominant (cultural) elite in society. Consequently, there is reason to suspect that Richard Rorty's modern-day pragmatism appeals to mainstream media scholarship in the United States, although Connolly (1983, p. 131) charges that Rorty's "language tranquilizes and comforts his fellow Americans, first by celebrating the technocratic values, self-conceptions, and economic arrangements operative in . . . American institutions and, second, by implying that once these endorsements have been offered there is not much more to be said." Indeed, as long as communication and media research continues to operate on the assumption that it is dealing with a pluralist society under free market conditions, there will be a rather limited reception of alternative visions or internal criticism of media institutions and their place in society.

Therefore, a rediscovery of pragmatism as a potential theoretical structure that accommodates notions of culture, communication, and democracy and provides a theory of social communication also offers a convenient explanation for the importance of the field. But it also requires the reassessment of original texts under the historical conditions of specific social, economic, and political processes in contemporary society.

The direction of communication and media studies in the United States may also have been determined by a clash between classical ideas about society as the site of the struggle of modernity (and the rise of individualism and rationality) and the knowledge about new media technologies that were capable of manipulating democracy and redefining the meaning of modern society. For instance, when the potential of destroying or severely changing a traditional attachment to the rationality of a print-oriented culture converts communication (media) research to a site of intellectual and emotional struggle, fostering an atmosphere of rejection, skepticism, or disbelief, the result is a distorted vision of the social and political potential of the new media that prevents inquiries into innovative alternatives for creating favorable conditions for a participatory society. Although second-generation scholarship, generated by individuals brought up in an age of cultural studies when questions of culture and cultural practice may replace the classical sociology of the mass media, could provide a more realistic (personal or experiential) view of the (electronic) media in the lives of people by reintroducing (or restoring) emancipatory powers to the individual, attachments to the past and political power of academic establishments are difficult to resist. In any event, the field of communication and media research in the United States has also failed to confront its own history and to reassess its position in the context of a larger culture, including the consequences of cooptation by the conditions of elite pluralism.

Neo-Marxist thought about communication and media in the United States, on the other hand, is indebted to a European tradition of social criticism that relies on structural conflicts or diverse cultural orientations, which has emerged from the historical changes in postwar Europe and the specific social and political conditions in the United Kingdom, France, or Germany, for instance. When the ideas of Western Marxism reached the United States, particularly since the 1960s, communication and media scholarship that was receptive to these ideas seemed to ignore or turn away from the experience of social criticism and radical thought in the United States and a tradition that had grown out of a direct reaction to the social and economic problems of the working class. In fact, the social history of the United States suggests that radical, socialist ideas have failed to inspire most Americans, including communication and media scientists, since notions of participation and community have retained their power as signifiers of contemporary culture. Searching for the reasons of such development, Schroyer asked, "can it be that 'socialism' or its moral equivalent, is actually contained within the utopian concept of 'Americanism' itself?" (1985, p. 284).

Nevertheless, the experience of the 1920s and 1930s provides a wide spectrum of radical dissent and the willingness to redress the ills of American capitalism, for example, poverty and a loss of social identity. The need for reliable information and the distrust of government and the press as sources and resources of social communication led to the rise of a documentary spirit that included progressive ideas and

Marxist critiques of society. Stott (1973) discusses the production of evidence about the conditions of existence in a variety of styles and through various media, presenting the diversity and the emotional richness of participation and illustrating the potential of a radical critique. There are several reasonable explanations for the failure of communication research to build on this tradition: a lack of historical grounding and the identification of the field with the ahistorical nature of social science research, a temptation to conform to intellectual fads concerning the treatment of new ideas about the role of communication and culture, and an inability to relate to the experiences of American radicalism that emerged from real-life conditions, and to build upon such work with an understanding of the nature of historical knowledge and its explanatory power. In addition, there remains a tendency in contemporary (so-called) critical communication scholarship to be caught up in itself, that is, to contemplate ideological differences as a (self-contained) academic exercise, while failing to consider the consequences of Marxism as a political movement, and therefore, opportunities for reconceptualizing media research or the writing of media history, for instance.

In addition, contemporary critics of communication and media theories have tended to embrace an analytical perspective that reduced media to a "site" within a myriad of cultural practices. They have found support in an intellectual tradition of social criticism that operates in its own history and responds to concrete political conditions that do not prevail in the United States. In fact, European thought in its latest neo-Marxist form "continues to lead the way to the problems and the problematization of American mass culture" (Hardt, 1988, p. 108). In addition, interdisciplinary excursions into the realm of culture and communication threaten to infringe upon the traditional sphere of media and communication research. For instance, when American literary criticism benefits from the work of Frederic Jameson who brought "political questions back to the discipline" (Buhle, 1987, p. 271), the theoretical discourse in communication (and mass communication) studies is, at best, marginally involved through the work of a few individuals whose interdisciplinary orientations produce insights into large theoretical issues involving semiotics, structuralism, and the demise of modernism. Indeed, the interdisciplinary consideration of communication, semiotics, the rediscovery of the importance of language as a philosophical concern, and an ever-widening search for the meaning of popular culture (media) may signal an end to "mass communication research" per se. Instead communication, and media as a particular manifestation of social communications, offer appropriate contexts for a study of society (and the development of social theories) that benefit from a variety of cultural, political, and economic perspectives.

Throughout the history of ideas about the nature of society and the role of communication (and media) in the emergence of a modern culture, social thinkers have turned their attention to the problem of democracy. However, there are ideological differences in their efforts to produce a sense of democracy, based upon specific considerations of language, communication, and community as prerequisite conditions for democratic practice. Thus, when pragmatist and reformist writers define the social idea of democracy in terms of communication as a binding force in society, they rely on assumptions about the potential ability of individuals to participate in society and the quality of discourse that reflect an almost mythical belief in the spirit of community. Dewey's ideal of democracy is not only "a way of life," but an environment "which provides a moral standard for personal conduct" (1963, p. 130).

These writers also share an understanding of the role of experts in shaping social and political agendas in light of the identification of science with the goals of democracy. The liberal-pluralist analysis of communication in contemporary society relates problems of democracy to political and economic issues of freedom of inquiry and dissemination of information within a commodity culture. The result is a critique of specific conditions that tends to reinforce established social or political institutions (and the ideology of the marketplace) with its appeals to corrective rather than disruptive action. Consequently, "communication revolutions" in American cultural history refer to scientific progress and the technological benefits of expanding markets rather than to a liberation of communication from the interests of the dominant system.

On the other hand, Marxist considerations of communication focus on the social or cultural conditions of individuals as members of working or middle-class cultures. Here the idea of democracy is an emerging practice grounded in the ability of people to share their experiences through communication and under conditions of freedom from domination and manipulation by specific economic or political interests. The problem of democracy and indeed, of community, is its identification with the discourse of the market and its dependence on the language of consumption. As long as social harmony is defined in terms of the relationship between supply and demand, and individual happiness is measured by the gratification of a need to possess and to consume, communication is reduced to a process of acquiring a sense of existence. The Marxist perspective recognizes the centrality of communication in the historical processes of alienation and emancipation, and regards the achievement of communicative competency as a prerequisite condition of democratic practice. Social communication and its institutionalization in cultural, economic, and political contexts—that is, the participation of individuals, the creation of a public sphere, and the relationship between the individuals and media—are the constituents of a Marxist discourse about the future of democracy.

And finally, there are other considerations that indicate a still different level of concern. The designation of culture—with its political and economic aspects—as the appropriate context for communication and media studies raises questions about the evolution of a Marxist perspective that emerges from a confrontation with the history of social criticism in the United States. They include the possibility of recognizing contemporary leftist social criticism as a continuation of an earlier tradition, the need to reconcile the ambitions of intellectuals with the importance of political practice, and the problem of defining the relationship between intellectual and social responsibility.

It is ironic that the preoccupation of intellectuals with an analysis of (popular) cultures has created explanations about contemporary society that remain inaccessible to people and therefore tend to lose their political potential. The reduction to jargon and theologies seems and inescapable consequence of organizational power, real or imagined. In his attack on American cultural idealism, Harris (1980, p. 284) writes that "the idealist expropriation of culture is not a matter of whim or taste but a recurrent product of persistent ideological and political conditions." In other words, "phenomena such as poverty, underdevelopment, imperialism, . . . ethnic and class conflict, exploitation, taxation, private property, . . . unemployment, or war . . . like everything else that is important to human beings . . . cannot be scientifically understood as manifestations of codes and rules" (1980, p. 285). Harris comments on a production of knowledge that has catered to the demands for facts, reducing historical and cultural processes to fit the needs for explanation and control.

Buhle (1987, p. 272) however, notes the failure of recent critiques of traditional social science practice, suggesting that the "tardy growth of cultural studies . . . seems to have yielded a theology of its own, as impenetrable to the uninitiated as the most exotic religious text and as precious to the initiates. This latter development has not been either democratic or particularly fruitful in any broader theoretical terms."

In either case, intellectual responsibility is discharged as an exercise in power over developing and sharing instrumental knowledge. Consequently, charges of intellectual elitism may further help isolate theoretical discourse from common, everyday existence and those who feel committed to the implementation of political alternatives.

Nevertheless, cultural studies as envisioned by Carey, for example, or as executed by those working in a Marxist tradition, combine into a persistent and powerful, if not persuasive reminder of the need to participate in the intellectual debates that are dominating the cultural and political discourse. The literature of mass communication theory and research in the United States has been void of any sustained participation in these debates which seem to have pushed the field (since the 1970s) into undesirable intellectual isolation. The frequently cited "Ferment in the Field" issue of the *Journal of Communication* (1983) may have been a breakthrough, but it hardly provides evidence of widespread participation in interdisciplinary explorations of communication and media issues.

The limitations of the field as a social scientific endeavor were recently confirmed by So (1988, p. 253), who concludes that (based upon a review of citations and cross-references) communication as a subfield, or a field with lesser status than other social scientific disciplines, operates with an "in-born constraint" and may be limited in its development. While the reasons for such a state of underdevelopment may involve the strength of other disciplines, particularly psychology and sociology, the lack of a vigorous exchange of ideas across disciplinary boundaries may also prove disastrous for the field. The results are already evident with a shifting emphasis to the scholarship in literary criticism, comparative literature, feminist studies, and other linguistic or ethnic interests as sources of cultural studies and loci of a contemporary discourse about media and communication.

Several years ago Lucien Goldmann (1976, p. 50) suggested that "those who will want to defend the humanist tradition, as well as the development of personal character and of the real intellectual level, must recognize that today the different aspects of the human problematic are more inseparable than ever before. Thus they gain nothing by acting in their own domain alone, because their action will be ineffective if it is not integrated into an overall struggle."

Although recent contributions in major communication journals, like *Critical Studies in Mass Communication* or *Journal of Communication,* are evidence of a new sensitivity towards incorporating debates on culture and communication as legitimate concerns of communication and media scholarship, editors of scholarly journals and national organizations should encourage interdisciplinary inquiries by redefining their mission as professional gatekeepers of their fields. With new journals entering the arena of cultural studies, and critical assessments of classical mass communication sociology becoming a professional ritual of sorts, traditional outlets for (mass) communication scholarship are challenged to reflect theoretical debates and methodological controversies to protect their claims as premier journals in the field.

Such conclusions shift the problematic of cultural concerns to the role of intellectuals, their allegiance to the interest of specific groups or classes in contemporary society, and their educational responsibilities, it raises questions of legitimation and emphasizes the importance of a moral grounding of critical discourse.

REFERENCES

Archer, M. (1988). *Culture and agency: The place of culture in social theory.* New York: Cambridge University Press.

Benedict, R. (1961). *Patterns of culture.* London: Routledge & Kegan Paul.

Bloom, A. (1987). *The closing of the American mind.* New York: Simon & Schuster.

Buhle, P. (1987). *Marxism in the USA. Remapping the history of the American left.* London: Verso.

Carey, J.W. (1989). *Communication as culture. Essays on media and society.* Boston: Unwin Hyman.

Connolly, W. (1983). Mirror of America. *Raritan, 3*(1), 124–135.

Dewey, J. (1954). *The public and its problems.* Chicago: Swallow Press.

Dewey, J. (1963). *Freedom and culture.* New York: Capricorn Books.

Dewey, J. (1966). *Democracy and education.* New York: The Free Press.

Douglas, M. (1966). *Purity and Danger.* London: Routledge & Kegan Paul.

Geertz, C. (1973). *The interpretation of cultures.* New York: Basic Books.

Goldmann, L. (1976). *Cultural creation in modern society.* Oxford: Basil Blackwell.

Habermas, J. (1971). *Knowledge and human interests.* Boston: Beacon Press.

Habermas, J. (1979). *Communication and the evolution of society.* Boston: Beacon Press.

Hardt, H. (1989a). *Behind the public sphere: Newsworkers, technology & media history.* Unpublished paper, presented at Journalism Research Colloquium, Dubrovnik, Yugoslavia.

Hardt, H. (1989b). The foreign language press in American history. *Journal of Communication, 39*(2), 114–31.

Hardt, H. (1989c). The return of the "critical" and the challenges of radical dissent: Critical theory, cultural studies and American mass communication research. In J. A. Anderson (Ed.), *Communication yearbook 12* (pp. 558–600). Beverly Hills, CA: Sage Publications.

Hardt, H. (1988). Marxist cultures: A review essay. *Journal of Communication Inquiry, 12*(1), 104–110.

Hardt, H. (1990). Paul F. Lazarsfeld: Communication research as critical research? In W.R. Langenbucher (Ed.), *Paul Lazarsfeld* (pp. 243–257, 303–306). München: K.G. Saur Verlag.

Harris, M. (1980). *Cultural materialism: The struggle for a science of culture.* New York: Random House.

Hirsch, E.D., Jr. (1987). *Cultural literacy.* New York: Houghton Mifflin.

Jacobi, R. (1987). *The last intellectuals: American culture in the age of academe.* New York: Basic Books.

Journal of Communication. (1983). *33*(3).

Lazarsfeld, P. (1941). Remarks on administrative and critical communications research. *Studies in Philosophy and Social Science, IX* (1), 2–16.

Leach, E.R. (1965). Culture and social cohesion: An anthropologist's view. In G. Horton (Ed.), *Science and culture. A study of cohesive and conjunctive forces* (pp. 24–38). Boston: Beacon Press.

Lippmann, W. (1922). *Public opinion.* New York: Harcourt Brace.

Malinowski, B.K. (1944). *A scientific theory of culture.* Chapel Hill: University of North Carolina Press.

Marcuse, H. (1968). *Negations: Essays in critical theory.* Boston: Beacon Press.

McLuhan, M. (1964). *Understanding media: The extensions of man.* New York: McGraw-Hill.

Mead, G.H. (1969). *Mind, self, and society. From the standpoint of a social behaviorist.* Chicago: University of Chicago Press.

Milliband, R. (1969). *The state in capitalist society: An analysis of the Western system of power.* New York: Basic Books.

Park, R. (1922). *The immigrant press and its control.* New York: Harper & Brothers.

Peters, J. (1989). Democracy and American mass communication theory: Dewey, Lippmann, Lazarsfeld. *Communication 11,* 199–220.

Rorty, R. (1982). *Consequences of pragmatism. (Essays 1972–1980).* Minneapolis: University of Minnesota Press.

Schiller, H. (1969). *Mass communication and American empire.* New York: Augustus Kelly.

Schroyer, T. (1985). Corruption of freedom in America (pp. 283–316). In J. Forester (Ed.), *Critical theory and public life.* Cambridge: MIT Press,

So, C.Y.K. (1988). Citation patterns of core communication journals. An assessment of the developmental status of communication. *Human Communication Research, 15* (2), 236–255.

Stott, W. (1973). *Documentary expression and thirties America.* New York: Oxford University Press.

Williams, R. (1961). *The long revolution.* New York: Columbia University Press.

7

Communication and Democracy: A Mandate for Procedural Invention

Brenda Dervin
Kathleen D. Clark
Department of Communication
Ohio State University

PURPOSE

The purpose of this chapter is to develop an argument which suggests that the current emphasis on macrolevel issues in discussions of "democratic" communication must be expanded to include emphasis on microlevel issues and, in particular, to include emphasis on the communicating procedures by which macro- and micro are linked. We argue that most discussions of democratic communication now focus on "whos" (who gets to speak, who has power) and "whats" (what is communicated) but now "hows (how do individuals connect to and make sense of self, other, society, culture, institutions; how do societies, cultures, institutions connect with individuals and with each other).

This chapter examines the causes and consequences of this deemphasis of the "hows" and challenges that failure to attend to the procedural linkages between macro- and microlevels seriously hampers our efforts to study and practice democratic communication. An alternative conception of communication-as-procedure is presented.[1]

THE PROBLEM: THE MISSING PROCEDURAL LINK

Calls for the "democratization of communication" frequently get lost in an eddy between two major streams of academic attention. Most theorists focus their attention on macrolevel structures in society, in particular, on the distribution of power and resources. In these discussion, "whos" and "whats" are emphasized: who has control of what media, what messages, what content. The "hows" of communicating—the procedures by which the communication is done—are deemphasized. The emphasis is placed on inputs and outputs. This stream of attention attempts to develop generalized understandings of democratic communication but these understandings do not include actual acts of communicating at the microlevel; the step taking which connects the macro to the micro and vice versa. For the purposes of this chapter, this stream will be labeled the macro approach.[2]

The second stream of attention seems to focus more directly on "hows" but in actuality still attends to macro issues without regard to how the macro- and microlevels link. This stream essentially sees democratic communication as participation that evolves from the bottom up in spontaneously created forms unique to specific moments in time and space. These forms are seen as arising culturally and cultural analyses are assumed to be the best frames for accounting for them. Emphasis is placed on cultural inputs and outputs. While "hows" get attention in this stream, the intent is not to arrive at understandings of individual acts of communicating at the microlevel or the step taking done by individuals that connects cultural input to output or vice versa. For the purposes of this chapter, this stream of attention will be labeled the cultural stream.

---

[1] We owe a particular debt to writings by Richard Carter (1989), John Dewey (1915), Paolo Freire (1970), Anthony Giddens (1989), Jurgen Habermas (1987, 1984, 1979), Stuart Hall (1989), Harvey Jackins (1974), Hamid Mowlana (1986), Jan Servaes (1986), and Majid Tehranian (1988, 1982, 1979). See references for citations. In addition, the discussions in Dervin, Grossberg, O'Keefe, and Wartella (1989), Volumes 1 and 2 were helpful. The ideas developed in this paper receive treatment in Dervin and Clark (1989) and Dervin (1990, 1989a, 1989b, 1983).

[2] For a good overview of various positions relating to democratic communication, see, in particular, *Communication Research Trends* ("Communication and Development," 1989).

Both streams of attention rise from the same ideas about communication and, in fact, from ideas about communication that they actively protest. Both acknowledge the mandate for dealing with pluralistic perspectives as a reality of the modern world, yet both end up studying communication without studying communicating and, thus, end up failing to enrich our understanding of how to deal with pluralism. The macro stream does so by assuming that equitable distribution of communication access and resources will lead directly to equitable communication ends. No human acts are conceptualized as intervening between structure and result. The communicating individual is essentially ignored.

The cultural stream, on the other hand, acknowledges all sorts of human acts but opts out into a solipsistic position. This position assumes so much uniqueness in these acts that no connections of understanding are sought between structure and act, act and consequence. Explanatory emphasis is placed on cultural uniqueness. Again, while the communicating acts of an individual may be described, they are not systematically addressed. Descriptions of individual acts are used to inform discussion of culture, not discussion of communication. The result is that individual acts of communicating are essentially ignored. In this way, no lessons can be derived that might help in the doing of communicating—the *hows*.

Ironically, both perspectives, while radically different in their assumptions, end up in the same place: The "how" of communication is left without systematic examination. And, somehow the structure (the system, institution, culture) is conceptualized as having some kind of mysterious being—an existence held in place by caveat. For the macro stream, the caveat is ownership and power and access. For the cultural stream, the caveat is culturally transmitted norms, rules, and understandings. Essentially the individual is ignored—as a communicating individual and as a communicating member of institution, culture, society. Both streams of emphasis disempower and rob the individual of the very pluralistic perspective that is the mandated focus of democratic communication.

It is important to note here that what we are proposing should not be construed as a return to "individualistic" ideas about communication. Rather, we are proposing that individuals constitute society/culture/institutions and these collective entities have no existence without the energizing behaviors of individuals. Thus, a formulation of communication must account for the individual. One of the questions we address is how it is appropriate to do this communicatively.

ROOTS IN NONCOMMUNICATION IDEAS
ABOUT COMMUNICATION

The caveats that drive the macro and cultural streams of attention described above are both rooted in ideas about communication that focus on transmission rather than dialogue. For one, power and ownership define the world; for the other, cultural rules and norms define it. Individual variation is deemphasized as are the means by which individuals connect themselves to and make sense of the world. An isomorphism is assumed between structure/culture and individual: the meaning making in the middle is left out.

The purpose of this chapter is not to suggest that either the macro or cultural streams of attention are wrong. Both must be given their due: Power and ownership do define the world; so do cultural rules and norms. But these elements are not *all* that define the world and they do not have a direct isomorphic relationship to individual behavior. Virtually all discussions of democratic communication acknowledge this, yet few do so as a central feature. It seems as if the problem of individuality is dealt with by opting out—either entirely into macro foci or solipsism.

The difficulty with this conception is that it is basically a noncommunicative way[3] of approaching the communication problematic. Individual human beings exist in structures, contexts, institutions, cultures. They are constrained and informed by these but never entirely. This is so because there is no complete isomorphism between structure, context, institution, culture, and the individual human mind. No individual human mind has direct access to "reality." Observation is always constrained by time, place, background, and individual perceptual limitations. While humans set up standards for judging whose observations are better, these standards are created and contested.

---

[3] This conceptualization of the communication procedure perspective rests heavily on the theoretical work of Richard Carter (see Carter, 1989, 1982, 1980, and, Carter et al., 1975, 1972). Carter (1980) states that collective behavior proceeds by and in step taking. He calls for inventive approaches to step-taking behavior in seeking the well-being of humanity, and suggests that the focuses of control are the specific place to intervene in a behavioral step in order to affect it. Carter (1982) suggests that communication produced by communicating may be connection, correspondence between two or more persons with respect to a shared condition, a focus of attention, a notion, an expression. Communicating may be focusing attention, cognizing about a focal condition, expressing oneself, or coding the expression. He notes that mass media and educational institutions can be seen as tools which respond to the need to deal with the amount of work associated with the communication among large numbers of people—the need to span space and time.

No matter how strong a culture, structure, institution, or context, there is always a mandate for the individual to make sense of the self's relationship to that culture, structure, institution, context. This intersection of self with structure (sometimes resulting in contests, sometimes in acculturation) is the stuff of myth, fable, and novels.

Both the macro and cultural streams of attention acknowledge these points. Yet, both end up studying pluralism and how humans deal with is not as a process but as end product. The macro stream looks at whose perspective wins; the cultural stream assumes culture wins. And the daily acts of communicating which form the web within which individual and structure/culture interact (contest, confuse, delimit) remain unattended.

This lack of attention to communicating is in many ways understandable. In one sense, the idea of communicating as dialogue is a relatively new idea for the species. Dialogue is not an issue when absolute power can punish any behavior regardless of whether its origins are based on misunderstandings. Dealing with human heterogeneity is not an issue when it is assumed that one central power holds the correct views of reality.

Any number of examples can be found to illustrate the point. In U.S. liberal democracy, for example, the founding fathers specified the structures they considered essential for democracy. Yet, few of these specifications pertained to communication per se. Their world view found no necessity because for them in an open marketplace of ideas, correct ideas would by some magical process win. And education was a path to achieving correct ideas. The possibility that there would be competing sets of "correct" ideas depending on one's time and place was not part of the framework. Also unimagined was the possibility that ideas, the products of communicating, are not properly treated as commodities if one is focused on communication.

While some have suggested that pluralism is the problem of the modern age, it cannot be said that the modern age invented pluralism. Rather, the species has arrived at a point, for a host of reasons, where traditional means of resolving conflicts do not work and where there are increasing demands for resolving conflicts as contact heterogeneity increases. At the same time, the species has arrived at a point where those subjected to authority more frequently question authority and, in particular, challenge authority's right to impose its own world view or assume homogeneity in world views. Unfortunately, however, we arrive as a species at this point without a robust history of experience with communication as dialogue, either as practitioners or as scholars.

LOSS OF THE INDIVIDUAL

We are further unhelpfully constrained by our attempt to avoid repeating past mistakes. We have been trying to stay away from any semblance of a return to ideas about communication that ignore structure, context, and history. The well-intentioned aim is to avoid a return to the now disavowed "individualistic," "personality," and "blame-the-victim" theories of communication. The irony in this is that we may have thrown the baby out with the bath water.

The "administrative" approach to the study of communication attempted to arrive at instructions that would allow communicators to transmit their messages to receivers completely, accurately, and with desired effect. This approach has been cast as the prototype of a nonpluralistic view of communication. Certainly, it exemplifies the transmission idea taken to an extreme in a manifestation that is unambiguously open to ideological attack. In a pluralistic world, it is considered inappropriate to ram your ideas down the throats of others. Further, focusing on individual behavior became synonymous with the "administrative" approach, so it has been ideologically incorrect, or at least difficult, to return attention to the individual.

Nonetheless, the ideological attack, however appropriate in many respects, results in a limited understanding of what is going on. Attacking the "administrative" approach solely on the grounds that it is nonpluralistic obscures the fact that models of communication based on ideas of campaigns or transmission constitute a weak conceptualization about communicating. The transmission model did not work very well either empirically or practically. It accounted for very little variance in human behavior and served badly as a model for communication design. It rarely was able to isolate strong communication effects and was unable to point to larger and stronger social forces.

Thus, there are two different, although sometimes overlapping, reasons for retreating from or rejecting the "administrative" approach: one ideological, the other theoretic. Ideologically, nonpluralistic ramifications condemned it. Theoretically, the inability to find strong effects condemned it. The ideological condemnations have received considerable coverage in the literature, but the theoretic condemnations require more attention than they have been given to date.

The question that must be asked is: Does our current understanding of the problematic of the individual in a communication context provide any useful guidance for study or practice? Most of our understandings of individual communication behavior have been derived from research and practice that has been transmission-oriented. If we assume that the transmission idea of communication is misguided and severely limited, then we must conclude that our ideas about individuality are also misguided and severely limited.

This conclusion is easier to accept when we focus on individual behavior per se. In rejecting the transmission model with its unfortunate link to the individual, the macro and the cultural streams have essentially rejected individual behavior as being an ideologically wrong site for attention. Both streams have implicitly accepted the idea that individual behavior at a level more micro than structure or culture is too chaotic for attention.

To briefly amplify this point consider these questions: What if, in actuality, the apparent chaos of individual behavior is a result of the application of inappropriate or wrong ideas about communicating to theorizing about individuals? What if it is not individuality that is chaotic but rather the paucity of our theorizings that leads to impressions of chaos?

An examination of past use of the transmission model suggests several stumbling blocks. First, we attempted to find constant impacts from message. This was inappropriate ideologically and weak theoretically. We then looked for constant impacts from culture or structure. This worked as long as we stayed at the macro level but fell apart at the micro level. We tried to differentiate people into subgroups based on differences we thought accounted for the plurality: sex, race, class, education, and so on. Again, this worked at the macro level but not the micro. From this experience we must conclude either that individual communication behavior is solipsistic or admit the possibility that there is something that eludes us. In order to do this, however, we must acknowledge the possibility that the fundamental idea that was found unacceptable about the concept of individuality—the idea that the individual can be treated as an atomized entity—is also the very same fundamental idea that sustains our retreat from individuality.

COMMUNICATION PROCEDURES: REINTRODUCING THE INDIVIDUAL IN A DIFFERENT FORM

The question becomes: Where does one look for something systematic about communication? Our attempts to find something systematic have all focused on states (rather than processes), on causes or on outcomes. All have deemphasized change over time. And, fundamentally, all have ignored the daily struggling step takings—sometimes arduous, sometimes routinized, but never entirely unproblematic—by which individuals make sense of and live in their worlds and by which structures, cultures, and institutions are introduced, maintained, and changed.

Is there something systematic about individual communicating that has eluded us because we have been looking in the wrong places? At states rather than process? At the individual human entity rather than at the step takings by which an individual connects to self, other, and society—and by which individuals attempt to connect society, culture, and institution to individual? In this chapter we suggest reintroducing the individual for consideration in communication theorizing but in a different manifestation: not as an individual per se but as an individual moment of communicating. The focus here is not on people (states) but on behavings (processes)—on acts of connecting and disconnecting, constructing and deconstructing, imagining and changing, on the communicatings which connect and disconnect individual, culture, institution, society. These moments of individual communicating are a manifestation of the structure or culture having its impact. These moments are also where we find the limits of impact.

A comparison may help. A macro or cultural perspective would expect that different people, classes, or cultures would decode messages differently. A communication procedure perspective would suggest that bringing a different sense-making procedure to bear is what makes a difference. For this second perspective it is not the state condition of being of a different culture or class that matters but rather the process condition.

The communication procedure perspective assumes that the individual giving meaning is actualized in behaviors—all manner of communicating behaviors. These behaviors include internal acts (observings, categorizings, definings, encodings, decodings, etc.) and external acts (talkings, gesturings, etc.). Each of these acts can be seen as a formal or informal routine—a step or series of steps. Some of these steps repeat the past while others break with the past. These behaviors apply to relating to self (remembering, forgetting, making up one's mind, changing one's mind, etc.), and to others (loving, hating, deciding, disagreeing, etc.). They apply to relating to individuals when seen independently as well as when constrained or limited by or enjoined by a collectivity. All these behaviors are driven by individual human consciousness (which may be operating consciously or unconsciously), the only site that directly drives individual behavior.

In this formulation, we recognize that individual behavior, constructed uniquely (at least in part) for each new moment of living, is susceptible to change as each individual constructs ways of dealing with the inherent unmanageability of reality. It is this individuality that appears chaotic. On the other hand, we assume that there is something systematic to be understood by looking at behavioral or procedural consistencies, rather than individual consistencies, by changing the focus from person to behavior, from state to process.[4]

COMMUNICATION-AS-PROCEDURE: A MANDATE FOR INVENTION

By leaving a focus on the individual as entity behind and introducing moments of behaving as carried out by individuals, we move to the idea of communication-as-procedure and the idea of procedure as the energizing linkage between the macro and the micro as well as the micro and the macro. A focus on communication procedure is not proposed as either ahistoric or acultural. Procedures are seen as themselves ideologically bound. They have social histories and purposes. They were invented (constructed) by human beings to serve needs at particular times and places. Because they are routinized and frequently ritualized, they can easily persist even after the social conditions of their origins disappear. Further, their impacts and the ways in which they have ideological force may be hidden in the same sense that it has been suggested that manifestations of power are often hidden.[5]

We have suggested above that the individual is actualized in behavior. We suggest that the structure (culture, institution, system) is actualized in behavior as well.[6] A social structure that is not reenergized regularly with acts of communicating dies; it simply does not exist. Structures are maintained, reified, rigidified, and changed through acts of communicating. Some of the acts are formalized and routinized. Examples of these include the systematic categorizations that journalists bring to reporting; the rules of parliamentary procedure used in many collectivities; the agenda setting mandated to those who run group meetings; the ways in which professionals elicit informa-

---

[4] White (1987, p. 14) argues that "instead of viewing the present occasion as continuous with a causally relation sequence of events, *kairos* [the will to invent] regards the present as unprecedented, as a moment of decision, a moment of crisis, and considers it impossible, therefore, to intervene successfully in the course of events merely on the basis of past experience. How can one make sense of a world that is eternally new simply by repeating the ready-made categories of tradition? Tradition must answer to the present, must be adapted to new circumstances that may modify or even disrupt received knowledge . . ."

[5] The conceptualization of power used heavily here is by Lukes (1974).

[6] Anthony Giddens (1984) discusses rules, procedures, and tactics as used by actors in the course of their everyday life to routinely negotiate the situations of social life. He argues that this routine use of rules, procedures, and tactics constitutes and reconstitutes social life.

tion from their clients. Other acts are less formal but still routinized. Examples include the aspects of reality which friends bring to attention in their daily greetings to each other; the ways in which people disagree; turn-taking behaviors in conversations; wearing clothing considered appropriate to an occasion.

We propose that by focusing on communication-as-procedure we can begin to unravel the problem of the elusive "communicating individual" and at the same time begin to rise to a higher level of theoretic abstraction where we will be able to reach for the lessons to be shared between our current seemingly disparate approaches to studying communication: political economy versus cultural studies; qualitative versus quantitative; and so on.

Further, we suggest this conceptual move will allow us to unravel a host of practical communication problems faced in attempts to arrive at more democratic forms of communication. One of these is the frequently observed phenomena whereby newly designed, supposedly more democratic structures decay over time so that eventually they look like the authoritarian structures that preceded them. In a communication-as-procedure formulation, one explanation for this is that in introducing change only new ideas of structure were attended to, while the actual procedures that would energize the structure and hold it in place were not.

Another practical concern is the problem of citizen participation in the collective. Without attention to procedure, participation is energized in old authoritarian forms. Over time, the relationship between the citizen and the collective deteriorates to a for-or-against procedural strategy. Examples here can be found in almost any individual's daily life: cooperating relationships at work disintegrate over time; egalitarian marriages fail. Myriad examples are available as well at the national level: The failure of U.S. leaders to hear the citizenry's position regarding the Vietnam War and the persistence of leadership's view that their views were the correct and only views; the decay of egalitarian ideas about citizen participation in China to old feudal procedures.

One important element of what is being proposed here is the idea that a communication-as-procedure approach introduces a consistency between theory and practice that allows the former to attend to where the action is in the latter. In this context attention can be placed not only on how structure restrains but how it frees; not only on how people are victimized but how they manage to find ways to *not* be victimized despite considerable odds; not only on how structural power limits potential but also on how individuals creatively empower themselves and how structures sometimes become empowering.

More fundamentally, however, this consistency between theory and practice allows the possibility that the practice of communicating can become not merely an "art" form, but rather a practice both informed by scholarship and by the understandings of practitioners. There are no end of important questions for which we need some understandings of the "hows" of communicating. A few examples: How does a leader facilitate pluralistic input? How can news writing be designed to help citizens inform themselves efficiently and effectively about others in a pluralistic world? How can we categorize documents in a retrieval system so they will be maximally useful to citizens mandated to participation in democratic decision making? How can we prevent old authoritarian forms from taking over even when we intend otherwise?

For the purposes of this chapter what is more important than the individual questions, however, is the central idea that a communication-as-procedure approach will help us bridge a gap between polarities in communication scholarship and practice that now impedes us: structure vs. individual; positivism vs. postmodernism; absolutism vs. relativism. For each of these oppositions, the polar ends are like opposite sides of the same coin. Each essentially assumes that heterogeneity means cacophony. And, since each rests its models of communication on state rather than process conditions, logically each can only end up in providing support for the assumption.

There is one additional bit of mischief which results—the idea that to focus scholarship on the invention of new communication forms is idealistic and utopian. A state view of communication necessarily leads to this conclusion for a state view searches for transmitted order. In doing so, a state view misses the daily inventings and creatings that are a mark of the highest qualities of the human species. The communicating steps that make up individual and collective life are all human inventions—some ancient, some recent. Some rigidify; some metamorphize; some appear and disappear like lightning. It is only by looking at communication as process, however, that the inventive character of the behavior that energizes individual and collective life comes into view.

A FRAMEWORK FOR THINKING ABOUT
DEMOCRATIC COMMUNICATION INVENTION

The communication-as-procedure perspective mandates that we focus on behavior at specific moments in time-space, but at the same time extract fundamental dimensions of these behaviors that are applicable across time-space. This idea will be illustrated here with a beginning framework. When one surveys the literature on democratic communication a number of dimensions or conditions can be extracted as necessary under one definition or another. Each of these conditions implies a set of communication procedures that can be observed, experimented with, or tested. The literature, however, has not focused on these procedures in systematic ways. What we are attempting in this section is a beginning model for doing so.

The fundamental question we are trying to answer is: What are the range of possible communication mandates of democratic communication? This leads us to a second fundamental question: What do people need to do communicatively to make sense of and participate in their worlds? Drawing heavily on the work of Carter[7], we propose a beginning template to organize our search for answers. This template, shown in Figure 4.1, proposes that we need to examine two dimensions of communicating: situation-defining strategies and communicating tactics. The essential idea is that what people do communicatively depends both on how they define their situations and on what they are attempting to do communicatively in these situations. Both situation-defining strategies and communicating tactics are defined as procedures because both involve behav*ings*. Strategies involve cognitive behavings while tactics involve communicative behavings.

The two procedural dimensions we have selected for development in this chapter are ones we propose as fundamental. We do not suggest they are the only fundamental dimensions to consider in a communication-as-procedure perspective. Rather, we suggest that they are illustrative of the kind of conceptualizing that we need to pursue.

In Figure 7.1, the vertical axis focuses on situation-defining strategies. The particular set of situation-defining strategies we have developed for use here focuses on how the communicating entity (individual or collective) sees itself at a specific moment relating to other communicating entities: What relationship to the world is the entity working on at that specific moment in time and space? In a world where sense is not given, every relationship involves daily acts of constructing via communicating. The individual needs to relate to self, to other individuals, to collectivities; collectivities also need to relate to self, and to individuals as well as other collectivities. For our purposes here, we will propose six different situation-defining strategies:

- INDIVIDUAL RELATING TO SELF: Here the individual is thinking, creating, observing, arriving at personal sense and understandings of self.

---

[7] See footnote 3.

Figure 7.1. An Example of a Communication-as-Procedure Framework Utilizing Two Procedural Dimensions: Situation-Defining Strategies and Communicating Tactics

Situation Defining Strategies	Communication Tactics								
	Attending	Creating Ideas	Finding Direction	Expressing	Finding Connection	Confronting Opposing	Mediating	Recalling	Undoing Rigidities
Individual relating to self									
Individual relating to other individuals									
Individual relating to collectivity									
Collectivity relating to self									
Collectivity relating to individual									
Collectivity relating to other collectivity									

- INDIVIDUAL RELATING TO OTHER INDIVIDUALS: Here the individual is relating to other individuals, learning about others, comparing self to other, connecting or disconnecting with others.
- INDIVIDUAL RELATING TO COLLECTIVITY: Here individual communicating focuses on participating in a collectivity which can move as one.
- COLLECTIVITY RELATING TO SELF: Here a defined collectivity is focusing on itself.
- COLLECTIVITY RELATING TO INDIVIDUAL: Here a defined collectivity is focusing on individuals.
- COLLECTIVITY RELATING TO OTHER COLLECTIVITY: Here one defined collectivity is relating to another defined collectivity.

It is important that these different situational definitions be understood as procedures for defining the situation. What this means is that, theoretically at least, the actor is free to apply any one of these strategies to any given situation depending on what the actor brings to bear cognitively when constructing a sense of the situation. This begins to allow us to focus on moments of behaving by individuals and collectivities rather than being limited to a static view of these merely as entities. Situation-defining strategies are proposed here as fundamental procedures in the sense that every collectivity that pursues democratic communication must necessarily account for each of the defining situations. The foci of communicating entities will vary depending on which of these defining strategies is adopted. The individual, for example, who is attempting to relate to self will differ communicatively than the individual who is attempting to relate to an other or collectivity. Likewise, the collectivity that is attempting to relate to self will differ communicatively from one that is attempting to relate to another collectivity.

In essence, the situation-defining strategy is a cognitive choice, sometimes individually produced, sometimes collectively produced. Other possible situation-defining strategies are, for example, assessments of situational constraint (e.g., how free the entity is to move) or situational power (e.g., how much power the entity has to define the situation). These alternatives are seen as examples of other fundamental situation-defining strategies. We are not incorporating these into our framework for the purposes of this chapter.

The importance of these defining strategies becomes clearer when we introduce the second procedural dimension, that of tactic. In order to construct and deal with their worlds human must necessarily perform different communicative tasks. One possible set of tactics to accomplish these tasks includes:

- ATTENDING to self, environment, each other, and collective being. This tactic involves generalized observing.
- CREATING IDEAS about self, reality, each other, institutions, collectiveness. We assume that since there is no isomorphic relationship between "reality" and individual, it is a human mandate to create ideas.
- FINDING DIRECTION. Determining possible directions in which to move, alone or together. Again, we assume that direction is not predetermined even in the most rigidly controlled collectivity. Even the implementation of societally homogenous direction requires individual and collective reenergization.
- EXPRESSING. Here the communicating activity is directed toward giving symbolic expression to individually or collectively created ideas.
- FINDING CONNECTEDNESS. Here the communicating activity is directed at getting connected to others—allies, comrades, interest groups, sympathizers, sources of ideas.
- CONFRONTING, OPPOSING. Here the focus is one entity contesting against other.
- MEDIATING. Here the focus is on compromising or otherwise resolving disagreements.
- RECALLING. Here the focus is on creating memory of own, other, or collective past and bringing memory to bear on the present.
- UNDOING RIGIDITIES. Here the focus is on a conscientizing process by which human entities come to grips with the rigidities with which they face life. We assume these rigidities have been induced in them by their experience, cultures, structures, and so on. During the conscientizing process rigidities dissolve and behavior becomes more flexible. This frees inventive potential.

We are not suggesting that these communicating tactics are the only ones necessary to democratic communication situations. We are proposing, however, that they are set of necessary tactics. By pitting these two sets of procedural dimensions against each other, we create the 56 cells in Figure 7.1. This chart is presented as a very fundamental illustration of a way to think about the communicating mandates of any human situation. Figure 7.1, therefore, provides a perspective for looking at how the microworld of individuals is connected to the macrolevel world of cultures, structures, and institutions, and vice versa. Thus, for example, in order for an individual to relate to his/her society and world, the individual needs to relate to self, others, and collectivities. Essential components of the individual's situation, as well, are how collectivities in that society relate to self, individuals, and each other.

Each of the cells is seen as a site for isolating communication behaviors—the communicating procedures performed at specific moments in time-space. The *situatedness* of this formulation is important and can be understood in two ways. One way involves understanding that life-facing involves daily constructings, even when some (or perhaps many or even all) of those constructings are repetitions of habitualized constructings used in the past. Since no moment in time-space has theoretically occurred before, each act of communicating is situated. The second meaning of situatedness refers to the idea that communicating behavior is situation-responsive. An inherent assumption of the framework represented in Figure 7.1 is that communicating tactics are potentially responsive to situation-defining strategies. How an individual creates ideas when relating to self potentially differs from how that individual may do so when relating to others or collectivities. As one example, the individual may use a wide-open categorizing strategy when relating to self but a highly closed and polarizing one when relating to others. Or, a collectivity may have developed formalized procedures for creating subtle variations in ideas when relating to individuals but gross differentiations when relating to other collectivities. Each of these means of creating ideas is seen as a communicating "how." Each is assumed to be an invention of past and/or present. Each is assumed to have the potential to become very rigidified so that the communicating entity never varies its tactic in a given kind of situation or, at an extreme, across all situations. At the same time each is assumed to have the potential for responsiveness; for being used or not used depending on how the communicating entity defines the demands of a current situation.

This framework is proposed as a guide to description; to examine how it is that humans now or in the past engaged in these communicatings. What are the ways in which attending is done when individuals are relating to themselves? How do these vary? Under what conditions? What consequences seem to relate to what ways of communicating? What are the ways in which attending is done when individuals are attempting to operate in collectivities? How do these vary? What consequences seem to relate to what ways of attending? The framework illustrated in Figure 7.1 is also proposed as a guide to invention: What alternative ways to communicating need to be invented in other for the species to move into the modern/post-modern age of democratic pluralism?

This latter point is important. Most of the work on democratic communication has limited to itself to understandings of the way things *are,* not the ways they *might be.* Yet clearly, humans now face communication demands for which the species is unprepared and for which humans have had little experience. Further, the traditional procedures of communicating established to handle problems of human heterogeneity in the past are less and less useful. These procedures were invented for particular time, space, and situation demands. They no longer function well because the time, space, and situation have changed. A primary change is the move from more homogeneous, more stable social contexts in which authoritarian procedures seemed to work reasonably well to more heterogeneous, less stable social contexts that demand procedures that the human species has not yet invented. One of the difficulties in understanding this point is that when authoritarian procedures are the operating communication procedures in a situation, it actually looks as if there are no communication procedures operating. In essence, the *hows* of those in authority are translated into *whats,* as if they are the nature of reality and not the behavings via which reality was constructed. With the demand for democratic communication that allows a plurality of voices to speak and be heard, the species must in essence make what has been hidden and assumed—that is, the hows of communicating—obvious and flexible.

This is what is meant by the title of this chapter: the mandate to invent. The question raised is what communication inventions have humans already created and used with what consequences? What inventions are now necessary because of changing species conditions?

PROCEDURE-LESS PROCEDURES

Before attempting to illustrate the discussion above with examples of some commonly used communication procedures, we must discuss what is perhaps the most visible manifestation of the fact that most formulations about communication structures and practice are actually noncommunicatively informed. If one starts with absolutist assumptions about the nature of reality and the nature of human observing, one arrives at a conception of communication that does not involve behavior: Ideas get into heads, messages get made, reality is assumed to be obvious. There is no need to talk about alternative ways in which people make observations, construct ideas, decide on directions, and so on. These are all given.

However, they are not given. But operating under assumptions that they are, we construct communication structures without attention to procedure: They are procedure-less. We will provide three examples:

media ownership structures; agenda-setting practices in organizations; and organizational member relationships to organizational leaders.

A current contest illuminated by studies of telecommunication is the structures of media ownership.[8] In the United States currently, it is assumed that privately owned media regulated via privatization and deregulation policies will allow people to hear the heterogeneity of understandings present in society. However, this structure is in one sense procedure-less because the problem of heterogeneity is resolved without explicit attention to the communication problematic. This problematic is: How can all individuals participate in the society using the media? How can they access the media and get on with attending, creating ideas, finding direction, confronting, opposing, mediating, recalling, and undoing rigidities as active members in the collectivity of a democratic society are supposed to do? The privately owned media regulated via privatization and deregulation policies basically assumes ownership and access is all that is necessary to yield heterogeneity of voice. Such a policy ignores, most obviously, the problem that only a limited number of voices can gain access and ownership. Even more important from a communication-as-behavior perspective is the fact that such a policy ignores the sense making that communicating entities must do to deal with a cacophony of diverse voices. Mere presence without procedures that allow comparison and comprehension is equivalent to nothing. So even if ownership and access patterns truly allowed diverse voices to speak, it can not be concluded that understanding of diversity would result.

Our second example involves agenda setting[9] which when examined from a communication-as-procedure perspective also remains essentially procedure-less. This means that agenda setting in organizations is usually accomplished in a noncommunicative or, at best, haphazardly communicative way—the leader or facilitator is given the power to set the agenda for all the others to follow. This agenda then channels attending, creating ideas, recalling, and expressing into particular conceptual frames, and so on.

Often, in an informal group, not specifically set up to accomplish a task, an agenda will play an unacknowledged role. If an informal group leader talks more, talks louder, has some tie of loyalty or influence with some other member of the group, reiterates a single point

---

[8] For examples of work that discuss this issue see Hachten (1982), Hamelink (1983), Head (1985), and Mowlana (1986).

[9] For various discussions involving agenda setting in organizations and groups see Dutton (1985), Hirokawa (1988), Poole and Roth (1989a, 1989b), and Stohl (1989).

of view, interrupts others, is viewed as having more power or authority than others, denigrates other ideas or expressions, holds the floor more often, captures the attention of others, then that leader's own personal, and perhaps unacknowledged, agenda will come to have a great influence on the group. Others voices will not be acknowledged, and over time, others in the group will learn to be silent or only to venture those utterances that they have learned are acceptable.

Our third example involves how individuals in collectivities relate to their leaders and to other members of the collectivity. These relationships are also often procedure-less. The member defers constructing power to the leader even, some research suggests, when the leader wants diverse input. Such deference is understandable given the nature of most power structures. From a communication-as-procedure perspective, however, it becomes important to notice that this is an arena in which behavior has rigidified. And, in the absence of an explicitly stated procedure that would work against this rigidity, again we find that power rules the day. Instead of procedure that mandates the individual and collective constructing and communicating, we defer to the right of power or authority to do the constructing and communicating: advertising dollars direct news values; powerful news sources define reality; the leader sets the group's direction; the personality of the journalist or leader takes precedence over ideas.

This challenge is seen as applying equally to situations where diverse voices are present and to those where they are not present. The former requires a more subtle analysis, however—an understanding that the mere presence of diverse voices that are allowed to speak as if diversity did not matter can result in cacophony rather than heterogeneity. In the presence of cacophony sense cannot be made and old rigidities take hold. The energization of the system is given over to the hands of power, hidden or obvious, routinized or capricious. Whichever communicating behaviors are used by power become the energizers. But since explicit attention is not paid to these procedures, we have labeled this phenomena as procedure-less procedures. This argument will become clearer as we proceed in the sections that follow.

EXAMPLES OF COMMUNICATION PROCEDURES

Theoretically, each of the 56 cells in Figure 7.1 could be filled with a set of communicating procedures. Figure 7.1 is proposed as a framework for discovery and exploration of description and invention. It is beyond our task at this point to discuss and fill in every cell. Instead, we will discuss examples of procedures for each of the situation-defining strategies in order to illustrate the potential of this approach for examining the way in which procedures serve to define relationships between the micro and the macro and vice versa and how procedures constrain or limit potentials for democratic communication.

Individual Relating to Self

This is the situational context in which it is most difficult to develop examples because views of reality based on positivist or authoritarian ideas actually do not propose the individual relationship to self as a communication problematic. Only when society sees the individual's behavior as intrusive has attention fallen here, usually cast off to the psychiatrist's couch or to a counselor or magician. There are examples however. One useful one is the "how" of creating ideas about one's existence in time.[10] Anthropological work identifies, for example, different ways in which people locate self in time: linear vs. cyclical for instance. Another useful example is the how of recalling—remembering what has occurred in the immediate or distant past. Tactics here deal with the "hows" by which people create narratives or stories about their lives and range all the way from methods of recording (e.g., the orally told folk tale vs. the journal or diary) to those "hows" that are creating a coherency to the story narrative. One more example is the "how" of deciding—choosing what road to travel.[11] Tactics might range all the way from chance (e.g., flipping a coin) to matrix-resolving (e.g., putting all options and all characteristics comparing options in a table) to wait and see (e.g., not doing anything and seeing if circumstances point to a direction).

While typically the tactics used as examples above have been seen as defining state characteristics of one culture versus another, from a communication-as-procedure perspective they are seen as processes, which are potentially changeable across changing conditions. Indeed, if an individual's behavior is rigidified into any one of the tactics in any given kind of situation, that has enormous implications for collective life. A rigid linear conception of time, for instance, has conse-

---

[10] Anthropological literature includes many rich examples of differences in communication between culture. See, in particular: Textor (1967), Murdock (1967), and Geertz (1973). A major difference is that anthropological discussion of communication behavior are usually presented as state conditions, not process conditions—assumed to characterize members of that culture across time and space.

[11] For some discussion of decision making, see Dutton (1985), Hirokawa (1988), Poole and Roth (1989a, 1989b), and Stohl (1989).

quences for how people are able to share ideas. It could lead, for example, to an approach to journalistic encoding behavior that permits bullet news. Or, if most individuals in a given culture define themselves in terms of cyclical time at all times, this has implications for the flexibility that culture is able to bring to bear on changing world conditions.

Individual Relating to Other Individuals

It is easier to find examples of procedures via which individuals relate to each other because the ways in which people think about and talk to each other have been important foci for the study of interpersonal communication, represented in research genres under such names as interpersonal perception or cognition, and conversational rules. In thinking about each other, for example, Rokeach[12] isolated cognitive tactics that he labeled generally as open- and close-mindedness. While he applied these to individuals as state conditions, for our purposes we will think of them as process conditions that may or may not be manifested rigidly in a given person or for a given person in given situations. Open-mindedness involves making fine gradations in distinguishing self from others while close-minded involved making gross and often polarized gradations.

The ways in which people attend to, share ideas with, make decisions, express, confront/oppose, mediate, and so on between each other are generally studied under the rubric called conversational rules. Conversational rules are informal sets of routines humans have developed in order to regulate communicating with each other. Rules govern turn taking, giving criticism, face-saving, who may speak when and how, who has authority, and cues about power and intimacy relationships.[13]

Two examples of conversation rules involve turn taking (how do we share ideas) and topic setting (how do we decide what to share ideas about). Literature on communicating between U.S. men and women shows, for example, that men capture a significantly greater share of the talking time and are significantly more likely to set the topic.[14]

---

[12] See Rokeach (1960).

[13] For examination of various aspects of conversation see Tracy, Van Dusen, & Robinson (1987), Knapp, Stafford, & Daly (1986), Yelsma (1986), O'Keefe and McCormack (1987), McLaughlin (1984), Goodwin, (1989), Kellerman and Lim (1989), and Tracy (1989).

[14] For discussion of conversation rules such as turn taking and topic setting, see Fitzpatrick (1983), Foss and Foss (1983), Nadler and Nadler (1987), Spitzack and Carter (1987), and Talley and Peck (1980).

Women, on the other hand, are more likely to interrupt, particularly with questions. Clearly such rule patterns, if rigidified, do not address a definition of democratic communication which suggests that the voices of diverse observers need to be heard.

The very concept of conversational rules suggests a repetitiveness to these behaviors, at least situationally (i.e., in a given situation, this is how one disagrees with another). Indeed, the literature on conversational rules suggests that the rules are learned out of consciousness. Virtually all children will learn the rules as they learn language and are heavily influenced by the family, community, and cultural environment in which they are raised.

Research focusing on conversational rules has in actuality given rather explicit attention to the long-term goal of improving communication by bringing rules to consciousness and modifying rules in order to achieve different communicative results. Conversational rules then are a crucial site for isolating communicating rigidities and reaching for greater communicative flexibility.

Individual Relating to Collectivity

Here the focus is on how the individual makes sense of and deals with his or her membership in a collectivity. Relatively little academic work has focused on this connection[15] although discussions of how members of organizations deal with leadership are relevant. What the literature suggests, as one example, is that many individuals in U.S. organizations focus their attending in collectivities on the leader— what the leader thinks, how the leader compares to self. Another example is how the individual attempts to make contributions to the group discussion. One tactic, a common one in U.S. group meetings, is for the individual to present his/her idea as an absolute position which does not need illumination or comparison with other ideas or clarification via example.

Both these examples focus on rigidified communicating procedures—attending which leaves the individual without ideas about members of the group other than the leader, or expressing that assumes absolute positions and leaves listeners unable to make sense of the ideas expressed on their own terms. For these examples, however, as with the examples in other sections above, theoretically the com-

---

[15] A number of how-to-do-it books are available, particularly those oriented to helping individuals achieve success in organizational settings. For overviews of academic work on organizational communication, see Jablin (1987) and Goldhaber and Barnett (1988).

municating tactics are responsive to changing situational conditions and communication mandates.

Collectivity Relating to Self

Parliamentary procedure[16] is perhaps the most well-known example of a collectivity relating to self communication procedure: a set of defined rules which set up a framework for discussion. Parliamentary procedure governs what shall be talked about, when, in what order, and for what actions and is used by such diverse collective bodies as the U.S. Congress and small clubs and organizations. Parliamentary procedure was developed to allow meetings of diverse individuals with diverse opinions to argue in an orderly and productive fashion and to reduce the likelihood that decision making would revert to a shouting match or blows.

Yet, at root, parliamentary procedure is a procedure based on transmission ideas about the communication problematic—the procedure rests on an ideology which suggests that correct ideas will surface and become clear in an open marketplace. For parliamentary procedure, meaning making is not considered. The procedure ignores, for example, the need for individuals to create ideas or understand how others came to have their ideas. In effect, parliamentary procedure confounds tactics into a process where people are required to be attending, creating ideas, finding direction, recalling, expressing, deciding, mediating, and confronting all at once.

As a result of these communicating constraints, only those individuals with already formed ideas can participate and only those willing to speak up will be heard. Further, only that part of thinking that has been defined as relevant by the collective is permitted to be voiced or heard. Each of these steps reduces the likelihood that a variety of views will be heard or that participants in the process who have not arrived with already formulated views will have the opportunity to contribute.

Another example of communicating tactics in the situational context of collectivity relating to itself is journalistic practice,[17] the set of hows by which an institution mandated to facilitate the sharing of

---

[16] For a concise description of parliamentary procedure see Stanley M. Ryan (1985) which summarizes the main points of the classic *Robert's Rules of Order Newly Revised*.

[17] See the following authors for discussions and descriptions of various journalistic practices: Katz (1987), Van Driel and Richardson (1988), Ettema and Glasser (1988), Bruck (1989), Jensen (1987), Kress (1986), Tuchman (1978), Altheide (1985), Hall, Christer, Jefferson, Clarke, and Roberts (1978), and Gitlin (1980).

ideas in the collectively goes about defining the nature of collective reality. Different journalists in different societies around the world all have some set of journalistic practices which they are required to follow.

Taking U.S. journalism as our example, we find a journalistic practice that conceptualizes itself as capable of accurate observation. Guided by such an ideology, this journalistic practice places high value on the idea that one well-trained journalist is an invaluable asset. From here, it is possible to create a "fact"-oriented journalism which implements the famous "5W" lead as well as a "personality" journalism which makes the journalist more· important than idea sharing. Further, since it is assumed that reality has a naturally given order that can be observed equally well by one well-trained journalist or another, the idea of bullet or spot news as journalistic practice takes root. Too, in a naturally ordered reality, history also is assumed as a noncontested given, so a journalistic practice that ignores history also takes root.

Another example in this situational context is the practice of public opinion polls.[18] Here, the collectivity assesses the opinions and inputs of individual citizens and collates them presenting them as the "collective mind." There are at least two problems with this procedure. The first is that the methods of conducting polls are generally derived from authoritarian assumptions—the individual is not genuinely asked how he or she understands the world. Rather the individual is typically asked to respond on a template which reflects how those in power understand the world. The second problem is that the procedure assumes that somehow the "collective mind" is adequately represented via a statistical amalgam of individual opinions. In reality, of course, there is no collective mind. The collectivity exists, as Dewey proposed, in communicating.[19] An idea created by a collectivity as a representation of the whole is always created via struggle—not only the struggle of contesting viewpoints, but the struggle of trying to understand others.

Collectivity Relating to Individual

Here we focus on procedures by which a collectivity (structure, institution) explicitly focuses on its relationships to individuals. Common examples are the host of service professions and organizations that

---

[18] For a critique of public opinion research, see Carter, Ruggels, and Simpson (1975), Dervin (1989b), Edelstein (1974), and Splichal (1987).

[19] See Dewey (1915) and also Rakow (in press).

human beings create to serve their individual and collective needs.[20] Two examples will be presented: one focuses on the formalized procedures that collectivities use in order to learn about individuals and their needs or how well their needs have been satisfied; the other focuses on the formalized procedures by which collectivities attempt to find something within its resources that is useful to the individual.

When an organization attempts to determine an individual's needs or satisfactions, the organization is dealing with essentially opposite sides of the same coin: What does the person need? Did we give the person what was needed? Yet, the literature shows that in actuality neither of these questions are often addressed by organizations. Instead, the questions become: What of the things we do do you need? Which of the things we do did you use? What of the things we do do you like?

The procedures as described here are widespread. Two examples: A doctor questions a patient about his or her health problem by asking the patient which of a series of health problems as defined by the system the patient has—Do you have x? Have you had y? Did your mother have z? Likewise, a librarian questions a patron about his or her information need by asking the patron a series of dichotomized questions designed to zero in on which part of the library collection meets the need—Do you want this or that? One or several?

Similarly, the doctor will assess how well the health care system did on a series of system-oriented measures: Did the patient get better? Was he or she cured? How long did he or she live? Did the patient follow orders? The library will assess how well it did by also asking a series of system-oriented questions. Do you like our book collection? Do we have enough of x? How often have you used us?

These procedures can be seen as all based on an absolutist world view. What those in power in the system see as valuable is deemed to be what is valuable. Use of these procedures has at least two consequences. One is that the way in which the system attempts to understand the individual in actuality deters understanding of the individual. The second is that the way in which the system attempts to evaluate itself using individual input reifies the system as it is now defined.

Another cut into the problematic of the collectivity relating to individuals is how the collectivity attempts to assist individuals in locating what they will find useful among the collectivity's resources. A prime example here is the category schemes in which communication

---

[20] For a review of literature pertinent to this section, see Dervin and Nilan (1986) and Dervin (1989a, 1989b).

systems store, retrieve, and transmit information. In journalism, for example, categories focus on local news, national news, entertainment, sports, and so on. In libraries, categories focus on hierarchically organized noun groupings as represented in Dewey Decimal or Library of Congress cataloguing systems. A third example is in database management systems where noun-oriented keywords are used as retrieval indexes.

What is interesting about all of these categorizations is that almost without exception it is assumed that the way in which the system categorizes is the correct way. No procedures allow for alternative categorizations or for users to move through a selection of alternative systems, some of which may be more relevant to particular users than others. Very little academic research has even been addressed to the question.

Collectivity Relating to Another Collectivity

Here we focus on the situation of one collectivity relating to another: organization to organization, state to state, nation to nation, alliance to alliance. Generally, such relationships are governed by law and agreement. Usually we do not think of these as communicative relationships. Rather the concerns have focused on the distribution of hard resources. In our recent history, however, we have seen instances where the problematic of the communication procedures by one collectivity is relating to another have received attention. A prime example is the call for a New World Information Communication Order by Third World and nonaligned nations.[21]

Criticisms, particularly against First World media, have focused on how Western interests control press services and use only western input when reporting on and defining other countries. Views of other countries are described as stereotyped and based on Western myths, misunderstandings, and purposive distortions. Alternatively, concern was expressed for how much of the media space in Third World and nonaligned nations is occupied by Western media products. A fundamental complaint is that Western interests prevent self-expression both intranationally and internationally.

From one perspective, this set of concerns fits best under the dis-

---

[21] For discussions of issues relating to this debate, see Argumedo (1981), Arusha Declaration on World Telecommunications Development (1985), Resolution of the Administrative Council of the International Telecommunication Union (1985), White (1987), Schiller (1978), Jayaweera (1987), and Servaes (1986).

cussion included earlier of procedure-less procedures. The First World nation position which argues that there ought to be no controls on freedom of the press is justified as the best way to produce a heterogeneity of voices. Clearly the justification is myth both when applied to international communication as well as when applied to intranation communication. From another perspective, however, what we see here is the implementation of noncommunicatively oriented media practice tactics. In the absence of explicit procedure, the procedures of stereotyping and polarizing become a normative part of a journalistic practice. The irony is that in most cases it is probably not intended. This is a good example of the problem of well-meaning systems decaying over time into authoritarian structures. Without explicit attention to the problematic of communication, there is no alternative. Any attempt to describe the world from one vantage point must necessarily be implemented narrowly and nonpluralistically.

SOME INVENTIONS

The examples given above of commonly used communication procedures have focused on procedures which are rigidly or mindlessly applied.[22] In some cases, the procedures are seen as state descriptions— the way, for example, people in a particular culture are. In other cases, the procedures are seen as the formalized rules by which communicating gets done. In other cases, the procedures seem to be haphazard results of assuming that communication is procedure-less. In all cases, however, the procedures have been described as being applied by a given communicating entity at all times, or a given communicating entity in all situations of the same type.

But the formulation presented in this chapter assumes that communicating is necessarily the most responsive and flexible of behaviors, that humans can change how they construct and deal with their worlds depending on the mandates of the situations in which they see themselves. In fact, this formulation assumes that such flexibility and responsiveness is a requisite for democratic communication no matter

---

[22] Many of the examples of inventions presented here have been developed and tested by Dervin and colleagues (see Dervin & Dewdney, 1986; Dervin & Nilan, 1986). Also utilized is the following: for inventions focusing on retrieval of information, Belkin (1978, 1982a, 1982b); for inventions relating to conscientizing. Freire (1970); for a variety of inventions focusing on interpersonal and group interactions aimed at undoing communicating rigidities, Jackins (1974); for journalistic inventions, Matta (1986); for the invention of "speak bitter, speak easy," Mao (Dreifus, 1973).

what definition of democratic is brought to bear and that there are communicative tasks that theoretically are mandated: Individuals need to construct ideas in order to move; collectivities need to allow individual members some level of understanding of each other; diverse viewpoints need to be represented efficiently; people need some mental hooks on which to hang their own understandings of the diversity within which they live; institutions need to understand the people they serve and find ways to effectively and efficiently help them as they wish to be helped; communication institutions need to find ways to display the diversity of opinion in the collective without opting out from the choices of power. How each of these communicative tasks may be accomplished is theoretically varied, across time and space and in response to ever-changing conditions.

The fact that we do not see a lot of flexible communication behavior around us does not deny the possibility. Part of the problem is that we have not been looking for it, focused as we have been on trying to find consistency across time in state conditions. Part of the problem is that we haven't conceptualized communication communicatively so that neither communication scholarship nor communication practice has served the species' need for invention very well.

There are, however, a variety of examples of explicit attempts to invent alternative communication procedures. At one extreme we have a host of examples of individual efforts at changing self, for example: learning to artfully mix abstract and concrete thoughts in messages, remembering to praise before criticizing, learning to ask questions before stating one's own opinion, or expanding the ways in which one categorizes the world. At the other extreme, we have examples of explicit efforts by collectivities to develop and use more effective communication procedures. A few examples of such inventions will be presented here as a means of displaying potentials.

The conscientizing process. In this approach, developed by Friere, procedures are instituted by which every group member can and must be heard until all have had a chance to say what they have to say. This procedure insists that all must speak everything they wish; that there is no reliance on loudest voice, squeakiest wheel, or power and authority. The conscientizing process continues, in essence, as long as necessary.

Agenda canvassing. In this approach, attributed historically to some groups of U.S. Native Americans, the chiefs brought to the meeting circle their agenda items. These were then canvassed without counterargument until all had proposed topics of discussion at which point the groups agenda was easily set by consensus.

Brainstorming. In this approach, one of the most frequent alternative procedural forms used in mainstream organizations, recognition is given to the idea that when an organization wants creative input different forms of communicating must be used than in the usual authority-run or parliamentary-procedure run meeting. In brainstorming, everyone is given a chance to speak and no one is allowed to criticize any idea. Further, ideas are recorded but without reference to who stated them thus preparing the way for a later evaluation phase which will not be met with defensive reactions.

Speak bitter, speak easy. In this approach, attributed to Mao, representatives of an "oppressed" group are given the floor to talk of their frustrations, angers, and hurts without interruption or comment by the "oppressor" group. The idea is that with these procedural controls, to speak bitter becomes easier.

Communication task assignments. In this approach, the assumption is that there are different communicative tasks to accomplish in any meeting and that this requires that some members of the group attend explicitly to the communicating process. Certain members of the group are given this assignment and given the right to interrupt the proceedings to call attention to events that need attention. Examples of such events include: a squabble when in effect the participants are arguing from different definitions; a point in time when only a few members of the group are participating; and, a point in time when participants are talking about different agenda items as if they were all the same.

Constructive criticism of the leader. In this approach, the procedure acknowledges how difficult it is for most people in most cultures to hear and act on criticism. For this reason, the procedure suggests that group members evaluate the leader by answering two questions: What has the leader done well? What could the leader do better?

Sense-making questions. In this approach, proposed as an alternative means by which professionals conduct needs assessments of individual clients/patrons/customers/users whom they serve, the professional's questions focus on learning and understanding what it is that brought the person to the system, what gaps the person faces, and what helps the person hopes to find. The questions, derived from an elaborate theoretic orientation to the problematics of communicating in systems, are seen as to going to the heart of what it is that brings a person to a system for help.

Pluralistic journalism. This proposal for journalistic practice attempts to incorporate into procedure the sense-making needs of members of the collectivity. The proposal mandates that 3–4 maximally different observers make observations and construct independent journalistic reports. They are then asked to explicitly address why they think their report differs from that of the other journalists. This latter material pertaining to understanding why observations are different allows readers to comprehend and make sense of heterogeneous voices. This proposal has been utilized in journalistic products created for a health clinic with enormous success.

User-based helps as retrieval tools. In this proposal, the readers of books (or articles) are asked to indicate how utilizing the materials helped them. The statements of the most recent group of readers are then made available to prospective readers as an alternative means for locating what would be useful to them. In one experiment, handwritten paragraphs were posted on a bulletin board; in another, they were pasted inside the book covers; in another, they were made available via computer. In all cases, readers were more likely to utilize these entry points than traditional ones.

Good news. In this approach, it is assumed that formalized discourse in society, via media, in organizations, and interpersonally, increasingly focuses on the negative and that individuals have trouble thinking and acting flexibly when weighed down in negativity. This procedure mandates that a group meeting, for example, require each group member to share positive news about self, organization, leader, world. In media, this procedure mandates that a portion of the coverage of all issues focus on the positive—accomplishments, instances of compassion and caring, examples of beauty and peace, or whatever is valued in that context.

All of the examples above share one thing in common—an acceptance of the dialogic nature of communication, the here-and-now making of meaning that involves continuing interaction between individuals, environments, and collectivities. By explicitly acknowledging the dialogic nature of communication, these inventions attempt to prevent or forestall the decay back into authoritarian power structures that confound even the most well-intentioned democratic communication designs. By acknowledging the dialogic nature of communication, these inventions also bring out for attention the ways in which micro and macro relate to each other, rather than assuming that these worlds are in opposition.

SOME PROBLEMS WITH INVENTION

The framework above is proposed as an example of a procedurally defined template for studying democratic communication. Studying is proposed both for descriptive and historical approaches: What *have* we done procedurally with what consequences at both macro and micro levels? Studying is also proposed as inventive: What *might* be done procedurally with what consequences at both macro and micro levels?

For the context of democratic communication, however, description and invention are not enough. A problem is allowing the system (i.e., the humans whose communicating behavior energizes the system) to accept new/alternative procedures. In this regard, one difficulty is that procedures are "rigidifed" into systems because they are ideologically bound. Another difficulty is that they are rigidified because they are behaviorally bound; embedded into repetitive behavioral patterns almost out-of-consciousness. Learning such patterns is easier than un-learning them.

The situationally defined strategy noticeably deemphasized in the examples above is that of individual relating to self. The communication tactic noticeably left out is that of undoing rigidities. Both cases demonstrate that as a species we have not paid explicit attention, either through research or practice design, to the need to build in procedures to deal with the fundamental intersection of situational strategy and communication tactic. Any time individuals singly or in collectivity come to a communicative moment, they are facing a new moment. This moment has not occurred before. It may be usefully addressed with tactics or strategies used in the past, but the communicating entities involved will be unable to perform responsively to the moment if they are not flexible and able to construct appropriate tactics and strategies. If they are hampered by rigidity, and our assumption is that it is part of the human condition to carry around rigidities, then it is impossible to proceed flexibly. We therefore assume that that necessity demands procedures for undoing these rigidities.

Yet, to allow procedures to keep pace with structural changes, the communication procedures that serve to energize structures must be amenable to change. This does not mean eliminating an "old" procedure, for the "old" procedure is seen as theoretically having utility depending on situational conditions. Rather it means removing the rigidity from the old procedure to allow for an increase in the diversity and flexibility of the communicative repertoire. The point is to make available to the communicating entity alternative communicating behaviors that can be brought to bear in the situation depending on how the situation is assessed.

The situation is made complicated because of the fact that the human's ability to change procedural skills depends not only on awareness of alternatives, but on the availability of repetitive practice. The way a human truly learns a behavior so that it becomes second nature is to perform it over and over again. Any procedure performed regularly will have power over a new procedure until that new procedure has been repeated enough to make it second nature—available for spontaneously rapid use. Therefore, to modulate a new procedure into a structure requires repetitive practice. The goal is to increase communicative capability.

Awareness of alternatives is not alone sufficient for the improvement of communicating capabilities. Since all structures are energized via communicatings performed by individual human beings either individually or in collectivity, what is envisioned here is a need both to increase awareness and to diversify habits. Increasing awareness is seen as the easier task since diversifying behavioral routines requires both practice and an acknowledgement of the anxiety and inefficiency that necessarily accompanies any behavior change process.

A further complication is that behavioral routines (particularly communication behavioral routines) are a site where oppressive or hurtful learning conditions are likely to show their damage.[23] As specified earlier under the tactic "undoing rigidity," if an individual is not flexible in a communication situation, that individual is unlikely to perform any of the tactics well. A crucial step that has not been given much attention (because the focuses of the macro and the cultural streams have been elsewhere) is the necessity to free current communicating habits from their rigidity. This freeing up of flexibility must be accomplished before appropriate communication tactics can even be learned, let alone practiced.

Behavioral routines, no matter what their sources, are often learned by humans while they are being systematically oppressed or hurt by the structures of their societies or systematically taught to

---

[23] The discussion of consciousness raising, conscientizing, and increasing communicative flexibility presented here rests heavily on works by: Breuer and Freud (1957), Freire (1970), Jackins (1974), and Rogers (1961).

oppress. The "essence" of psychoanalytic theory and research suggests that behaviors learned in such oppressive and hurtful circumstances are not available to change simply as a result of awareness and practice. Rather, the behavior will be habitualized in a qualitatively different way.

Behaviors that become habitualized without oppressive or hurtful circumstances surrounding their acquisition are easily observed by actors and reasonably amenable to change via practice. This is because they are in the realm of consciousness where awareness of them is stored both digitally and analogically. In contrast, behaviors that are learned in oppressive and hurtful circumstances are not easily observed by actors are performed out of consciousness, and awareness of them is stored only analogically. An important aspect of what is being proposed here is that we are challenging the assumed-to-be unconsciousness of the performance of communicating procedures (e.g., the rules and norms of cultures). We are suggesting that unconsciousness, an inability to be aware of behavior, is a special case involving learning which was in some way oppressive or hurtful. What this means is that the habitualization of the behavior is deeply enmeshed with acceptance of oppression and hurt and with the inability to think and observe that results from oppressive and hurtful circumstances.

Behaviors habitualized in this way need more than thought and practice to make them amenable to change. The actor must go through a self-controlled consciousness-raising process. The actor may artfully use others (as confidants, counselors, spiritual leaders, etc.) during this process but, as the essence of psychoanalytic theory suggests, the process is a self-controlled one, an act of individual emergence from past circumstances.

Most societies have very few existing procedures for what is regarded here as a fundamentally requisite tactic. Communication research has paid little attention to this concern since Western societies have, in essence, relegated the world of the "subjective" to the psychiatric couch and out of the system mainstream. A possible exception to this may be entertainment media programs which studies show have at times served therapeutic and conscientizing functions.

A crucial element of the perspective on communication proposed in this chapter, then, is the idea that in establishing democratic means of communicating it will be necessary to assist communicating entities in this process by incorporating conscientizing tactical procedures. This undoing of rigidities is seen as a necessary part of attempts to gain greater flexibility—in essence, to become more communicatively competent. Further, the capacity for communicative competence is seen as inherent in the human species and necessary to the implementation of democratic communication designs in whatever definitional context they are proposed.

REFERENCES

Altheide, D. (1985). *Media power.* Beverly Hills: Sage.
Argumedo, A. (1981, Summer). The new world information order and international power. *Journal of International Affairs,* pp. 179–188.
Arusha Declaration on World Telecommunications Development. (1985, May 30). At the First World Telecommunications Development Conference, Arusha, Tanzania, pp. 1–15.
Belkin, N.J. (1978). Information concepts for information science. *Journal of Documentation, 34*(1), 133–143.
Belkin, N.J., Oddy, R.N., & Brooks, H.M. (1982a). ASK for information retrieval: Part I. Background and theory. *Journal of Documentation, 38*(2), 61–71.
Belkin, N.J., Oddy, R.N., & Brooks, H.M. (1982b). ASK for information retrieval: Part II. Results of a design study. *Journal of Documentation, 38*(3), 145–164.
Breuer, J., & Freud, S. (1957). *Studies in hysteria* (ed. and trans. by J. Strachley). New York: Basic Books.
Bruck, P.A. (1989). Strategies for peace, strategies for news research. *Journal of Communication, 39*(1), 108–129.
Carter, R. (1989, May). *What does a gap imply?* Paper prepared for panel, "Finding a More Powerful Analytic for Comparative Research: Using the Gap Idea in Cross-Cultural Research," Intercultural and Development Communication Division, International Communication Association meeting, San Francisco, CA.
Carter, R. (1982). *Button, button.* . . . Seattle, WA: School of Communication, University of Washington.
Carter, R.F. (1980, December). *Discontinuity and communication.* Paper written for the seminar on communication from Eastern and Western sponsored by the East-West Communication Institute, East-West Center, Honolulu, HI.
Carter, R.F., Ruggels, W.L., Jackson, K.M., & Heffner, M.B. (1972). Application of signaled stopping technique to communication research. In P. Clarke (Ed.), *New models for mass communication research* (pp. 5–44). Beverly Hills, CA: Sage.
Carter, R.F., Ruggels W.L., & Simpson, R.A. (1975). *Minding society.* Paper presented to the AEJ meeting, Ottawa, Canada.
Communication and development. (1989). *Communication Research Trends, 9*(3). (A Quarterly Information Service from the Centre for the Study of Communication and Culture.)

Dervin, B. (1990). Comparative theory reconceptualized: From entities and states to processes and dynamics. *Communication Theory, 1*(1).

Dervin, B. (1989a). Users as research inventions: How research categories perpetuate inequities. *Journal of Communication, 39*(3), 216–232.

Dervin, B. (1989b). Audience as listener and learner; teacher and confidante: Measuring and being measured by the audience. In R. E. Rice & C. Atkins (Eds.), *Public communication campaigns* (2nd ed., pp. 67–86). Newbury Park, CA: Sage.

Dervin, B. (1983). Information as a user construct: The relevance of perceived information needs to synthesis and interpretation. In S.A. Ward & L.J. Reed (Eds.), *Knowledge structure and use: Implications for synthesis and interpretation* (pp. 153–183). Philadelphia, PA: University Press.

Dervin, B., & Clark, K.D. (1989). Communications as cultural identity: The invention mandate. *Media Development, 36* (2), 5–8.

Dervin, B., & Dewdney, P. (1986). Neutral questioning: A new approach to the reference interview. *RQ, 25*(4), 506–513.

Dervin, B., Grossberg, L., O'Keefe, B.J., & Wartella, E. (1989). *Rethinking Communication, Volume 1: Paradigm issues.* Newbury Park: CA: Sage Publications.

Dervin, B., Grossberg, L., O'Keefe, B.J., & Wartella, E. (1989). *Rethinking communication, Volume 2: Paradigm exemplars.* Newbury Park, CA: Sage Publications.

Dervin, B., & Nilan, M. (1986). Information needs and used. *Annual Review of Information Science and Technology, 21,* 3–33.

Dewey, J. (1915). *Democracy and education.* New York: Macmillan.

Dreifus, C. (1973). *Women's fate: Raps from a feminist consciousness raising group.* New York: Bantam.

Dutton, W.H. (1985). Decision-making in the information age: Computer models and public policy. In R. Finnegan, G. Salaman, & K. Thompson (Eds.), *Information technology: Social issues, a reader* (pp. 181–190). Sevenoaks, UK: Hodden and Stoughton.

Edelstein, A. (1974). *The uses of communication in decision making: A comparative study of Yugoslavia and the United States.* New York: Praeger.

Ettema, J.S., & Glasser, T.L. (1988). Narrative form and moral force: The realization of innocence and guilt through investigative journalism. *Journal of Communication 38*(3), 8–26.

Fitzpatrick, M.A. (1983). Effective interpersonal communication for women in the corporations: Think like a man, talk like a lady. In J. Pilotta (Ed.), *Women in organizations: Barriers and breakthroughs* (pp. 73–84). Prophet Heights, IL: Wayland Press.

Foss, K.A., & Foss, S.K. (1983). The status of research on women and communication. *Communication Quarterly, 31,* 195–204.

Freire, P. (1970). *Pedagogy of the oppressed.* New York: Seabury Press.

Geertz, C. (1973). *The interpretation of culture.* New York: Basic Books.

Giddens, A. (1984). *The constitution of society: Outline of the theory of structuration.* Cambridge: Polity Press.

Giddens, A. (1989). The orthodox consensus and the emerging synthesis. In B. Dervin, L. Grossberg, B.J. O'Keefe, & E. Wartella (Eds.), *Rethinking communication, Volume 1: Paradigm issues* (pp. 53–65). Newbury Park, CA: Sage.

Gitlin, T. (1980). *The whole world is watching: Mass media in the making and unmaking of the new left.* Berkeley, CA: University of California Press.

Goldhaber, G.M., & Barnett, G.A. (1988). *Handbook of organizational communication.* Norwood, NJ: Ablex.

Goodwin, C. (1989). Turn construction and conversational organization. In B. Dervin, L. Grossberg, B.J. O'Keefe, & E. Wartella (Eds.) *Rethinking Communication, Volume 2: Paradigm exemplars* (pp. 88–102). Newbury Park, CA: Sage.

Habermas, J. (1984). *Theory of communicative action I: Reason and the rationalization of society* (T. McCarthy, trans.). Boston: Beacon Press.

Habermas, J. (1987). *Theory of communicative action I: Lifeworld and system* (T. McCarthy, trans.). Boston: Beacon Press.

Habermas, J. (1979) *Communication and the evolution of society* (T. McCarthy, trans.). Boston: Beacon.

Hachten, W.A. (1982). *The world news prism: Changing media, clashing ideologies.* Ames, IA: The Iowa State University.

Hall, S. (1989). Ideology and communication theory. In B. Dervin, L. Grossberg, B.J. O'Keefe, & E. Wartella (Eds.), Rethinking communication, Volume 1: Paradigm issues (pp. 40–52). Newbury Park, CA: Sage.

Hall, S., Chrichter, C., Jefferson, T., Clarke, J., & Roberts, B. (1978). *Policing the crisis: Mugging, the state, and law and order.* London: Macmillan.

Hamelink, C.J. (1983). *Cultural autonomy in global communications.* New York: Longman.

Head, S.W. (1985). *World broadcasting systems: A comparative analysis.* Belmont, CA: Wadsworth.

Hirokawa, R.Y. (1988). Group communication and decision-making performance: A continued test of the functional perspective. *Human Communication Research, 14*(4), 487–515.

Jablin, F.M., Putman, L.L., Roberts, K.H., & Porter, L.W. (1987). *Handbook of organizational communication.* Newbury Park, CA: Sage.

Jackins, H. (1974). *The human situation.* Seattle, WA: Rational Island Publishing.

Jayaweera, N. (1987). Rethinking development communication: A holistic view. In N. Jayaweera & S. Amunugama (Eds.), *Rethinking development communication* (pp. 76–94). Newbury Park, CA: Sage.

Jensen, K.B. (1987). News as ideology: Economic statistics and political ritual in television network news. *Journal of Communication, 37*(1), 8–27.

Katz, J. (1987). What makes crime "news"? *Media, Culture, and Society, 9,* 47–75.

Kellerman, K., & Lim, T.S. (1989). Conversational acquaintance: The flexibility of routinized behavior. In B. Dervin, L. Grossberg, B.J. O'Keefe, &

E. Wartella (Eds.), *Rethinking communication, Volume 2: Paradigm exemplars* (pp. 172–187). Newbury Park, CA: Sage.

Knapp, M.L., Stafford, L., & Daly, J.A. (1986). Regrettable messages: Things people wish they hadn't said. *Journal of Communication, 36*(4), 40–58.

Kress, G. (1986). Language in the media: The construction of the domain of public and private. *Media, Culture, and Society, 8*, 395–419.

Lukes, S. (1974). *Power: A radical view*. London: The MacMillan Press Ltd.

Matta, F.R. (1986). Alternative communication: Solidarity and development in the face of transnational expansion. In R. Atwood & E.G. McAnany (Eds.), *Communication and Latin American society: Trends in critical research, 1960–1985* (pp. 190–214). Madison, WI: The University of Wisconsin Press.

McLaughlin, M. (1984). What conversationalists know: Rules, maxims, and other lore. *Conversation: How talk is organized*. Beverly Hills: Sage.

Mowlana, H. (1986). *Global information and world communication: New frontiers in international relations*. New York: Longman.

Murdock, G.P. (1967). *Ethnographic atlas: A summary*. Pittsburgh: University of Pittsburgh Press.

Nadler, M.K., & Nadler, L.B. (1987). Communication, gender and intraorganizational negotiation ability. In L.D. Stewart & S. Ting (Eds.), *Communication, gender & sex roles in diverse interaction contexts* (pp. 119–134). Norwood, NJ: Ablex.

O'Keefe, B.J., & McCormack, S.A. (1987). Message design logic and message goal structure: Effects on perceptions of message quality in regulative communication situations. *Human Communication Research, 14*(1), 68–92.

Poole, M.S., & Roth, J. (1989a). Decision development in small groups IV: A typology of group decisions paths. *Human Communication Research, 15*(3), 323–356.

Poole, M.S., & Roth, J. (1989b). Decision development in small groups V: Test of a contingency model. *Human Communication Research, 15*(4), 549–589.

Rakow, L.S. (in press). Information and power: Toward a critical theory of information campaigns. In C.T. Salmon (Ed.), *Information campaigns: Managing the process of social change* (Vol. 18, pp. 164–184). Newbury Park, CA: Sage Publication Annual Review.

Resolution of the Administrative Council of the International Telecommunication Union. (1985, May 30). At the First World Telecommunications Development Conference, Arusha, Tanzania, pp. 1–15.

Rogers, C. (1961). *On becoming a person: A therapeutic view of psychotherapy*. Boston: Houghton Mifflin.

Rokeach, M. (1960). *The open and closed mind: Investigations into the nature of belief systems and personality systems*. New York: Basic Books.

Ryan, S.M. (1985). *Parliamentary procedures: Essential principles*. New York: Cornwall Books.

Schiller, H.I. (1978). Decolonization of information: Efforts toward a new international order. *Latin American Perspectives, 16, 5*(1), 35–48.

Servaes, J. (1986). Development theory and communication policy: Power to the people! *European Journal of Communication, 1,* 203–229.

Spitzack, C., & Carter, K. (1987). Women in communication studies: A typology for revision. *Quarterly Journal of Speech, 73*(4), 401–423.

Splichal, S. (1987). 'Public opinion' and the controversies of communication science. *Media, Culture, and Society, 9, 237–61.*

Stohl, C. (1989). Understanding quality circles: a communication network perspective. In B. Dervin, L. Grossberg, B.J. O'Keefe, & E. Wartella (Eds.) *Rethinking communication, Volume 2: Paradigm exemplars* (pp. 346–360). Newbury Park, CA: Sage.

Talley, M.A., & Peck, V.R. (1980). The relationship between psychological gender orientation and communication style. *Human Communication Research, 6,* 326–339.

Tehranian, M. (1988). Information technologies and world development. *Intermedia, 16*(3), 30–38.

Tehranian, M. (1982). Open planning: The uses of communications in participatory development. *Development and Peace, 3,* 60–70.

Tehranian, M. (1979). Communication and international development: Some theoretical considerations. *Cultures, 6*(3), 29–37.

Textor, R.B. (1967). *A cross-cultural survey.* New Haven, CT: HRAF Press.

Tracy, K. (1989). Conversational dilemmas and the naturalistic experiment. In B. Dervin, L. Grossberg, B.J. O'Keefe, & E. Wartella (Eds.), *Rethinking communication, Volume 2: Paradigm exemplars* (pp. 411–423). Newbury Park, CA: Sage.

Tracy, K., Van Dusen, D., & Robinson, S. (1987). "Good" and "bad" criticism: A descriptive analysis. *Journal of Communication, 37*(2),46–59.

Tuchman, G. (1978). *Making news: A study in the construction of reality.* New York: The Free Press.

Van Driel, B., & Richardson, J.T. (1988). Print coverage of new religious movements: A longitudinal study. *Journal of Communication, 38*(3), 37–61.

White, E.C. (1987). *Kaironomia: On the will to invent.* Ithaca, NY: Cornell University Press.

White, R.A. (1987, May). *Progress toward a new world information and communication order: A third world perspective.* Unpublished paper, Centre for the Study of Communictaion and Culture, London.

Yelsma, P. (1986). Marriage vs. cohabitation: Couples communication practices and satisfaction. *Journal of Communication, 36*(4), 94–107.

8

Cultural "Dependency," "Diversity," "Identity," "Imperialism" or "Synchronization"

Jan Servaes
Department of Mass Communication
Catholic University of Nijmegen
The Netherlands

INTRODUCTION

Modernization and dependency continue to be the two most common views on development for social change, in general, as well as in the field of communication for development (or development communication, or even international communication for that matter) in particular.

The *modernization theory*, developed during the late 1940s and 1950s, states that the problem of underdevelopment or "backwardness" can be solved by a more or less mechanical application of the economic and political system in the West to countries in the so-called Third World. It starts from the assumption that the difference between the First and the Third World is one of degree rather than of kind. The *dependency theory*, on the other hand, emerged in the mid-1960s. It has to be interpreted as a critique on the modernization perspective, initially mainly formulated by Latin American social scientists. This dependency approach formed part of a general structuralistic reorientation in the social sciences. Contrary to the modernization scholars, who concentrated on the analyses of the nation-state, the "dependistas" were primarily concerned with the effects of dependency in peripheral countries, but implicit in their analysis was the idea that development and underdevelopment must be understood in the context of the world system. They argue that the domination of the Periphery by the Center occurs through a combination of power components, that is, military, economics, politics, culture, and so on. The specific components of the domination of any nation at a given point of time vary from those of another as a result of the variations in numerous factors, including the resources of the Center powers, the nature or structure of the Periphery nation, and the degree of resistance to domination. However, generally speaking, both modernization and dependency scholars start from a primarily economically oriented analytical method.

Since the late 1970s, the above two development paradigms have come under attack in academic circles. Contrary to the more economic and political oriented views of the modernization and dependency theories, one started to argue that there is no universal path to development, that development must be conceived as an integral, multidimensional, and dialectic process that can differ from one community to another. The basic assumption is that there are no societies that function completely autonomously and that are completely self-sufficient, nor are there any communities whose development is exclusively determined by external factors. Every community is dependent in one way or another, both in form and in degree. Thus, one sought a framework within which both the so-called Center and Periphery could be studied separately and in their mutual relationship, that is, an external as well as internal analysis. This also implies that the problem of development is a relative one, and no part of the world can claim to be developed in all respects. Therefore, this view argues, the discussion on the degree and scope of inter(in)dependence is connected with the content of development: need-oriented, endogenous, self-reliant, ecologically sound, and based on participatory democracy and structural transformations. The common starting point here is the examination of the changes from a "bottom-up" perspective, from the self-development of the local community. I have defined this new perspective on development as *"multiplicity in one world"* (for more details, see Servaes, 1987, 1989b).

After a brief overview of a number of interrelated dialectic-analytical "aspects" which together, in my opinion, constitute the essence of this "multiplicity" paradigm, and a general assessment of the so-called "cultural imperialism" perspective, I will discuss a number of aspects to outline a new research framework which is presently being used to study the interrelationship between culture and communication in Thailand (see Boonyaketmala, 1985; Servaes & Malikhao, 1989, Servaes, 1990a, 1990b).

ONE WORLD, MANY CULTURES

First a few words about the "novelty" of this multiplicity paradigm and its consequences for the study of communication and development problems. The impetus for this new approach stems from at least two interdisciplinary theories: the mainly economic *world system analysis* and the anthropological *"coupling" of production forms* approach. The best-known representative of the former trend is Immanuel Wallerstein, who argues that the fundamental traits of the capitalist world system since the 16th century have remained virtually unchanged, that a small number of Center countries enter into functional relationships with peripheral and semiperipheral nations, that the developmental dynamic is determined internally and not externally. According to other authors (see, e.g., Thomas, 1984; Vogler, 1985) the interpretations of this group seem to stress the dynamic of the capitalist system onesidedly as a universally explanatory principle. From the latter viewpoint it is more a matter of *multiple dynamic*: in the margin of the capitalist system, all kinds of pre- or noncapitalistic organizational patterns maintain their own coherency and significance. It is not surprising that this view prevails among anthropologists, especially those who are doing research in Africa (Fonkoue, 1985; Meillassoux, 1986). For it is precisely in Africa where old forms of organization, however much transformed, still seem to form a real "obstacle" to the effects of capitalist relationships. These forms of economic organization and production are often defined by the term *"conviviality."* In this respect, two research areas from the work of these anthropologists are important: their studies on the organization and development of local groups, communities and social structures in general; and their analyses of the so-called "informal sectors" in society. They stress the special autonomy of superstructural institutions in the precapitalist forms of production and also the coupling of forms of production and its particular role after decolonization has gained the upper hand. From this, it appears that all kinds of noneconomic factors, such as cultural principles like kinship and religion, that gave the old forms of production form still have a direct influence in this coupling.

CULTURE AND CULTURAL IDENTITY

The concept of culture has long been virtually ignored in the development debate. Only in the above multiplicity paradigm, the concept of
culture has come into the picture.

Culture can be defined as a social setting in which a certain reference framework has taken concrete form or has been "institutionalized" and orients and structures the interaction and communication
of people within this historical context. This intrinsic bond with a society whose actions are full of value makes all social facts cultural
goods. For social facts like institutions, behavioral patterns, norm systems, structures, and societal models are construed and cultivated in
the light of certain values, preferences, or options that have developed
in a society in response to certain common needs or problems. Under
the concept of culture one therefore also means material and immate-
rial aspects of a certain way of life, past on and corroborated via socialization processes (e.g., school, media, church) to the members of
that society. This process through which knowledge is transmitted is
never linear. It is linked to power in conscious and unconscious ways;
it is sporadic and ubiquitous and transcends national and "cultural"
boundaries. It not only concerns decisions about good and evil and so
on, but also the way we eat, live, or dress. Three empirical dimensions
can be distinguished in such reference frameworks: a world view
(Weltanschauung), a value system, and a symbolic representation.

In this regard the term *cultural identity* refers to two complementary phenomena: on the one hand an inward sense of association or
identification with a specific culture or subculture, on the other hand
an outward tendency within a specific culture to share a sense of what
it has in common with other cultures and of what distinguishes it
from other cultures. However, since the needs and values that various
cultural communities develop in divergent situations and environments are not the same, the various cultures also manifest a varying
"identity." Like all social processes, this process is not purely rational
or a preplanned event. Thus, culture must be seen as the unintended
result of an interweaving of the behavior of a group of people who
interrelate and interact with each other.

At the same time, cultural identity can be interpreted and applied
in a suppressive or negative as well as liberative or positive way. Roy
Preiswerk (1980), for instance, attempted to evaluate the degree and
level of cultural identity, self-reliance, and basic needs in a multiple
development perspective. A positive-liberating interpretation of the
concept of cultural identity may, among other aspects, imply a posi-

tive orientation toward historical values, norms, and institutions; the resistance to excessive external influence; the rejection of values, institutions, and forms that destroy social cohesion; and the adaptation of forms of production so that they favor the specificity of human and local social development. On the other hand, a negative-dominating interpretation of cultural identity may include the use of so-called traditional values and norms, or arguments emphasizing the cultural "uniqueness" to legitimize marginalization or the existing status quo. Both processes could be at work simultaneously (for more details, see Servaes, 1989a).

POWER AND EMPOWERMENT

This perspective builds also on newer insights about power relationships adopted from European poststructuralist thinking. Contrary to the traditional, static interpretation of power, authors like Michel Foucault, Anthony Giddens, or Jurgen Habermas advocate a *more dialectic, dynamic and multicentered perception of power factors.* In the context of communication for development this implies that also counter power or empowerment from a bottom-up or grassroots perspective has to be taken into account. In general, one can distinguish between three problem areas in regard to power relationships: the mutual dependency between the macro-level of the society or a given system and the micro-level of the social actions involved; the position and the autonomy of the subject, and the relationship of domination, dependency and subordination versus liberation, selective participation and emancipation of power and interest contra positions.

The main factors of this new perspective are so-called *new social movements* with a concern for public issues like ecology, social justice, peace, education, civic action, and so on. Building on Habermas's (1981, 1985) research program I contend that the new social movements in the West, such as the women's movement, the environmental movement, and the peace movement, are not primarily oriented to problems that concern the distribution of material wealth but resist the *colonization of the life world.* They advocate a society where the blind dynamic and the imperialism of the independent subsystems of economy and state are subject to the normative restrictions of a "life world" in which communication processes can develop again in full freedom. Although Habermas mainly focuses on modern Western societies, I argued elsewhere (see Servaes, 1988) that his theoretical insights transcend this context and have a more global or universal "appeal," that is, are also relevant for Third World environments because this type of social groupings transcends the notion of political parties as traditionally understood and conceived. The guiding principle of these social movements is to proceed from the grassroots upwards, from a bottom-up perspective, rather than from the top downwards as is the case in the classic power structure that disregards the views of the masses and is therefore elite-oriented. The most effective forms of mobilization of these social movements are rooted in popular culture expressions.

DEPENDENCY AND CULTURE

Nowadays, as many scholars argue, we stand within the rather paradoxical situation that, as the Third World begins to emancipate itself economically and politically, cultural dominance increases. While the former colonialist was largely out to plunder economically profitable areas and showed only moderate interest in political administration, the technological evolution of the communication media have contributed to a cultural and ideological dependence.

Johan Galtung (1980) distinguishes between four *mechanisms of imperialism*: exploitation, penetration through a bridgehead (i.e., the peripheral elite), fragmentation, and marginalization. While exploitation is seen as the major source of inequality in this world, the three other mechanisms can be conceived as supporting factors, though not all are necessary. In other words, their influence can be both direct and indirect, either of an objectively measurable or subjectively perceptible nature. Therefore, Cees Hamelink (1983) gives preference to the concept of *cultural synchronization* above the more common "cultural imperialism" idea. In his opinion, cultural imperialism is the most frequent, but not exclusive, form in which cultural synchronization occurs. For cultural synchronization can take place without any overt imperialistic relations.

Building on this notion of cultural synchronization, one can distinguish between different *modes of influence* by the degree of intentionality which precedes them or with which they are accepted. According to Oliver Boyd-Barrett (1982), the international communication process consists of four major interrelated components: (a) the shape of the communication vehicle, involving a specific technology at the consumer end, and a typical range and balance of communication contexts; (b) a set of industrial arrangements for the continuation of media production, involving given structural relationships and financial facilities; (c) a body of values about ideal practice; and (d) specific media contents. Lee (1980), among others, adds a fifth component when emphasizing the importance of historical analysis.

Scholars who are particularly interested in studying the so-called "shape of the communication vehicle" (see, e.g., Katz & Wedell, 1977) would argue that radio and television were mainly developed in the United States specifically as one-way communication media for domestic distribution. Yet neither of these features were absolutely necessary as technological or market terms. This one-way character of broadcasting media—that is, the goal of nonstop broadcasting, the orientation towards a large, mass audience, and the striving for up-to-the-minute news—has become the dominant "shape" for the rest of the world. This standardization is sustained by a technological infrastructure developed largely in the United States. Although some developing countries have begun to manufacture their own receiver sets, all are dependent on imports for the expensive production and distribution technology, supplied by transnational companies. The organizational and financial structure, which lies behind the shape of a communication vehicle, is equally subject to export and dissemination. The form of the export or dissemination is not always direct, but may be of an indirect nature through advertising, technology transfer, the control of banking facilities, the dissemination of values or contents, and so on. (For a general appraisal, see, e.g., Becker, 1984, or Hancock, 1984.) It is in the software (programming), management, and evaluation domains where the threats to cultural autonomy and local adaptations are most acute because once a nation accepts another's concepts of what constitutes "professional," "responsible," or "appropriate" use of any communication medium, its room for cultural adaptation and experimentation may be seriously compromised. Such values of practice can be either explicit and visible rules of behavior in media organizations or implicit assumptions. Examples of values of practice include the idealized principles of "objectivity" and "impartiality" in news reporting, assumptions about the most appropriate forms of technology for specific media tasks (e.g., in encouraging the adoption of educational TV by developing countries); assumptions about what constitutes a "good" TV series. Another example of how Western values of practice can be exported and disseminated is through training and education (more details in Golding, 1977, and Jakubowicz, 1986).

As has been pointed out already, the number of people who have been doing research within this cultural dependency perspective is large. Some researchers focus on a particular medium, others on a specific geographic area. Both approaches have also been combined, either from a general standpoint, or by way of a case study. However, the most outstanding work in this tradition that has had the greatest influence on the international scene is the study by the International Commission for the Study of Communication Problems, edited by Sean MacBride (1980).

THREE "SCHOOLS"

Looking for the underlying theories in the cultural dependency field, one could broadly distinguish between three "schools" which all stem from more general theoretical and methodological approaches within Marxism: the culturalists, the political economists, and the structuralists.

First are the *culturalists,* who interpret culture, communication, and ideology rather idealistically and autonomously. They sympathize with the instrumentalist view which states that the media are actively engaged on behalf of a ruling class in suppressing or diverting opposition and reinforcing the ruling ideology. It attempts to establish with some empirical precision the links that bind the state power and the media together. Secondly, there are the *political economists,* who, as materialists, are more concerned with the political and economical base in which culture and communication occur. They work within a more structuralist view that analyses how the economic forces in the media favor resistance to fundamental social change, mainly because of a combination of market forces, operational requirements, and established work practices. The key in this view is ownership; its focus is thus more on economic structures than ideological content of the media. Thirdly, there is a more *structuralistic* view that concentrates more on the ideology and content of the media itself. The difference from the above views, especially the political-economist, lies in the recognition of a greater degree of "autonomy" of the cultural superstructure from the economic structure. Therefore, it is precisely the theoretical insights of this latter school that have contributed to the search for the new perspective on communication for development, that is, the multiplicity paradigm.

However, also this third school should not be looked at in a monolithic way. It has led to a number of subdivisions. Some authors (e.g., Grossberg, 1984; Hall, 1980; Jouet, 1981; Thompson, 1984; White, 1985) have been trying to bring some order in this variety. In general, three trends could be distinguished: a structuralist-materialist trend, a structuralist-culturalist trend, and an anthropological trend. According to the *structuralist-materialist* view the task of a materialistic theory of ideology is twofold: to investigate the origin and change of ideologies and to devise a relational schema indicating dominance, interdependence, and subordination between ideologies. Research in the origin and change of ideologies must start with an analysis of the processes of change in the structure of a particular society in relationship to its natural environment, that is, the reproduction conditions of already present ideologies must be identified. These changes form the material foundation for the rise of new ideologies. The ideological order of power, control, and dominance present in every society has two components: maintenance of a certain discourse and the use of nondiscursive, material forms of reward and sanction. This ideological order is structured in ideological apparatuses, which can be considered clusters of discourse and material practices. Since these ideological apparatuses are the result of class struggle, a distinction must be made between the ideological, dominating apparatuses of the ruling class and the ideological counterapparatuses of the suppressed class. The second *structuralist-culturalist* trend has become wellknown because of the studies done at the Centre for Contemporary Cultural Studies in Birmingham. The attempt is made to expand the concept of culture to the ways of life of all classes and to select these "lived cultures" as the object of study. Thus, they reject, with their new definition of culture, the distinction between "high" and "low" cultures, and give descriptions from the bottom with a minimum of theoretical clarity and consistency. The stress is also placed on texts as the object of culture analysis. They reduce meanings to the social experiences of an individual or a collective that form the origin of each assignation of meaning. Thus, it is held that the various historical cultural contents express the communal values and world view of class. The concepts of conscientization, experience, and collective action play an important role here. The third, and as yet the least profiled trend, can be called the *anthropological* trend, because it draws its concepts and analytical methods from cultural anthropology and ethnology. This group proceeds from the thesis that a particular culture must be studied in its totality, that is, as a way of life with a specific meaning, value, and belief pattern that typifies that particular society or local entity. The communication media are then considered institutions by which the new meaning systems are transmitted in a ritual manner in a community. Media like television thus fulfill the role of the tellers of myths and stories. The culture of a nation is interpreted as structured around myths that can be both cosmic and national. They function on a nonintentional, symbolic level and only come to the surface at times of national crisis, rapid social change, or exterior threat.

BLAMING THE "OUTSIDERS"

Though the cultural dependency perspective has contributed a great deal to a more appropriate assessment of the real situation in most Third World cultures, it can, with its stress on external explanatory factors, be considered the antithesis of the endogenously oriented modernization paradigm. But, as both mostly use economic variables, the difference is minimal in regard to the content of development. Just as the dependency theory flows from dissatisfaction with the modernization paradigm, the critics of the dependency point of view charge that it is not capable of adequately explaining the complex post-colonial reality.

Common criticisms are (see, for instance, Blomstrom & Hettne, 1984; Chilcote & Johnson, 1983; Narula & Pearce, 1986; Servaes, 1983): (a) A lack of internal class and state analyses within the Periphery that inhibits development of the productive forces. It is impossible to develop explanatory models without looking at the development of the global framework of power relations as a whole. (b) The excessive economic, static, and monolithic approaches that are often unable to explain and account for changes in underdeveloped economies over time. This implicitly accepted static and ahistorical view largely ignores the historical manifestations of imperialism and is in danger of becoming mere empty and highly abstract formulae. It prevents dependistas from explaining why and how stages and phases succeed one another and encourages a "third worldist" ideology that undermines the potential for international solidarity by lumping together as "enemies" both the center and the periphery in the Center. (c) A naive view of production forms which locates the force of capitalist development and underdevelopment in the transfer of the economic surplus from the Periphery to the Center, and therefore fails to differentiate capitalist from feudal or other precapitalist modes of controlling the direct producer and appropriating the surplus. (d) An overstress on the external variables as the cause of underdevelopment and dependency tends to focus on the metropoles and international capital (the so-called existing international division of labour), as they are "blamed" for poverty, stagnation, and backwardness, instead of on local class formation. This misdirects political action, producing pessimism and political complacency on the part of actual or potential revolutionary or liberative movements. (e) An erroneous evaluation of the internationalization of capital and production which holds that industrialization and thus "development" cannot take place in the Periphery, in the face of growing evidence to the contrary. The existing obstacles to development are due less to imperialist—Third World relationships than to the internal contradictions of the Periphery itself. (f) Finally this view of dependency, translated in political terms, primarily serves the interests and desires of the Third World bourgeoisie. While overstressing the contradictions on the international level the "dependistas" take little account of the contradictions on the national level between, on the one hand, the nation-state and the media structure and, on the other hand, the government and the public at large.

BEYOND CULTURAL DEPENDENCY

Many authors, among them also advocates of the cultural imperialism approach, have also recognized these shortcomings at the level of international communication research and urged that the approach be redefined and reexamined. Tracey (1985, p. 44), for instance, argues that "the level of analysis employed for understanding the implications of the mass media at the international, as opposed to the national and individual level, has remained frozen at the stage of intellectual development achieved by communications [sic] research in the first three or four decades of this century."

Generally, research into cultural dependency patterns is limited to *quantitative* and objectively measurable results. This kind of study demonstrates how much information, recreation, advertising, capital, software, and hardware are exported versus imported and also that there is an unbalanced communication flow between the Center and the Periphery and also causes intraregional and intranational disparities (between rural and urban areas, between linguistic and ethnic majorities and minorities, between rich and poor groups of classes, etc.). In general, most of the dependistas immediately take it for granted that, together with the high volume of Western media products, a conservative and capitalistic ideology and a consumption culture is transmitted and established. In this sense, they challenge the points of departure of the modernists and, in particular, those of the diffusion theorists who assume that the media play an important role in processes of social change. The *qualitative* impact and consequences of this dependency relationship, however, are often overlooked. For one also needs more detailed information on the qualitative aspects, such as, cultural and ideological components or the impact of external (mainly Western) influences on local communities. How these unequal processes affect, for instance, the culture, ideology, and identity of the local population in the long term. (Some reservation must be made for the problem of the production of news, which has already been analyzed in detail, both quantitatively and qualitatively. But, in view of its specific character, the findings derived are difficult to generalize.)

Such a view ignores some of the basic truths about communication, as they are developed in the multiplicity paradigm. Far from being a top-down phenomenon only, foreign mass media interact with local networks in what can be named a *coerseductive* (for coersive/seductive) way, and, therefore, have radically different effects and meanings in different cultural settings. Far from being passive recipients, audiences are actively involved in the construction of meaning around the media they consume. At a more theoretical level, *Habermas' theory of communicative action* could once again be taken as an example. It eloquently reveals the ambivalent character of mass communication. Media create a hierarchicalization of the communicative processes because they create lines of communication from the Center to the Periphery and from top to bottom. At the same time, the mass media are directly linked to the rational structure of the communicative action. They are not detached from it, like the subsystems of power and money, but they embody generalized forms of communication. In so doing, they remain, for their functioning, ultimately dependent on bipolar positions of communicatively gifted actors. Herein, according to Habermas, lies their ambivalence, which was not perceived by the Frankfurt School. A pluralistic and democratic use of mass media is far from being achieved at this time, he states, but it does belong to the real possibilities of the mass media.

As documented by Alrabaa (1986), Boyd (1984), Laing (1986), Mattelart (1983), Tracey (1985), Ugboajah (1985), or Wang (1984), one can observe at least *two interrelated developments*. First, there is a tendency to import cultural content and develop local imitations, and, second, many Third World communicators and organizations are using the imported media technologies to attempt to forge a more autonomous culture, independent of but, at the same time, borrowing from the Western culture. The idea of an international media software convergence is, therefore, rendered weak. Furthermore, as is the case in the West, one observes that, in spite of the better production quality, the majority of local audiences prefer programs produced in their own culture. This happens for at least two reasons: language and cultural affinity. Therefore, imported media can have a *boomerang effect,* conveying precisely the opposite consequence to that presumed by purveyors or observers on the surface. For instance, in his interesting analysis of the role of the Portugese language during the era of Portuguese colonialism in Africa, De Sousa (1974, p. 125) concludes that "in a dialectic process, the very Portuguese language that served the colonial power as an instrument of alienation was being used against it as a vehicle for ideas that preached emancipation from colonial domination."

At a more structural level, an important transition taking place in many countries is the strengthening of the traditional culture at grass-roots level. "Traditional" should not be viewed here in a conservative-repressive but progressive-emancipative way. Therefore, one can observe the growth of *dualistic communication structures.* Adaptation of traditional media for education and social action are encouraged because of their cultural values and their inexpensiveness: "Folk media are grounded on indigenous culture produced and consumed by members of a group. They reinforce the values of the group. They are visible cultural features, often strictly conventional, by which social relationships and a world view are maintained and defined. They take on many forms and are rich in symbolism" (Ugboajah, 1985, p. 172). A logical approach for societies and cultures that are concerned about the hegemony of culturally imperialistic Western media, therefore, could be to develop sets of "alternative," "countercultural," or "de-mythologizing" integrated media that could use external media technologies and products for radically different purposes (such as those described by Mattelart & Siegelaub, 1979, 1983; Nettleford, 1979; Tehranian, 1984; or in the special issue on "People's Power" of *Media Development,* 1988). Video and audiocassettes especially are generally explicitly mentioned for their "emancipative" potentials. They are rather cheap and consumer friendly on the one hand, and are less easy to control and censor by authorities on the other hand. Nevertheless, Boyd and Straubhaar (1985, p. 19) warn against too much optimism:

> While the view of Third World audiences as passive may no longer be accurate, the concepts of media dependency on foreign sources and a one-way flow of information may be exacerbated by VCRs. Given an apparently widespread trend toward entertainment in audience choices, this apparently greater freedom of choice may turn out to be only a greater freedom to select from pirated Western-produced television or film material. Cassettes may extend the present imbalance in the flow of films and television programs from developed to developing countries,

even in those countries where such imported content is banned or limited in broadcasting. The tendency of most cassette material to be pirated may also disrupt the existing levels of film and television production in the Third World. When copies are made illegally, no royalties are paid to the producer. This reduces the financial base of Third World production companies. Some Third World governments that count on maintaining political control, at least in part through control of communication media, are also discomfited by VCR's erosion of their control over television content. Not only might viewers ignore government-guided newscasts and development messages, but they may select illegally imported material that is considered immoral or politically subversive.

CONCLUSION

In accordance with the findings of other scholars (see, e.g., Fisher & Harms, 1983; Graff, 1983), I wish to summarize the above described changes in the field of communication for development and its consequences for communication research as follows:

1. The growth of a deeper understanding of the *nature of communication* itself: Early models in the 1950s and 1960s saw the communication process simply as a message going from a sender to a receiver (that is, Laswell's classic S-M-R model). The emphasis was mainly sender- and media-centric; the stress laid on the freedom of the press, the absence of censorship, and so on. Since the 1970s, however, communication has become more receiver- and message-centric. The emphasis is more on the process of communication (that is, the exchange of meaning) and on the significance of this process (that is, the social relationships created by communication and the social institutions and context which result from such relationships).

2. A new understanding of *communication as a two-way process:* The "oligarchic" view of communication implied that freedom of information was a one-way right from a higher to a lower level, from the Center to the Periphery, from an institution to an individual, from a communication-rich nation to a communication-poor one, and so on. Today, the interactive nature of communication is increasingly recognized. It is seen as fundamentally two-way rather than one-way, interactive and participatory rather than linear.

3. The trend towards *participatory democracy:* The end of the

colonial era has seen the rise of many independent states and the spread of democratic principles, even if only at the level of lip service. Though often ignored in practice, democracy is honored in theory. The world's communication media are still largely controlled by governments or powerful private interests, but they are more attuned to and aware of the democratic ideals than previously. At the same time, literacy levels have increased tremendously, and there has been a remarkable improvement in people's ability to handle and use communication technology. As a consequence, more and more people can use mass media and can no longer be denied access to and participation in communication processes for the lack of communication and technical skills.

4. Recognition of the *imbalance in communication resources:* The disparity in communication resources between different parts of the world is increasingly recognized as a cause of concern. As the Center nations develop their resources, the gap between Center and Periphery becomes greater. The plea for a more balanced and equal distribution of communication resources can only be discussed in terms of power at national and international levels. The attempt by local power elites to totally control the modern communication channels—press, broadcasting, education, and bureaucracy—does not longer ensure control of all the communication networks in a given society. Nor does control of the mass media ensure support for the controlling forces, nor for any mobilization around their objectives, nor for the effective repression of opposition.

5. The growing sense of *transnationalization and cultural synchronization*: Perhaps the greatest impetus towards a new formulation of communication freedoms and the need for realistic communication policies and planning have come from the realization that the international flow of communication has become the main carrier of transnational cultural synchronization. This cultural synchronization can take place without perceptible dependent relationships.

6. A new understanding of what is happening within the boundaries of the *nation-state*: One has to accept that "internal" and "external" factors inhibiting development do not exist independently of each other. Thus, in order to understand and develop a proper strategy one must have an understanding of the class relationships of any particular peripheral social formation

and the ways in which these structures articulate with the Center on the one hand, and the producing classes in the Third World on the other. To dismiss Third World ruling classes, for example, as mere puppets whose interests are always mechanically synonymous with those of the Center is to ignore the realities of a much more complex relationship. The very unevenness and contradictory nature of the capitalist development process necessarily produces a constantly changing relationship.

7. Recognition of the 'impact' of *communication technology*: Some communication systems (e.g., audio- and videotaping, copying, radio broadcasting) have become cheap and so simple that the rationale for regulating and controlling them centrally, as well as the ability to do so, is no longer relevant. However, other systems (for instance, satellites, remote sensing, transborder data flows) have become so expensive that they are beyond the means of smaller countries and may not be "suitable" to local environments.

8. A new understanding towards an *integration* of distinct means of communication: Modern mass media and alternate or parallel networks of folk media or interpersonal communication channels are not mutually exclusive by definition. Contrary to the beliefs of diffusion theorists, they are more effective if appropriatally used in an integrated fashion, according to the needs and constraints of the local context. The modern mass-media, having been mechanically transplanted from abroad into Third World societies, enjoy varying and limited rates of penetration. They are seldom truly integrated into institutional structures as occurs in Western societies. However, they can be effectively combined, provided a functional division of labor is established between them, and provided the limits of the mass media are recognized.

9. The recognition of *dualistic or parallel communication structures*: No longer governments or rulers are able to operate effectively, to control, censor, or to play the role of gatekeeper with regard to all communications networks at all times in a given society. Both alternate and parallel networks, which may not always be active, often function through political, sociocultural, religious, or class structures or can be based upon secular, cultural, artistic, or folkloric channels. These networks feature a highly participatory character, high rates of credibility and a

strong organic integration with other institutions deeply rooted in a given society.

REFERENCES

Alrabaa, S. (1986) Western mass media hegemony over the Third World. *Communication. 12*, 1.

Becker, J. (Ed.). (1984). *Information technology and a new international order* Lund: Studentlitteratur.

Becker, J., Hedebro, G., & Paldan, L. (Eds.). (1986). *Communication and domination.* Norwood, NJ: Ablex.

Blomstrom, M., & Hettne, B. (1984). *Development theory in transition. The dependency debate and beyond.* London: Zed.

Boonyaketmala, B. (1985). *The political economy of cultural dominance, dependence and disengagement. The transnationalized film industry in Thailand (1897–1984).* PhD Department of Political Science, University of Hawaii.

Boyd, D. (1984). The Janus effect? Imported television entertainment programming in developing countries. *Critical Studies in Mass Communication, 1,* 379–391.

Boyd, D., & Straubhaar, J. (1985). Development impact of the home video cassette recorder on Third World countries. *Journal of Broadcasting & Electronic Media, 29*(1), 5–21.

Boyd-Barrett, O. (1982). Cultural dependency and the mass media. In M. Gurevitch, T. Bennett, J. Curran, & J. Woollacott (Eds.), *Culture, society and the media.* London: Methuen.

Chilcote, R. R., & Johnson, D. (Eds.). (1983). *Theories of development. Mode of production or dependency?* Beverly Hills: Sage.

De Sousa, E. (1974). *Portugese colonialism in Africa.* Paris: UNESCO.

Fisher, D., & Harms, L.S. (Eds.). (1983). *The right to communicate: A new human right.* Dublin: Boole Press.

Fonkoue, J. (1985). *Difference et identite.* Paris: Silex.

Galtung, J. (1980). *The true worlds. A transnational perspective.* New York: Free Press.

Golding, P. (1977). Media professionalism in the Third World: The transfer of an ideology. In J. Curran, M. Gurevitch, & J. Woollacott (Eds.), *Mass communication and society.* London: Arnold.

Graff, R. (Ed.). (1983). *Communication for national development. Lessons from experience.* Cambridge: Oelgeschlager, Gunn & Hain.

Grossberg, L. (1984). Interpreting the "crisis" of culture in communication theory. *Critical Studies in Mass Communication, 1.*

Habermas, J. (1981). *Theorie des kommunikativen Handelns I+II,* Frankfurt: Suhrkamp.

Habermas, J. (1985). *Der philosophische Diskurs der Moderne.* Frankfurt: Suhrkamp.

Hall, S. (1980). Cultural studies: two paradigms. *Media, Culture and Society, 2,* 1.

Hamelink, C. (1983). *Cultural autonomy in global communications. Planning national information policy.* New York: Longman.

Hancock, A. (Ed). (1984). *Technology transfer and communication.* Paris: UNESCO.

Jakubowicz, K. (1986). Broadcasting and cultural identity in Black Africa: Can they go together? *The Third Channel, 2,* 1.

Jouet, J. (1981). Review of radical communication research: The conceptual limits. In E. McAnany, J. Schnitman, & N. Janus (Eds.), *Communication and social structure.* New York: Praeger.

Katz, E., & Wedell, G. (1977). *Broadcasting in the Third World. Promise and performance.* Cambridge, MA: Harvard University Press.

Laing, D. (1986). The music industry and the 'cultural imperialism' thesis. *Media, Culture and Society, 3,* 331–341.

Lee, C.C. (1980). *Media imperialism reconsidered. The homogenizing of television culture.* London: Sage.

MacBride, S. (Ed.). (1980). *Many voices. One world. Communication and society. Today and tomorrow.* Paris: UNESCO.

Mattelart, A., & Siegelaub, S. (Eds.). (1979). *Communication and class struggle* (Vol. 1). Paris: IMMRC.

Mattelart, A., & Siegelaub, S. (Eds.). (1983). *Communication and class struggle* (Vol. 2). Paris: IMMRC.

Mattelart, A. (1983). *Transnationals and the Third World. The struggle for culture.* Boston, MA: Bergin & Garvey.

Meillassoux, C. (1986). *Anthropologie de l'esclavage.* Paris: Presses Universitaires de France.

Narula, U., & Pearce, W. (1986). *Development as communication. A perspective on India.* Carbondale: Southern Illinois University Press.

Nettleford, R. (1979). *Cultural action and social change. The case of Jamaica.* Ottawa: International Development Research Centre.

Preiswerk, R. (1980). Identite culturelle, self-reliance et besoins fondamentaux. In P. Spitz & J. Galtung (Eds.), *Il faut manger pour vivre.* Paris: Presses Universitaires de France.

Servaes, J. (1983). *Communication and development. Some theoretical remarks.* Leuven, Belgium: Acco.

Servaes, J. (1987). *Media aid. Naar een 'ander' communicatie- en ontwikkelingsbeleid.* Leuven, Belgium: Acco.

Servaes, J. (1988). *Communication, development, and new social movements. A European perspective.* Paper International Communication Association (ICA) Conference, New Orleans, LA.

Servaes, J. (1989a). Cultural identity and modes of communication. In J. Anderson (Ed.), *Communication yearbook* (Vol. 12). Beverly Hills: Sage.

Servaes, J. (1989b). Shifts in development and communication theory: With a brief discussion of its communication policy and planning consequences. In B. Dervin & M. Voigt (Eds.), *Progress in communication sciences* (Vol. 9). Norwood, NJ: Ablex.

Servaes, J. (1990a). Technology transfer in Thailand: For whom and for what? *Journal of Contemporary Asia, 20*(2), *277–287.*

Servaes, J. (1990b). Unmasking the Thai smile. Interpersonal communication in Thailand. In K. Renckstorf & J. Janssen. (Eds), Communicatiewetenschappelÿke Bÿdragen 1989–1990. Nijmegen, The Netherlands: ITS.

Servaes, J., & Malikhao, P. (1989). How 'culture' affects films and video in Thailand. *Media Development, 36*(4), 32–36.

Sinclair, J. (1986). Dependent development and broadcasting: The Mexican Formula. *Media, Culture and Society, 8.*

Tehranian, M. (1984). Dependency and communication dualism in the Third World. With special reference to the case of Iran. In G. Wang & W. Dissanayake (Eds.), *Continuity and change in communication systems: An Asian perspective.* Norwood, NJ: Ablex.

Thomas, C. (1984). *The rise of the authoritarian state in peripheral societies.* London: Heinemann.

Thompson, J.B. (1984). *Studies in the theory of ideology.* Cambridge: Polity Press.

Traber, M. (Ed.). (1988). Communication—People's power. *Media Development, 35, 1.*

Tracey, M. (1985). The poisoned chalice? International television and the idea of dominance. *Daedalus, 114, 4.*

Ugboajah, F. (Ed.). (1985). *Mass communication, culture and society in West Africa.* Munich: Saur.

Vogler, C. (1985). *The nation state. The neglected dimension of class.* Hants, England: Gower.

Wang, G., & Dissanayake, W. (Eds.). (1984). *Continuity and change in communication systems: An Asian perspective.* Norwood, NJ: Ablex.

White, R. (1985). *The significance of recent developments in the field of mass communication.* Paper Sommatie 1985, Veldhoven, The Netherlands.

Part II

Studies in Communication and Democracy

9

Introduction: Studies in Communication Democracy

Janet Wasko
Dept. of Speech
University of Oregon

The decade of the 1980s proved only to reinforce the connection between democracy and communications. Certainly this was a most timely theme for the 1990 Congress of the International Association for Mass Communication and for this volume.

The issue of democratic communications takes on vital importance in the wake of popular movements that swept Eastern Europe in the waning months of 1989, leaving the Stalinist legacy buried beneath the rubble of the Berlin Wall. What started out as democratic movements calling for a free press and other basic reforms ended by toppling governments in Poland, East Germany, Czechoslovakia, and Romania. In less than six months, a tidal wave of unarmed civilians did more for democracy than all of NATO's warships, tanks, combat aircraft, and nuclear warheads had done in 40 years. While similar motivations prompted student demonstrations in the People's Republic of China, albeit with much different results, the movement has also produced radical changes in the Soviet Union.

What final shape these new reforms and new governments will take is not certain. But what is certain is that, at least in Eastern Europe, existing governments were overthrown by ordinary people using extraordinary courage—and mass communications. Without the use of the printed word, information broadcast via the airwaves, and other means of communication, those popular movements may not have succeeded.

Another development of the 1980s was the expansion of information and communication technologies, that is: satellite systems, home
video, cable, and so on. The link between these technologies and democracy became another key issue of the 1980s. The possibilities for
technological democracy seemed especially attractive in Western
countries, where media concentration continued at an accelerated
pace. The irony was especially heightened in the United States, where
voter turnout for Presidential elections was the lowest of 28 "democratic" countries.

The virtues of electronic or technological democracy were applauded
during the decade by numerous authors, such as Pool (1983), Toffler
(1980), and Dizard (1989), who argued that new communication technologies would provide more information and entertainment to more
people, thus stimulating a more democratic environment. Still others,
including Webster and Robins (1986), Schiller (1984), Hamelink (1988),
Reinecke (1984), and Mosco (1989), identified problems with the direction of new technological developments, stressing political, social, and
economic factors that tend to inhibit democratization.

Meanwhile, issues related to democratic communications introduced by the MacBride Commission in the 1970s, were revived at the
end of the 1980s. The MacBride Roundtable on Communication, representing communication professionals and nongovernmental organizations, met in Harare, Zimbabwe, in October 1989, and called for a
revitalization of the principles of the New World Information and Communication Order. The Harare Statement, adopted unanimously by
the group, notes that "the mass media could play a more decisive role
in furthering the democratic process, in the realization of peoples'
rights to self-determination and in the quest for peace and international understanding." The statement also emphasizes that the key to
these efforts is participation, including "access to the media, people's
right of reply, and their involvement in the decision making processes."

And finally, communication democracy was the aim of grass roots
organizations and citizens groups (such as the Union for Democratic
Communications, in the United States and Canada), and the focus of
several collections by communication scholars and activists (see
Raboy & Bruck, 1989; Wasko & Mosco, 1992).

In Part I, the authors stressed the fundamental relationship between democratic societies and democratic communications. In other
words, it is impossible to consider the concept of democratization of
communications without examining the democratization of society as
a whole. Though various components of such systems have been identified, we still don't have a clear map of the road to true communication democracy. Raymond Williams's observation—cited by several

authors—is again appropriate: A democratic communication system must be discussed and imagined, as none currently exist. Slavko Splichal further argues that it is necessary to work out democratic communication systems through criticism of theories and systems. Theories of communication democracy, then, must be considered along with empirical studies that analyze concrete problems encountered in efforts to democratize communication and society.

So, we continue this critique with the next group of articles that discusses the democratic characteristics of specific communications and information systems and presents case studies of communications democracy.

Several themes are explored in this section:

1. The problems of promoting democratic communications in the face of opposition to communication rights and democratic potential of communication systems. The media's representation of democratic communication and the right to communicate is one of the problems identified.
2. The assessment of communications democracy in specific national and regional communication systems. Different conceptions of democracy and the role of communication are considered in different settings, such as Austria, Malaysia, South Pacific, and South Asia.
3. The role of new technologies in strengthening or weakening democracy. The democratic possibilities for new communication systems are analyzed and critiqued.
4. The need for government to communicate to citizens in democratic systems. Guidelines and problems are presented.

In the first article, Colleen Roach outlines the problems of gaining acceptance for the "right to communicate" in the United States. In the 1980s, both the press and government officials denounced the concept, which was promoted as part of the New World Information Order, as radical and subversive. Roach documents the contradictions in the U.S. position, as well as the misrepresentation of the debate in the U.S. press. She also ties in the concepts of "right to know" and "right to culture," and finally raises questions pertaining to the role of the nation-state in the discussion of cultural and communication rights.

The nation-state also is relevant to Mustapha Masmoudi's discussion, as he analyzes aspects of government communication and information policy. He identifies differences between the various sectors of government, suggesting that one of the "laws of democracy" is that the role of communications is to clarify, and that political information should contribute to democratizing society and better understanding between governments and citizens.

Robert Jacobson points out, however, that "good government" is not enough for democracy, and reminds us that information technologies have historically been associated with power. He examines the concepts of reciprocity and interactivity, and argues that "reciprocity—a back-and-forth giving and taking, moderated by all participants in a discourse to their mutual advantage . . ." is a requirement for democratic technology, while interactive systems may only provide an illusion of democracy. Jacobson then focuses on the interactive and reciprocal characteristics of certain new information technologies, especially computer bulletin board systems.

In the next article, Peter Bruck discusses the need to rescue the concept of civil society (especially as it relates to communications media) not only as separate from State authority, but also from the restraints and dynamics of capital. He reviews the recent efforts of citizens' movements in East Central Europe to rearticulate civil society in their rejection of restrictive Communist governments. He further argues that West Central European countries have been uninspired by these movements. On the contrary, neoconservative politics reign in these countries, especially in the area of communications, where, in Austria, for example, media concentration is at an all-time high and the idea of democratization has come to be defined as "the widest possible consumer choice." Both of these trends are common to many Western countries, where Bruck's conclusions are appropriate: "The term civil society then needs to designate not only the social space free and independent of the legitimation and control needs of the State, but also free and independent of the accumulation needs and commodification dynamics of capital." Certainly this warning is applicable in both the East and West, but is especially urgent in light of Eastern European countries' reformulation of social systems, in general, and communications systems, in particular.

Binod Agrawal traces the introduction of new communications technologies in the plural civilizations of South Asia, noting that this rapid development must be analyzed within the context of a sociocultural and historical framework. He categorizes different views on the issue as technopositivist, technoneutral or technonegative, and argues that technonegativism is most applicable in the case of India, for instance, where new technologies, especially satellite broadcasting, "has reduced the possibility of people's participation, thereby, weakening democracy."

Meanwhile, Peter Gerdes considers the concept of democracy in the South Pacific area, where he observes a strong oral tradition and a consensus approach to maintaining social order. Gerdes's study emphasizes the importance of analyzing concrete cases in the question of communication democracy, for, as in the South Pacific, there are places where media may not be so essential to the democratic process. He also points out that the Western media have not learned to respect democracies that are different. This is certainly an important lesson for any academic discussion of communication democracy, as well.

Peter Gerdes's chapter reminds us of the continuing complex and difficult issues associated with the notion of democratic communications. While we have offered no concrete proposals to assure democracy or democratic communications systems, at least this volume has been an attempt to grapple with these issues, and to further discuss and imagine such systems.

REFERENCES

Dizard, W. (1989). *The coming information age.* New York: Longman.
Hamelink, C. (1988). *The technology gamble.* Norwood, NJ: Ablex.
Mosco, V. (1989). *The pay-per society.* Toronto: Garamond.
Pool, I. de Sola. (1983). *Technologies of freedom.* Cambridge, MA: Harvard University Press.
Raboy, M., & Bruck, P.A. (1989). *Communication for and against democracy.* Black Rose Books.
Reinecke, I. (1984). *Electronic illusions: A skeptic's view of our high-tech future.* Harmondsworth: Penguin.
Schiller, H. (1984). *Information and the crisis economy.* Norwood, NJ: Ablex.
Toffler, A. (1980). *The third wave.* New York: Collins.
Wasko, J., & Mosco, V. (1992). *Democratic communications in the information age.* Toronto: Garamond Press.
Webster, F., & Robins, K. (1986). *Information technology: A Luddite analysis.* Norwood, NJ: Ablex.

10

Reflections on Communication and Cultural Rights and the Rights of Peoples

Colleen Roach
Department of Communication Arts and Sciences
Queens College
City University of New York

AMERICAN OBJECTIONS TO THE RIGHT TO COMMUNICATE

Jean d'Arcy (1969), the late Frenchman who was considered the father of the right to communicate, began his foreword to a book on this subject by quoting from Bertolt Brecht:

> Radio must be changed from a means of distribution to a means of communication. Radio would be the most wonderful means of communication imaginable in public life, a huge linked system—that is to say, it would be such if it were capable not only of receiving but of transmitting, of allowing the listener not only to hear but to speak, and did not isolate him but brought him into contact. (d'Arcy, 1977)

Given that Jean d'Arcy thus traces the ideological lineage of the right to communicate back to Brecht, is it surprising that in the 1980s this concept would be roundly denounced by the United States press and government officials as both radical and subversive?

U.S. objections to the right to communicate surfaced during the 1980s, when it was viewed as a key component of the movement for a New International Information Order (NIIO). As such, the right to communicate, like all of the other subissues of the NIIO debate (such as the social responsibility of the media, national communication policies and the protection of journalists) was denounced for promoting government control of the media (Roach, 1987).

The following editorial, widely syndicated in American newspapers in 1983, is a typical representation of how this attack was presented in the press:

> Sounds very good—unless you understand that this [the right to communicate] means that any radical group can command as much space in any publication or as much air time on any radio or television station it wishes. This means an end to private ownership of the means of communication. It means that these media become organs of official propaganda . . . UNESCO must back off. Control is not the answer. ("Freedom to Communicate," 1983)

However, in addition to this general attack on the right to communicate, American spokespeople also criticized it for another reason: It was viewed as one of the "people's rights" (or "rights of solidarity") that UNESCO began supporting in the 1980s. Hence, the right to communicate became enmeshed in the larger East/West controversy over "collective rights vs. individual rights."

In UNESCO's Second Medium-Term Plan for 1984–1989, approved at the 1982 General Conference, special attention was paid to the "rights of peoples," which were even mentioned in the title of Major Program XIII: "Peace, International Understanding and the Rights of Peoples." Moreover, this program is described in this official document, approved by the Organization's Member States, as representing "the culmination of the approach underlying the Medium-Term Plan" (UNESCO, 1983, p. 53).

Although the connection between the right to communicate and "people's rights" was not made explicit in the various Communications Resolutions of the General Conferences in the 1980s, an attempt was made to establish such a link in UNESCO's Draft "Program and Budget for 1984–85," which was also subject to approval by the Member States. The American ambassador to UNESCO, Jean Gerard (1983), did not hesitate to criticize this linkage at a meeting of the Executive Board, held in June 1983: "I have serious reservations about the introduction in the Communication chapter of the concept of the 'new rights of solidarity' (paragraph 3130). This seems to parallel some other liberties taken with language at UNESCO; liberties which have caused long and serious arguments" (Gerard, 1983, p. 12).

In spite of the fact that this "language" disappeared from the Final Document approved by the 1983 General Conference, the controversy over the right to communicate and the "rights of peoples" persisted, as demonstrated in the following AP coverage (October 25, 1983) of the 1983 General Conference:

> The right to communicate has become the centerpiece for the New World Information and Communication Order UNESCO is trying to establish gradually. It is one of the "collective or people's rights," that have fueled a major controversy at the organization. Many non-industrialized nations maintain that peoples' rights should have equality with individual human rights. Western nations maintain such a concept could be used by authoritarian governments.

CONTRADICTIONS OF THE AMERICAN POSITION ON THE RIGHT TO COMMUNICATE

The American position on the right to communicate completely ignores the historical evolution of this concept. Had the American press and diplomats done their homework, they would have easily discovered the Western origin of the right to communicate. As already indicated, this notion was sired in 1969 by the late Jean d'Arcy, an important figure in French media circles and the president of the London-based International Institute of Communications (IIC). In the early 1970s, the IIC (then known as the International Broadcast Institute) sponsored several meetings where the right to communicate was introduced and evaluated by international researchers (Fisher, 1982).

Another important series of meetings on the right to communicate was held in the 1970s at an American institute which was established by an act of Congress: the Honolulu-based East/West Center at the East/West Communications Institute. Because of their research in Hawaii, L.S. Harms and Jim Richstad (1977), two American academics, became closely identified with work on this notion.

In their prefatory remarks to one of the most important early reference works on the right to communicate, Harms and Richstad made a surprising revelation. In delving into the conceptual roots of work on this new right, the two authors make an important reference to a well-known American pioneer in the field of communications: Harold Lasswell. According to Harms and Richstad, Lasswell delivered a paper in Honolulu in 1973 (Lasswell, 1972) that provided a conceptual basis for the right to communicate. In an apparent departure from his "source-receiver" communication paradigm that had been so influential for over 45 years, Lasswell was now presenting the outline of a participatory model. This new model was to be based upon a "horizontal," "nonlinear," "multiway" mode of communication, notions that later became standard terms of reference in describing the goals of the right to communicate (Harms & Richstad, 1977, pp. 4–5). Harms and Richstad also noted that during this early period Wilbur Schramm remarked that he felt "The right to communicate is still a skeleton without flesh . . . but nevertheless something that deserves our most serious thought" (Harms & Richstad, 1977, p. 10).

Although Brecht would probably not be a happy bedfellow with Lasswell and Schramm, it is nonetheless significant that one finds an undeniable American involvement in the origins of the right to communicate. Moreover, by way of context, it should also be noted that both myself and other authors have pointed out similar American contributions to other issues associated with the New International Information Order debate (Roach, 1987; Nordenstreng, 1984).

In addition, the Western contribution to the right to communicate was openly admitted by Leonard Sussman (1983), an early and adamant critic of both UNESCO and the NIIO:

> The concept of this still theoretical "right" originated in the West, as did most human rights guarantees now written into universal covenants . . . Though most of the theoretical work on the formulation of this "right" in international law has been done in Europe and the U.S., the developing countries fully support the general approach.

UNESCO's involvement in advancing this principle can also be directly traced to a Western initiative. It was Sweden that introduced, at the 1974 General Conference, a resolution calling for study and definition of the right to communicate. Moreover, another U.S. ally, the Netherlands, strengthened this resolution by adding an amendment that the "right of participation" should be a key element in examining the right to communicate (Harms & Richstad, 1977, p. 7).

It should also be stressed that from the mid- to late 1970s, the United States did not voice any opposition to the right to communicate, which is certainly not surprising given the Carter administration's policy on human rights. We have examined three documents of this period that can be taken to represent official American thinking on various aspects of the NIIO debate: the "Kroloff-Cohen Report on the New World Information Order," presented to the Senate Committee on Foreign Relations in 1977; an internal document submitted by the U.S. delegation to UNESCO entitled "Recommendations for the Final Report of the International Commission for the Study of Communication Problems," issued in 1978; and Congressional hearings on "UNESCO and Freedom of Information" held in 1979. None of the documents even mentions the right to communicate. In contrast, what may be considered as a "semi-official" American report on the NIIO (insofar as it was financed by the USIA) speaks at some length of the right to communicate. However, in "The United States and the Debate on a New World Information Order," published in 1978, one finds a clear endorsement for work on this concept. In introducing the section on this new right, the report stresses that it is primarily to be seen as an extension of Article 19 of the Universal Declaration of Human Rights. It is well known that Article 19, which mentions the freedom for individuals to seek, receive, and impart information, is widely hailed by Western diplomats as the most important section of this declaration. Interestingly enough, the only negative reaction to the right to communicate in the USIA-financed report is the following statement: "The effort has been criticized by some for being overly idealistic" (Academy for Educational Development, 1978, p. 104).

How then does one account for the American vilification of the right to communicate in the 1980s? First and foremost, we must return to our point of departure: The official American effort to present every concept linked to the NIIO debate strictly in terms of "government control of the media." Although this strategy was certainly operational more often than not during the Carter years, it was elevated to the ranks of an all-embracing sacred doctrine by the Reagan administration. Common-sense considerations as well as historical perspectives fell by the side during the 1980s (Roach, 1987). The attempt to link the right to communicate to Communist doctrine is particularly ludicrous since the Soviet opposition to this concept was not only well known but published in the text of the MacBride Report.[1] Lastly, as already indicated, the United States opposed the right to communicate in the 1980s because of its linkage with a new generation of "people's rights," a subject to which we now turn our attention.

PEOPLE'S RIGHTS

During the 1980s, the conflict over UNESCO's support for a new generation of "people's rights" led to an American boycott of the term "people." The controversy over people's rights in the 1980s was acted

---

[1] The Soviet representative on the MacBride Commission officially dissented from a one-and-one-half page reference to the right to communicate in the Final Report: "The right to communicate is not an internationally accepted right on either a national or international level. Therefore it should not be discussed at such length in such a way in our report" (UNESCO, 1980, p. 172).

out mainly in the Social Sciences Sector of UNESCO, which has responsibility for carrying out the Organization's mandate in the area of human rights. The polemics reached a peak at the 1983 General Conference when the organization passed Resolution 13.1 on "Peace, international understanding, human rights and the rights of peoples. . ." U.S. opposition to people's rights was based upon the stated belief that such a concept neglected the individual, and actually referred to government or State rights.

"The people" are invoked by governments throughout the world to legitimize their actions. And, as evidenced in former President Reagan's State of the Union addresses in 1987 and 1988, it is not difficult to find examples of speeches of American government officials delivered for home consumption that make ample use of the term "people," in sharp contrast to the apparent American allergy to the term when it appears in international fora. Such a discrepancy would undoubtedly be explained by notions of legitimacy: It is legitimate in the Western world for governments to speak in the name of the people, whereas Communist States had traditionally been regarded as illegitimate precisely because they did not speak in the name of their people. A perfect example of such schematic thinking is to be found in Leonard Sussman's (1983) definition of "the people, the people's rights" in his Glossary of International Communications. Sussman's entry makes a distinction between usage of these terms in the First and Second Worlds. Not surprisingly, in the First World "the people are the ultimate governors," and "sovereignty rests with the people (not with the State as a corporate entity)". In contrast, in the Marxist Second World, "To support their legitimacy Marxist governors claim they act in the interests of the people, though they do not submit their leadership or policies to direct tests of the will of the people."[2]

Such a characterization, useful as it may be for understanding why "people's rights" became anathema to U.S. policy makers, does not account for the just use of the term "people" and the concept "rights of peoples" within the United Nations system. Once again, there is a historical trajectory that has been completely ignored by both Suss-

---

[2] The fact that the "will of the people" has played no small role in modifying Eastern European political developments in the late 1980s diminishes the force of the American attack on Soviet legitimacy. But a caveat is called for: The presentation in the West of Eastern European social movements as "people's movements" deserves careful analysis. This analysis should pose questions such as the following: If these movements or important segments thereof begin to reject the marketplace, will they still be presented as "peoples' movement"? Are there not very negative aspects of "peoples' power" unleashed by these movements, such as anti-semitism? Are the peoples' movements in Eastern Europe the same as those in Third World countries?

man and U.S. officials. The concept of "people's rights" can actually be traced back to the very foundation of the United Nations in 1945. The constitution of the United Nations begins with the famous phrase, "We the peoples of the United Nations . . ." Article I, Section 2 of the UN Constitution, which lays out the purposes of the organization, makes clear reference to the notion of "peoples": "To develop friendly relations among nations based on respect for the principle of equal rights and self-determination of peoples." Article 55 of Chapter IX repeats this reference to "the self-determination of peoples" in connection with International Economic and Social Cooperation.

These constitutional references to the "self-determination of peoples" played their most important role in legitimizing the decolonization movement of the 1960s and 1970s. The enunciation of the principle of self-determination found its most concrete and explicit formulation in the Declaration on the Granting of Independence to Colonial Countries and Peoples, adopted by UN General Assembly Resolution 1514 (XV) of December 1960. This Declaration, which makes ample use of the term "peoples," was seconded by a host of other UN Resolutions throughout the period of the 1960s and 1970s. Article I of the United Nations International Covenant on Civil and Political Rights, passed on December 16, 1966, states as follows: "All peoples have rights of self-determination. By virtue of that right they freely determine their political status and freely pursue their economic, social and cultural development." Hence, the "rights of peoples" in the 1980s can trace a direct lineage back to an historical process: the decolonization struggles of the 1960s and 1970s (Fenet, 1982; Jouve, 1983; "Droits de l'homme," 1984).

Consequently the American refusal of the term "people" in the United Nations is tantamount to a denial of this very same historical process. In light of the demands generated by the decolonization movement—notably the New International Information Order and the New International Economic Order—it is not surprising that the implicit reference to this movement in the term "peoples" would be dismissed out of hand. This dismissal should be seen for what it is: An inherent rejection by wide sectors of the American ruling class of the decolonization process in the Third World.

And yet it would be a mistake to assume that the U.S. opposition to the "rights of peoples" represents a position of consensus, even within establishment circles. In 1984, the "rights of peoples" was one of many issues examined by the U.S. National Commission for UNESCO in order to determine whether there were grounds for an American withdrawal from the Organization. The National Commission's Report (which came out strongly against withdrawal) pointed out that the "rights of peoples" were certainly in keeping with American traditions.

> The term "rights of peoples" is not in itself objectionable. In fact, it can and should be defined to reflect the traditional concerns of the US: for example, the rights of peoples includes self-determination, as American as Woodrow Wilson's Fourteen Points. The rights of peoples should be combined with individual rights, rather than reflect a dichotomy. (U.S. National Communion for UNESCO, 1984, p. 12)

The National Commission then went on to quote a staff study of the U.S. House of Representatives Committee on Foreign Affairs that summarized a series of reasons why the U.S. should not unilaterally oppose "people's rights." The first three reasons are as follows:

> First, debate on people's rights may be inevitable, as noted above, but such a debate does not necessarily diminish the legitimacy of individual human rights . . . Second, the whole issue of people's rights and human rights and the long-term implications they raise for U.S. foreign policy in a pluralist, complex, interdependent world deserves considerably more attention than mere opposition to people's rights. Otherwise, how can the United States and its Western allies manage and influence the debate and its outcome? Third, U.S. categorical opposition to people's rights and support for individual human rights runs the risk of denying our own recognition of certain group rights such as the right of self-determination . . . (U.S. National Commission for UNESCO, 1984, pp. 12–13)

The National Commission's Report might have added that in rejecting people's rights American diplomats have also turned their backs on the very history of the United States. Need we be reminded that the American constitution opens with "We the people," and that the term "people" is used throughout the writings of early colonial figures such as Alexander Hamilton, James Madison, and Thomas Jefferson?

One of the most important political speeches of the 19th century went down in history precisely because of its eloquent invocation of the people. We are speaking of Abraham Lincoln's famous Gettysburg Address of 1863, delivered during the Civil War:

> That we here highly resolve that those dead shall not have died in vain; that this nation, under God, shall have a new birth of freedom, and that government of the people, by the people, for the people shall not perish from the earth.

Official objections notwithstanding, in more recent history "the people" has remained a popular concept in both academic and legal works. The classic American work on freedom of the press, written almost 40 years ago, bears the title of *The People's Right to Know* (Cross, 1953). The Supreme Court, in one of the most important communications decisions of the 1960s, also validated the spirit if not the letter of "people's rights." In the landmark "Red Lion decision" of 1969, which upheld the Fairness Doctrine, the highest court of the land unanimously decided that the rights of the audience took precedence over those of broadcasters:

> The people as a whole retain their interest in free speech by radio and their collective right to have the medium function consistently and with the ends and purposes of the First Amendment." (Red Lion vs. FCC, 1969)

Although the Fairness Doctrine was abolished by the Federal Communications Commission in a deregulation sweep in 1987, the Red Lion decision is still quoted by those who advocate its reestablishment.

Even some of the most severe critics of the right to communicate do not hesitate to invoke "the people" when it serves their purposes. The famous "Talloires Declaration," adopted by the press of the "free world" in May 1981 makes reference to "the people" and their rights:

> We believe, however, that the people's interests . . . are better served by free and open reporting (Paragraph 5). . . . The people's right to news and information should not be abridged. (Paragraph 9)[3]

THE EMERGING "RIGHT TO KNOW" IN THE UNITED STATES

In spite of the American attack on the international movement for a right to communicate in the 1980s, the Reagan administration's efforts to control and censor information on the domestic front produced a call for a very similar right: the right to know. One of the backers of this right has been Senator Paul Simon, Chair of the Senate Subcommittee on the Constitution. In March 1988, the following state-

---

[3] The Talloires Declaration was adopted at a conference held in May 1981 in Talloires, France. The meeting was co-sponsored by the World Press Freedom Committee (WPFC), an American lobbying group for the media. Since the mid-1970s, the WPFC has served as an umbrella organization for attacks on UNESCO and the NIIO.

ment of Simon was entered in the Congressional Record under the title of "The Right to Know: Preserving Self-Government and Public Accountability":

> A people deprived of information about their government and the world around them are constrained by their ignorance. Their choices are limited by what they are permitted to know. Without knowledge, the sovereignty of the people cannot be fully and freely exercised. (Congressional Record, 1988)

Simon also entered in the Congressional Record a lengthy article by Christopher Harvie of the Advocacy Institute. Harvie's article provides a detailed summary of how the American people's right to know was violated repeatedly by the Reagan Administration in the name of secrecy and national security. The biggest foreign policy scandal of the 1980s, the Iran-Contra affair, was condemned for flouting the "people's right to know":

> Most recently, the Iran-Contra affair has illustrated with terrible clarity that the citizenry will suffer such "misgovernment" when the people's right to know is ignored ... The Iran-Contra affair violated the principal tenet of democratic self-government: the consent of the governed. Democracies are governed by consent, not coercion; that principle is violated when the public is deceived or kept in the dark about fundamental policy matters. (Congressional Record, 1988)

The rest of Harvie's article offers a thorough overview of the numerous ways in which the information rights of the citizenry were trounced during the Reagan years, including the privatization and classification of government information, and restrictions on the publication of academic and scientific research. Numerous statements from the writings of the Founding Fathers are quoted to emphasize the fact that public access to information was intended to be a bedrock of U.S. democracy (Demac, 1988).

There is other evidence of an increasing consciousness that the present information policies of the U.S. government and American media industries assault the "right to know." A nonprofit research library and information center known as "Data Center" has undertaken a "Right to Know Project" that so far has resulted in the publication of two volumes of articles documenting the ways in which the flow of information to the public has been curtailed in recent years (Horn, 1985, 1988). Like Christopher Harvie of the Advocacy Institute, the "Right to Know Project" anchors its work in a legalistic framework, in particular the First Amendment to the Constitution. Another group, which has taken out half-page ads in several publications entitled "The American People's Right to Know" is the National Emergency Civil Liberties Committee. Like the Data Center Project, the Committee has a legalistic framework: It also places the "right to know" within the context of the American constitution.[4]

THE RIGHT TO CULTURE

Although the Right to Communicate and the Right to Know are of unquestionable relevance to peoples in both the developing and developed worlds, there is another right which could perhaps subsume these rights or take on added significance in the decade of the 1990s: the right to culture.

The right to culture is sanctified in a number of instruments of international law, most notably the Universal Declaration of Human Rights (1948) and the International Covenant on Economic, Social and Cultural Rights (1966). Article 27 of the Human Rights Declaration is noteworthy for its emphasis on the participatory aspect of culture: "Everyone has the right freely to participate in the cultural life of the community, to enjoy the arts and to share in scientific advancement and its benefits." Although the International Covenant on Economic, Social and Cultural Rights has not been ratified by the United States, its provisions do offer some directions on how cultural rights should be enforced. Wolfgang Kleinwachter has pointed out that this covenant "defines very clearly the rights and responsibilities of both the individual and the government" (Kleinwachter, 1988, pp. 9–10). However, although the covenant does make a preambular reference to individual duties both to other individuals and the community to "promote and observe the rights mentioned in the covenant," almost all of the 15 articles give precedence to State responsibilities and duties. Nonetheless, it is very significant that the first item of the first article invokes a third social actor whose identity is distinct from individuals or the State: the people. Article 1 reads: "All people have the right of self-determination. By virtue of that right they freely determine their political status and freely pursue their economic, social and cultural development."

The African Charter on Human and People's Rights (which was adopted by the Organization of African unity in 1981 and entered into

---

[4] The National Civil Liberties Committee may be contacted at the following address: 175 Fifth Ave., New York, NY 10010.

force in 1986) achieves a better balance of the cultural rights of both individuals and peoples. Article 17 refers to the right of individuals "to participate freely in the cultural life of the community," but Article 22 provides that "All peoples shall have the right to their economic, social and cultural development with due regard to their freedom and identity . . ."

Since the United Nations has proclaimed the 1990s as the "World Decade for Cultural Development," international activities centering around the meaning and exercise of the "right to culture" are certain to proliferate. Already there has been an important cultural debate launched on the concept of "Eurocentrism." It is indicative of the kind of thinking in international development now taking place that Samir Amin (1989), one of the Third World's leading economists, whose work was a reference point for North/South economic debates of the 1970s, has most recently turned his attention to questions of cultural domination. Amin's latest book, entitled simply *Eurocentrism,* rejects the antiuniversalist cultural assumptions of the West and calls for a non-Eurocentric version of world history.

Within the United States, the issue of Eurocentrism has often been played out in the universities, where demands for cross-cultural curricula have coalesced in the building of new multiethnic coalitions that cut across nationalities, as well as the student-professor divide. After months of strife in 1988, one of the country's premier academic institutions, Stanford University, remodeled its core curriculum along less Eurocentric lines. The polemics over culture have been fueled by several factors, one of which was the publication of two books in the late 1980s calling for a "re-emphasis" on Western classics in the American educational system: E.D. Hirsch's *Cultural Literacy* and A. Bloom's *The Closing of the American Mind* (Hirsch, 1988; Bloom, 1987). Hirsch' work, subtitled "What Every American Needs to Know," argues that at the root of U.S. educational problems lies a lack of shared knowledge and information, possession of which would give people "cultural literacy." His solution is preservation of "mainstream culture" through a nationally established core curriculum. An idea of what this would emphasize can be gleaned from the appendix to his book, which contains a list of nearly 4,000 facts, concepts, and sayings that "culturally literate" Americans should know. The blatantly Eurocentric bias of this list, as well as Hirsch's palpable distrust of multilingual and multicultural education reveals the true objective of his argument: to restore respect for Western civilization within American education. One of the strongest critiques of Hirsch's work is its implication "that blacks and other minorities will continue to suffer social and economic disabilities as long as they fail to obtain cultural literacy" (Clark, 1988). Bloom's theses present a much more sweeping indictment of the American educational system, particularly insofar as its "purity" has been tainted by what he perceives to be the aftereffects of the 1960s. He is against feminism, affirmative action for minorities, and in favor of the restoration of philosophy (Western, of course) as the core principle of American education. His ideas have been mainly criticized for their elitism and his deification of Western-based education.

Another factor that has influenced the upsurge of interest in cultural expression has been the undeniable increase of incidents of racism in urban and university communities around the country. These incidents, a legacy of the conservative climate of the Reagan era, illustrate with great clarity how demands for cultural recognition are linked to oppression.

Support for a "right to culture" in the United States has, however, so far not resulted in the kind of coalition that backs the "right to know." One could say that the "people" voicing cultural demands are primarily ethnic or racial minorities, or in certain cases activist artists who are bypassed by the power politics of policy making at the national and local level.

Nonetheless, there are a certain number of progressive groups attempting to promote new thinking and practices on the cultural rights of people living in the United States (including both minorities and larger segments of the population). One such group is the Alliance for Cultural Democracy (ACD), an organization devoted to cultural pluralism, and the integration of cultural, political, and economic struggles. The ACD is multiethnic and very much rooted in local community grassroots activities.[5]

One of the ACD's projects is a Draft Declaration of Cultural Human Rights, which is a statement of principles and actions designed to guarantee the cultural rights of all peoples. The ACD's Declaration contradicts the notion that progressive forces never think in practical terms, since it highlights support for a truly public cultural policy:

> We believe that written and unwritten policy must acknowledge that all people are entitled to their rights: to participate in setting policy for those public service institutions that affect their lives; to a democratic tax structure that equitably returns tax dollars and services to commu-

---

[5] The ACD may be contacted at the following address: Alliance for Cultural Democracy, P.O. Box 7591, Minneapolis, MN 55407. Information on the ACD's Draft Declaration on Cultural Rights may be obtained by writing one of the following individuals: Judy Branfam, 327 Summer St., 3rd floor, Boston, MA 02210; Lisa Maya Knauer, 88 2nd Ave., No. 6, New York, NY 10003.

nities; to public support for local initiative in solving problems of local concern in all arenas from education to economic development to public art.

BEYOND THE NATION-STATE?

Much of the discussion on cultural and communication rights has taken place within the context of nation-states and intergovernmental organizations. However, it should be recognized that the increasingly important movement to go "beyond the nation state" may have a direct impact on further development of concepts such as the right to communicate and the right to culture. Of course, as most political theorists would acknowledge, the "beyond the nation-state" debate is cyclical: it reappears at regular intervals in history. However, what seems to distinguish the present era is that there is a real momentum to go beyond the nation-state that is fueled by grass-roots actions and not just academic theories. In addition to Eastern European events, two of the most important political processes of the 1980s were mass-based movements that, however short-lived, did demonstrate the reach of "people's power": the overthrow of the Marcos regime in the Philippines and the student/worker democracy movement in China. Although neither movement, particularly that in China, lends itself to easy analysis, it is certain that the worldwide public fascination with these events was prompted by the "spectacle" of people actually going out into the streets and, against tremendous political odds, taking control of their lives.

The worldwide peace movement, which is based on grass-roots activities around the globe, has for some time been moving beyond the nation-state. Although the recent acceleration of this trend has many intellectual variants, which range from calls for the consolidation of international law, to proposals for local autonomy, "the people" are going ahead with many different kinds of activities that openly bypass national governments. This is particularly true of many of the recent U.S. citizens' initiatives for promoting peace with the people of the Soviet Union.

The "beyond the nation-state" discussion has direct relevance to the conceptualization of people's rights. Although the most recognized work on people's rights has been done within intergovernmental organizations, such as the Organization of African Unity (OAU) or UNESCO, there has also been an attempt to define this "new generation of human rights" in terms that are not State-centric. In 1976 the Italian Lelio Basso Foundation for the Rights of Peoples sponsored a meeting in Algiers that brought together both representatives of National Liberation Movements and international legal specialists sympathetic to the notion of people's rights. The result was an endorsement for a concept of international law that went beyond national governments. Although the Algiers Declaration endorses, in preambular fashion, the human rights instruments of the United Nations, its own treatment of human rights begins and ends with "the people." Moreover, these rights are not qualified, as in the OAU document, by mention of "respect for State laws."

The specific historical context of the Algiers Declaration was the 1970s denunciation of the political, economic, and military oppression of Third World peoples by neocolonialism. Therefore its primary concerns are with the rights of liberation such as "the right to existence," "the right to political self-determination," and the "economic rights of peoples."

However, the significance of the Algiers Declaration transcends its particular historical moment. It not only endorses the political and economic rights of peoples but also the "right to culture." Section IV states:

> Every people has the right to speak its own language and preserve and develop its own culture, thereby contributing to the enrichment of the culture of mankind. (Article 13)
>
> Every people has the right to its artistic, historical and cultural wealth. (Article 14)
>
> Every people has the right not to have an alien culture imposed upon it. (Article 15)

What should be stressed is that the truly radical aspect of this Declaration (and the movement that supported it) was its deliberate attempt to go beyond the nation-state as the final arbiter of people's rights. Richard Falk, of Princeton University, has written that the Declaration "posits a claim that rights can be authoritatively formulated by populist initiative and do not depend on government initiative" (Falk, 1981, p. 51).

Writing in particular on the needs of the Third World in international law, Falk holds that the United Nations, which is made up of governments, cannot address the fundamental structures of domination through which capitalism operates:

> It becomes clear that governments cannot be entrusted with the rule of serving as the guardian of fundamental human rights. In this regard,

the whole tradition of international law is to some extent regressive in the current era. Even the United Nations is an organization of states in which the interests of people are misleadingly assumed to be legitimately represented by governments . . . the widespread character of repression attendant upon the current stage of capitalist development makes it naive to expect any international institution composed of states to safeguard in a genuine way the fundamental rights of people. (Falk, 1981, p. 191)

Faced with the State limitations of the United Nations, Falk (1981, p. 190) posits that the people "must insist upon their own legitimacy as a source of rights, even as against the state."

Although the Algiers Declaration was written in a Third World context, its truly radical notion of "people's rights" may have relevance for movements in the United States such as those outlined above. It is one thing to frame the "right to know" and the "right to culture" within a legalistic context whose legitimacy ultimately derives from the State. If people actually begin to believe, however, that their information and cultural rights do not depend on this Higher Authority, but on themselves, it would be the beginning of a new political era.

REFERENCES

The Academy for Educational Development. (1978). *The United States and the debate on the world information order*. Washington, DC: Author.

Amin, S. (1989). *Eurocentrism*. New York: Monthly Review Press.

Bloom, A. (1987). *The closing of the American mind*. New York: Simon and Schuster.

Clark, C. (1988). Ideas, history and the crisis in education. *Radical History Review*, No. 42.

The Congressional Record. (1988, March 4). Washington, DC.

Cross, H.L. (1953). *The people's right to know*. New York: University Press.

d'Arcy, J. (1969, November). Direct broadcast satellites and the right to communicate. *EBU Review, 118*, 14–18.

d'Arcy, J. (1977). Foreword. In *Evolving perspectives on the right to communicate*. Honolulu: East-West Center, East-West Communication Institute.

Demac, D.A. (1988). *Liberty denied: the current rise of censorship in America*. New York: PEN America Center.

Droits de l'homme, droits des peuples. (1984, February). Dossier in *Le Monde Diplomatique*, Paris.

Falk, R. (1981). *Human rights and state sovereignty*. New York: Holmes and Meier.

Fenet, A. (Ed.). (1982). *Droits de l'homme, droits des peuples*. Paris: PUF.

Fisher, D. (1982). *The right to communicate: A status report* (UNESCO Reports and Papers on Mass Communication No. 94). Paris: UNESCO.

Freedom to communicate. (1985, June 29). *Daily American.* West Frankfurt, IL.

Gerard, J.B.S. (1983, June 7). *Statement on the UNESCO draft program and budget: 1984–1985 (22C/5).* 116th Session of the Executive Board.

Harms, L.S., & Richstad, J. (Eds.). (1977). *Evolving perspectives on the right to communicate.* Honolulu: East-West Communications Institute.

Hirsch, E.D., Jr. (1988). *Cultural literacy: What every American needs to know.* New York: Vintage.

Horn, Z. (Ed.). (1985). *The right to know* (Vol. I and II). This publication, as well as information on the "Right to Know" Project, may be obtained by writing to the following address: Data Center Products and services, 464 19th St., Oakland, CA 94612.

Jouve, E. (1983). *Le tiers monde dans la vie internationale.* Paris: Berger-Levrault.

Kleinwachter, W. (1988). The right to participate in the cultural life of society. *Media Development, SSSV*(4), 9–10.

Lasswell, H.D. (1972, September). *The future of world communications: Quality and style of life* (Papers of the East-West Communication Institute, No. 4). Honolulu: East-West Communications Institute.

Nordenstreng, K. (1984). *The mass media declaration of UNESCO.* Norwood, NJ: Ablex.

Roach, C. (1987). The U.S. position on the New World Information and Communication Order. *Journal of Communication, 37*(4), 36–51.

Roach, C. (1987). The position of the Reagan Administration on the NWICO. *Media Development, XXXIV*(4), 32–37.

Sussman, L. (1983). *Warning of a bloodless dialect: Glossary for international communications.* Washington, DC: Media Institute.

UNESCO. (1980). *Many voices, one world (MacBride report).* Paris: UNESCO.

UNESCO. (1983). *Second-medium term plan (1984–1989)* (4XC/Approved). Paris: UNESCO.

U.S. National Commission for UNESCO. (1984). *What are the issues concerning the decision of the United States to withdraw from UNESCO.* Washington, DC: Author.

11

Power, Communication, and Democracy

Moustapha Masmoudi

⌐We should not ignore the link that exists between political orientations of a state and its information policy. In fact, mass media constitute the mirror in which these orientations are reflected, and the microscope which allows us to pay attention to any national activity.⌡

In a parallel direction, the intervention of public opinion in the course of public affairs is acquiring more and more scope. While this public opinion is generally specific because it either reads or watches the screen, mass media are generally behind the evolution recorded in all fields.

Therefore, a modern state can only last through permanent communication between citizens and the various wheels of power. But any state communication is not necessarily governmental. To understand this point, we must keep in mind the difference between the three powers: the executive, the legislative, and the judiciary.

This type of communication is amenable to the government, to parliament, to central or regional administration, to political parties, and so on. It bears, in itself, all the specificities, strengths, and weaknesses of the governmental system it is supporting. It derives from the same theoretical concepts, but the mechanisms of its practice differ from one stage to another. Consequently, it would be interesting to analyze the constants and to put the results of this empirical statement within the reach of future communicators.

INFORMATION AND EXECUTIVE POWER

It is advisable to distinguish between governmental communication and administrative information. In fact, press releases announcing electrical power cuts, newsletters concerning the organization of work within hospitals, advertising campaigns undertaken by publishing establishments, as well as other practical pieces of information are echoes of governmental efforts. But they cannot be compared to governmental information.

The same holds true in respect to municipal communications. On a daily basis, measures adopted by local or rural councils are communicated to the press. These pieces of information are of immediate interest to citizens, and attract their attention just as much as major international events.

Besides these various aspects, governmental information should be better placed in relation to the part to be played by the Head of State.

Governmental Information

Typical governmental information mainly emanates from the Council of Ministers' deliberations.

According to Jeffries (1985), General Manager for the Information Central Office in Great Britain, this type of information informs citizens of actions undertaken by the Government on their behalf, explains how the government spends tax money and tells them how the government operates to protect the nation and citizens against physical and economic dangers, as well as why it undertakes such actions. According to Jeffries, people are neither ready to react positively nor to cooperate with measures they do not understand, nor with those that have no connection to their personal needs or with national interest.

Thus, it is a question of providing media and people with accurate and correct information on the political actions and decisions of the government in a degree compatible with national security.

With the generalization and improvement of communications, people have become saturated with information of all kinds. Government should compete to attract citizens' attention by resorting to the same tactics and the same techniques used by any other organization. Jeffries adds that the message that the government wishes to convey is not always one that people want to hear. How to pay one's taxes, housing shortages, unemployment, sickness, old age, pollution, and international tensions—such is the substance of official communications. Indicating that the message is issued by the government will not necessarily enlarge its audience nor ensure its credibility.

What must be done within a country's government where public opinion is enlightened in order to preserve the democratic institutions of that country? The answer to this British question came from the Federal Republic of Germany. Wolfgang Bergsdorf (1985), director of the Board of Press and Information in the federal government, summarized a response in five parts: (a) the absolute preeminence of values answerable for Justice, Peace, or Independence; (b) the signals and symptoms of crisis, famine, disasters, acts of victory, whatever generally presents an interest to mass media, (c) novelty of events, (d) political success (vote gains), and (e) the status of a communication originator, or in other words, the higher the hierarchical rank, the more impact for the communication. Normally, Bergsdorf explains, political governmental communications should observe at least two of these five rules.

Bernard Tricot (1985) states that the durability of governmental communication is one of its conditions of success. So is the capacity for swiftness, whether it is a matter of taking the lead, replying, or explaining. Unfortunately, he adds, we know that the state is becoming a machine, more and more difficult to master.

In any case, it is in the general interest for government to animate state communication. This communication should not constrain action, but on the contrary, should facilitate and prepare it, and achieve results.

According to Tricot, equilibrium is the spokesman's mission. He or she should exist for himself, appear as he actually is, without substituting himself to anybody, fight for governmental policy, contribute to secure the unity of governmental expression, remind ministers—who may forget—the requirements for good communication, and know the professionals of the written and audiovisual press.

According to Bergsdorf, the Minister of Press and Information is responsible for presenting and explaining constitutional goals and measures adopted by the government and that are beyond the competence of only one minister or that concern several areas. It is also this Minister's duty to coordinate public relations between ministries, whenever it is a matter of general policy.

In parallel with this organization, we find a certain modernization of operating processes. In some societies the state would sometimes act like a company, through advertising campaigns. Also noticeable is the development of communication through images, signals, and symbols. This communication should be less abstract or cerebral and transmitted through such signals and symbols. This implies a real creativity that cannot be entrusted to commercial agencies because it deals with the State image and requires a great deal of tact and perception.

⌊More precisely, election campaigns in Occidental countries and the use of television by presidential candidates have prompted concern over the impact of the media. Both a presidential candidate or a president in power who has in mind to renew his or her mandate, need media in all its forms, but, in particular, television.⌋

In some Occidental countries, this medium has become the absolute weapon of candidates to the Presidency. According to research by "Media France Intercontinents," television carried the 1988 campaign in the United States, without facing any other kind of competition. The era of large public meetings is over, and even the role of print journalists has been reduced.⌊Candidates daily cover hundreds of kilometers to appear on the evening TV news. It is a matter of creating "photo opportunities" and choosing a sequence from a well-staged playlet, with a short sentence summarizing the message.⌋*

During the American campaigns, the same investigator adds, the key man for each party is the communication consultant who has the ultimate responsibility of choosing the form of the message and who, thereby, inevitably intervenes on the political scene itself.

In this respect, election campaigns are dissociated from governmental information; moreover, presidential information has its own mechanisms and conception.

Presidential Information

What must this information represent for a Head of State? How will he/she use it? Is there any presidential communication specific to developing countries and another exclusive to developed countries?

The answer to these questions depends on the context in which presidential authority is exercised, and which may change according to the form of government. Between a presidential regime and a parliamentary one (republican or monarchical), the content of the information related to the Head of State is completely different; the nature of responsibilities, the election terms, or the hereditary character change the content of the message and the means of action.

Bruce Fein (1985), a former general counsellor to the U.S. Federal Communications Commission, considers that "an elected Head of State has the right to attempt to persuade his nation and that such a formulation of his policy must have the citizens' strong support." Fein further explains that the President, the chief of the executive, does not seek to communicate with citizens, make them understand his or her policy, ask for their support, or explain that his or her initiatives risk being effective, if the citizens themselves do not stand against the adverse parties of the President. The issue is to tell citizens who elected or appointed him or her, what he or she expects to do, and what are his or her problems or difficulties.

As Andre Fanon (1985), a former French minister (RDR), asserts: "I would not say, even if I were of the opposition, that the government is misusing television: it is its vocation to do so. . . ."

From another point of view, Tricot notes that the Head of State remains the symbol not only of the nation, but of society, its beliefs, and its ways of life. As a direct chief of the Executive and its administration, he or she is more than just a manager, but takes an oath to preserve, protect and defend the constitution. His or her speeches are inspired either by governmental actuality, by national celebrations, or both. He/she chooses from former times what may justify or illustrate present courses of action, according to the times and their problems.

When circumstances become dramatic, Heads of State also endeavor to give rise not only to communication, but to a kind of national communion. The goal is for the public to feel that such an expression of a message is beyond the government's plan.

The problems these days, however, is to know how to use media without exaggeration. How to win a capital of images and at the same time avoid the saturation effect on TV viewers? The technique of inserting images that do not catch the eye but that may enter the individual's subconscious, is beginning to spread in advertising a commercial product or promoting a politician's profile. Naturally, in politics, the process of seduction or insight into human psychology is essential, but one should know how to avoid the traps of perversion and manipulation.

Moreover, the knowledge of public opinion is an important element in leading a nation. It is a question of knowing the evolution of conjuncture, and above all, following the evolution of this opinion. Nevertheless, it is necessary to learn how to precede events, react in time, and avoid being the prisoner of these surveys.

PARLIAMENTARY COMMUNICATION

Is the development of governmental communication detrimental to parliamentary activity? We might be tempted to answer this question in the affirmative, since the abundance and the rapidity of governmental information have certainly weakened the role played by members of Parliament as messengers between the city and their respective regions. The question is to whether legislative communication has developed on its own.

In fact parliamentary communication policy should aim at three objectives: (a) to promote the image of Parliament as one of the essential powers and consequently consolidate the democratic nature of the regime, (b) to extend the effect of governmental communication, and (c) to contribute to civic education by the popularization of laws and various juridical clauses.

According to Edgar Faure (1985), the essential means of communication in a democracy is Parliament. He indicated that the essential criterion for a decision is parliamentary debate. Parliament is like a tribunal—a place where matters are studied sufficiently to draw out solutions.

There are cases when power should not be influenced by public opinion (for example, giving up the idea of setting up a nuclear power station). Generally, a normal parliamentary debate should create adequate communication between public opinion and political power, to allow the latter to know to what extent it may or may not face scrutiny by the public.

Before being a place where government explains and proposes, however, parliament is a center of expression, where members want as large an audience as possible. It is no longer sufficient for the audience to have access to tribunes, or for the Official Gazette to publish (with inevitable delay) the reports on debates, or for parliamentary debates to become the topic of statistics and comments. Members of Parliament want to multiply the written and oral opportunities, and their goal is to question the executive (Tricot, 1985). They want Parliament to expand through radio and television.

According to Fein, there is TV coverage of all debates in the U.S. Congress on a cable channel called C-Span. Citizens can spend 24 hours a day following this exclusive coverage of the work of members of Congress. In addition, in some larger states, Congressional representatives receive funds (up to half a million dollars) to communicate with citizens directly. Some of these funds are allocated to sample surveys that attempt to find out how people feel about various decisions. Finally, whenever the members of Congress wish to communicate with citizens from their electoral districts, they may send letters free of charge.

In other respects, it is commonly admitted that parliamentary control is not necessarily practiced with the possibility of overthrowing the Congress. There are no parliamentary means of getting rid of the President or of any of his or her collaborators, as discussed by Zouhair

Mourhaffer (1987). Even in Great Britain's parliamentary system, the same author recalls that since 1895 the Ministers' Cabinet has withdrawn only twice after defiance votes in the House of Commons.

Blamont (1987) explains that control is oriented more towards reciprocal information rather than setting governmental responsibility in action. In fact, an effective system of information allows Parliament to intervene, inflect some governmental action, or sway the electorate.

The main point is that the written and audiovisual press reserve a great deal of space and time throughout the year for this important information, unfortunately without taking advantage of the interesting information they may obtain from a plenary session. Correspondents become saturated during long sessions and sometimes neglect the gist of the matter; the ultimate loser is the public who may be deprived of an interesting political chronology of events.

Deliberations within permanent commissions constitute an important source of information for all members of Parliament, according to Moudhaffar. These commissions are the link between Parliament and government and they have several trump cards at their disposal to perform their information mission. The specialization of their fields allows them to exert a definite control over ministerial departments. Through their various reports, they inform parliament and, indirectly, public opinion.

But the question is still open concerning the secrecy of the work performed by these commissions. In fact, the confidential nature of their work authorizes members of Parliament to have available to them information of great interest. Nevertheless, this advantage only partly compensates for the ignorance of the real contribution provided by members selected for commissions' work and their contribution to the enrichment of the texts as presented by the Executive. Laurent Fabius (1988), President of the French National Assembly, feels that the assembly should be more expansive towards society and more transparent. He wonders why some important sessions of parliamentary commissions are not open to the press. Anyway, in countries with great parliamentary traditions, discussions about this matter are still going on between partisans and opponents.

Lastly, we should emphasize the necessity of solidarity and complementarity that should exist between the powers on which any democratic regime is based. It is commonly admitted that a long time goes by between an official governmental statement, which will be on the front page of newspapers after a meeting of the cabinet council, and the time when the anticipated measures become applicable. A long time is needed between parliamentary debates and the publication of decrees. In this case, information on work performed by commissions and during parliamentary debate is necessary to secure the relay and avoid any gap between a political decision and its implementation.

All these considerations should induce Parliaments in newly democratic countries to define what a parliamentary information policy should be with much more clear-sightedness and to carefully watch its application.

COMMUNICATION OF POLITICAL PARTIES

Political communication in public life is proteiform. There is a common factor between various types of communication; each type of communication is original.

For Denis Baudouin (1985), the main point at the level of parties is propaganda; in fact, it is obvious that a political party, while explaining its program and its aims, makes its favored policy the most attractive. Consequently, taking the lead should be emphasized, while demonstrations should be simplified to encourage the participation of the electorate. Nowadays, this orientation should be moderate, otherwise the party runs the risk of not being credible and could lose its followers.

In pluralist regimes, political parties cannot pretend to express all the aspirations of the country. However, bringing its communication policy into play, the government must refer to the governing party or to the parties of the majority systems.

When there is a majority party, its communication and that of the government, taking into consideration all the national preoccupations, could be the same. Nevertheless, in some aspects, the dominating political formation could also escape the government's vigilance, if the latter lacks the former's competence. In such a case, both communication policies will be distinct, while being more or less concerted.

"Most probably there will be political parties for still a long time to come," notes Edgar Faure, but the existing technology is such that important modifications could be made. It is possible for political parties to change their motives and their significance. Instead of parties relying on theoretically opposite doctrinal choices, there will be parties relying on an exchange of teams, as in the case of sporting events. It is a question of the image conveyed. Showing programs of this kind is the most effective way to attract the electorate. A 15-minute speech transmitted in the best way possible—that appears to have the best image, even if it does not convey the essential point—may have more impact than anything else during an electoral campaign. However, this would not be the kind of communication suitable for governmental action.

The nature of information within a party, even if it is the governing party, should come from a flexible and pragmatic concept. With the prospect of elections, the representatives of a governing party should appear as new and as imaginative as their opponents and adopt all means that will allow them to win the electors' confidence.

INSTRUCTIONS

The debate concerning the relationship between media and government has aroused the interest of several investigators. The International Commission for the Study of International Communication Problems (CIC), created by UNESCO in 1977, presented thoughts on this topic.

The Commission unequivocally condemned any attack whatsoever on the freedom of information or on the freedom of circulation between societies. It was recommended that the obstacles and restrictions due to the concentration of ownership of public and private information bodies, and private or official advertising should be subject to special investigation.

It was argued that freedom would gain over respect and dignity if it is associated with the will of acting in a responsible way. The Commission considered the principle of responsibility as fundamental; it should be conceived as an indispensable corollary to the principle of freedom.

According to the Commission, no government should be the judge of what people need to know or say. Any indoctrination is never without a break, and experience shows that a permanent monologue does not succeed in obliterating criticism or in abolishing any freedom of judgment. But the Commission allowed the State, taking these exceptions into account, the use of media by public services and all concerned partners, and the right to establish certain regulations even if the information system belongs to the private sector.

Formal and informal systems of education should essentially encourage the creative use of communication and develop a sense of criticism among people. It is a matter of constructing a model of communication that should be humanist and democratic, not meant for a nonmercantile elite, where the center of gravity of the authorities moves on from government to public opinion.

If it is possible to go beyond the present distribution of roles, whereby media give and people receive, and to set up a more equitable dialogue between equals by integrating citizens in the process of making decisions, the public opinion would become a conscience aware of public affairs and, with the experience of social practices, work in view of the democratization of social life and a better understanding between governments and citizens. This is indeed the most noble aspect of political information.

What is necessary is to discover some constants that would facilitate the task of those who should explain the fundamental choices of society. Any Head of State or government is invited to decide, according to what he or she considers necessary for the country, an option which might be unpopular. But, then, it is his or her task to explain the reasons and the expected results. The access to all means of the system should be within his or her reach. It is obvious that media so far have been at the disposal of the opposition, but a balance should be achieved.

This balance will never be accomplished in the absolute sense. If we do come close to it, it will not be permanent, as there is no equilibrium mechanism. Thus, the role of communications is to clarify. This is the law of democracy.

REFERENCES

Baudouin, D. (1985). *La Communication Gouvernementale,* pp. 163–166. Edition de l'Institut de la Communication Sociale.

Bergsdorf, W. (1985). *La Communication Gouvernementale,* pp. 73–88. Editions de l'Institut de la Communication Sociale.

Blamont, E. (1987). *Juris classeur administratif & politique,* pp. 32, 102.

Fabius, L. (1988, August 24). *Le Monde.*

Fanon, A. (1985). *La Communication Gouvernementale,* pp. 37–40. Edition de l'Institut de la Communication Sociale.

Faure, E. (1985). *La Communication Gouvernementale,* pp. 237–247. Edition de l'Institut de la Communication Sociale.

Fein, B. (1985). *La Communication Gouvernementale,* pp. 55–62. Edition de l'Institut de la Communication Sociale.

Jeffries, S. (1985). *La Communication Gouvernementale,* pp. 89–96. Edition de l'Institut de la Communication Sociale.

Mourhaffer, Z. (1987). *Leqislative power in Maqhreb.*

Tricot, B. (1985). *La Communication Gouvernementale,* pp. 111–126. Edition de l'Institut de la Communication Sociale.

12

Reciprocity Versus Interactivity: Principles of Democracy and Control for an Information Age

Robert Jacobson

Technology, to a great extent, determines the discourse among citizens and between citizens and their rulers. Who manages the technology and, in turn, the discourse? Today, many social resources and much energy are invested in novel applications of information technology, or "new media," for managing communication in both the private and public spheres.

For millennia, technologies of information have fulfilled a hegemonic purpose. State "information technology" in its most primitive forms (public pageants, religious spectacles, mechanical visual and acoustic devices for transmitting alarms and commands) and more recent manifestations have been used to gain and hold power (Mumford, 1970). The sociopolitical role of radio and television, inventions of the 20th century, is now a favorite topic of critical theorists (for example, Schiller, 1972; Epstein, 1974; Ewen & Ewen, 1982; Radical Science Collective, 1985). Scholars ponder the effects of modern broadcast one-to-many technologies: Do they amplify or diminish political awareness? For the media industry and the political interests it serves, these opinions are irrelevant. The broadcast media work. The order survives, and profitably, too.

Less celebrated are the reciprocal (one-on-one) information technologies. Most common among these are the universally available mail and the ubiquitous telephone. Reciprocal information technologies, too, have a political dimension. Those who participate in their use determine, to a greater or lesser extent, the time and manner of the discourse on which they as communicators embark. They create a context for their discourse that may, in the proper historical circumstance, enable a critical perspective to emerge. Reciprocity—a back-and-forth giving and taking, moderated by all participants in a discourse to their mutual advantage—is an underappreciated property of empowering communication processes. It is reciprocity that a democratic technology must engender and sustain, and it is reciprocity as a design criterion that this paper mainly examines.

Habermas (1975), Forester (1989), and their philosophical comrades (Forester, 1985) are concerned that no genuine political change can proceed so long as communication in the public sphere is distorted to serve the rulers. Habermas and Forester conceive of an authentic communication, a pure discourse of "straight talk," as a way to identify differences within a society—the first step toward social emancipation. For this they prescribe unconventional uses of conventional broadcast information technologies (particularly radio and video) (for example, Habermas, 1979). These social theorists deal at a high level of abstraction and seem unaware of an imminent explosion of even more powerful information technologies that may confound their strategy for communication-assisted political change.

"Interactive" technologies involve the recipient of a message with the source of the message. A message is received and an action is requested or required. It may be as simple as replying with another message or initiating an action that results in a positive outcome for the source—money is deposited in a bank, a job gets done, a person purchases a vacation or a video program, and so forth. The degree of involvement and autonomous action permitted the recipient depends on what the source wishes to accomplish. Interactive communicators, employing globalized telecommunication networks, may have broad reach, but they engage participating "users" on an individual basis. The participant in an interactive communication may feel that the exchange of information taking place between the participant and the "host" is very personal. In fact, the same exchange probably is taking place between several thousand or even millions of participants and the host. It is this *apparent* experience of private, personal communication that is the most dangerous power of interactive media: to give the participant an illusion of control that masks the deliberately managed nature of the exchange.

Interactive media may appeal to democrats who despair of finding much succor in the conventional broadcast media. Many expect to find in interactive media an antidote to the broadcast media's anesthetic properties (Barber, 1984). But this hope, too, may be illusory.

In the United States, the birthplace of interactive media, the management of electoral activity by clever politicians and parties armed with computer databases and direct-mail machinery is commonplace (Forbes, 1988). Not only individuals but whole neighborhoods and nongeographical interest groupings are "targeted" by pollsters and politicos. Once their driving fears or aspirations have been identified, these communities are deluged by "junk mail" and "junk phone calls" (mass-produced and uninvited, spurning reciprocity), radio and television advertising, and managed news designed to provoke a specific political response. The intensity of these communications is creating skepticism among citizens regarding the political process and cynicism regarding the managers themselves.

Unfortunately, representative democracy requires a great deal of management. There is enough discontent available to keep every representative and bureaucrat busy. In a complex society, bearing this collective weight is beyond the ability of political managers. Then a crisis of confidence sets in and agreed-upon rules may be suspended, leading to political tumult. It is far better for the state to head off discontent at an early stage, by engaging citizens in activities that drain their political energy.

This is where the new, interactive media—in the familiar controlling, managing mode of broadcast media—are most dangerous. They are perfect tools for producing homogeneity among a populace, capable of holding the "mob's" attention (a power frequently denoted as reaching the "lowest common denominator") continuously. Efforts are already underway to graft behavioral science to computer science, to produce irresistible "virtual environments" within which people can literally lose themselves. Put to the purpose of preserving the social *status quo*, the interactive media can compel or induce constant cooperation—much as rats are compelled to run a maze to escape pain, or induced to do tricks for food—blotting out self-awareness, and stealing time that might otherwise be devoted to positive action. In time, even conceiving of changing "the way things are" may become an obsolete behavior as the interactive compulsiveness of the these media become irresistible.

On the other hand, some forms of interactive media (at least theoretically) contain the seeds of a truer democracy. These are the reciprocal manifestations of these media, autonomous telephone and computer "communities" that could more faithfully fulfill the revolutionary aspirations of the American Way of Independence or, in Europe, that tumultuous year of 1848, when bourgeois order finally replaced kingly prerogative as the tyrant of daily life.

It must be acknowledged, first off, that the established order's desire to maintain itself, albeit in a dynamic, rather than static, form—always adapting to face new challenges—prejudices the future. The established order prefers a "technology gamble" to a "social gamble": That is, the established order would prefer to take a chance on the effects of new technology puts to its own purpose, rather than allow society to take a chance on a new order (Hamelink, 1988). Even if the technology gamble is likely to be deadly to human beings, the environment, or both (jeopardizing a common future), it is preferable, for those who rule, to taking a social gamble that may produce positive technological outcomes but that brings with it the end of the current regime.

Technology produced in this context will incorporate an inherent bias toward convention (Forty, 1986) and control (Wicklein, 1981; Reinecke, 1984). Consultants promote this controlling use of information technology (though often with a "human face") (Diebold, 1983)—for example, by calling for technological alternatives to overly regimented, productivity-lessening applications (Zuboff, 1988). Traditional research in communication lends itself to this purpose, by studying how to "improve" the essentially broadcast nature of interactive media (Rice, 1984): increasing the involvement of workers, for instance, with systems that are designed ultimately to maintain the asymmetry that favors an employer over its employees. Similar research is ongoing in the asymmetrical world of producers and consumers (Strauss, 1983).

On the information sciences side, a new body of human-computer interaction research—or "usability" research—is refining, slowly, the efficacy of the contact between human beings and interactive systems. On its face, this research is purely technical, to make better functioning information systems. But the usability scientists and engineers work for firms that provide technology to hierarchical institutions (corporations, government, and especially the military) whose basic purpose is control and coordination. The activities of the usability researchers, while fascinating, may simply lead to more effective systems of electronic entrapment.

In a satire by former Pantheon editor Tom Egelhardt, The Saatchi Institute for Well-being and Human Development, an affiliate of the transnational Saatchi & Saatchi advertising agency, reports on research carried on by unnamed advertising agencies to study "virtual and hyperspatial modes of transport for bringing the potential consumer directly to the ad" (Engelhardt, 1989). This entails the simulation of electronic environments in which the information system user experiences more acute "sensory" stimuli than are available in the material world. What makes Engelhardt's satire effective is that research of this type is probably taking place, but how much? We may not know until it is upon us.

All of this points to the conclusion that, unless a new tack is taken, the future manifestations of interactive technology, far from being "technologies of freedom" (Pool, 1979) may instead become "technologies of control" (Wilson, 1988).

And so, back to reciprocity, the essential quality of democratic communications. Reciprocity is realized on the margin of information technologies, where individuals band together to create communities of common interest and intent. It is best demonstrated in action.

Reciprocity coexists with interactivity in the computer bulletin board system (or BBS). A simple affair, the BBS is an electronic *agoura*—a modern version of the Greek marketplace and forum—maintained in the memory of a personal computer. It is reached via a computer, telephone, and modem by its "residents." Thousands of computer bulletin boards have now sprung up in North America, Japan, and Europe. Therein hundreds of thousands of amateur and professional computerists find a rare opportunity to coselect their fellow communicants and, equally rare, the ability to partake of fair, authentic, and balanced communications—reciprocal communications.

Special software, now available in a host of varieties, enables the bulletin board system operator, or "sysop," to construct public meeting places, discrete conference halls wherein people of like mind—fans of poetry, sports, science, public affairs, or any of a number of issues—can gather to inform and debate one another, and even private conference rooms where people of a particular orientation (partisan, sexual, or other) can openly converse on matters that a larger community might criticize or mock. In most bulletin boards, it is also possible for individuals to "chat" with one another for entertainment or to organize a common activity. A very attractive feature of BBSs is their ability to store computer programs that some participants "upload" so that others may share them, at little or no cost. (Textual, graphical, and audio programs comprise this wealth, as well as traditional computer utilities.) The real heroes on BBSs are those who share their thoughts and programs. Another breed of heroes are those who offer support to those in need of personal help, humor in hot situations (when participants irrationally "flame" against one another), or insight to a particularly knotty problem.

Successful sysops allow their participants great latitude in designing the bulletin boards. Community rules are proposed by the participants; their violation is a matter of public censure, possibly banishment from the community (often causing personal distress for the exiled). These rules are like a constitution. The basic elements of fair play form their inner core, but these rules are malleable in the face of popular calls for their alteration. Many sysops host live gatherings, face to face (or "f-t-f" as BBS lore has it), that serve to break down the barriers of anonymity and build a commitment to the community, its purposes, and its rules (Rheingold, 1986).

Not all bulletin boards are benign. In the United States, tales of Nazi and police "red squad" BBSs are legion; a few, discovered by the press, stand in for a supposed many. Nor are BBSs themselves invulnerable to sociopathic interference: Computer "viruses," damaging programs, occasionally show up to waylay the unwary. But the ratio of socially positive, esteem-building, and empowering bulletin boards far exceeds the handful of hells in which lost souls plan a fascist future, and sysops are increasingly adept at fending off the assaults of "crackers" who find joy in spreading chaos.

Today, some bulletin boards are evolving into much larger entities, regional communities numbering in the thousands of participants. One of these, acclaimed for its exceptionally democratic style of management and cornucopia of original, progressive thinkers, is The WELL (Whole Earth 'Lectronic Link), a spinoff of the Whole Earth Catalog movement run with the same countercultural esprit and energy that characterized the late 1960s (but with a great deal more insight and discipline). Over 6,000 participants, mainly clustered in the San Francisco Bay area, inhabit The WELL, discussing more than 150 topics ranging from intellectual and mystical examinations of "mind" to urban politics, global affairs, and parenting. Today, The WELL's membership spreads around the world via telephone and computer networks, and links are being established with similar systems in other cities and overseas. In fact, this movement toward integration is one of the most discussed topics on The WELL, as participants struggle to balance the desire for a broader outlook with care for the specialness of localism that sustains friendships beyond the electronic medium.[1]

Other super-BBSs, like Econet and Peacenet in the United States, and RURTEL and others in Britain and Europe, sustain specific political and cultural movements that could not otherwise easily coordi-

---

[1] The WELL, in which the author and other WELL participants developed many of the ideas expressed in this paper, is available worldwide via the USENET and uucp computer networks. It can also be dialed directly at (01) (415) 332-6106 (modem settings: 1200 baud, 7E-1). The "Global" conference is particularly well-suited to international discussions.

nate their members and activities. USENET, an amorphous, globe-girdling network of computerists, is jointly owned and operated by its millions of users worldwide, who employ USENET for professional and personal communication.

These systems are organic in origin, autonomous in operation, and often focused on local or regional affairs; many are distinctly populist. They stimulate communal identity, if not political action. One may wonder how democracy-serving the smaller interactive media really are when, for many participants, the most often-used BBS apparati are "chat lines" and similar diversions. The exclusive use of these features, by containing the participant in commonsensical, mundane interactions, can reify the *status quo* in a very personal way (in terms which occasionally tend toward the overtly abusive and sexist). Nevertheless, there is in these smaller systems, at least, a latent power to challenge hegemony and mobilize collective action.

Increasingly, however, national and international entities (including transnational information corporations like IBM and Reuters) are offering similar interactive media for public use. In operation, these systems resemble their simpler antecedents. However, where the small systems often are operated by volunteers, usually for little or no profit, the large systems are intended to be very profitable. They are not designed with democracy in mind. Already, on some of these systems (like the IBM/Sears collaboration, Prodigy), efforts have been made to standardize and sanitize their customers' conversations. Participants may be guided toward "electronic malls" wherein they are tempted to part with their money, in the easiest fashion, merely by pushing a button (Mosco, 1989). Prodigy, for example, exposes its customers to an advertisement on every screen of text or graphics, except on the BBS simulators it reluctantly provides at its customers' request.

This tendency toward control has been even more pronounced in the plans of privately owned utilities and governmental administrations to operate nationwide interactive information systems: Political and cultural censorship are built in as a matter of deliberate design. Reciprocity, on the other hand, is excluded.

The design and presentational style of these large systems strictly limits customer interaction and exchange. The few radicals who can afford these systems and who, more importantly, can put up with their managed channels of exchange, defend pockets of resistance via chat lines and private mail. But the mere act of mentioning another computer communication system on CompuServe, the largest existing commercial system, is enough to have one's account terminated; other commercial systems are equally harsh with dissenters. Nevertheless, these systems are popular because, in return for submission to the corporate politbureau and its regulations, they can gain access to information and personalities that, increasingly, are no longer in the public domain but only available at a price.

As commercial computer networks are integrated on a large scale, the small, autonomous systems are coming under pressure to conform to the "big boys" standards. For example, in the United States, many of the small media are being solicited to make use of telephone company "gateways" through which telephone customers may one day be able to access dozens of information services. For this opportunity to compete for a much larger market (which may effect its own changes), the small media must adhere to the technological and content standards set by the gateway owners.

The gateway owners discourage autonomy and absolutely prohibit information content that is agitational. Sexual conduct, which Wilhelm Reich identified as a precursor to critical political awareness, is equally discouraged. (Even in France, where romance is the national treasure, forces on the Right are attempting to "clean up" the innuendo and suggestiveness of the relatively unmonitored national Minitel service.) Above all, the gateway owners seem intent on replicating the crippled communications that result from the mass media, only with a "participatory" twist. This does not bode well for democratic uses of technology.

And, even now, the technology factories are preparing newer, more powerful media. These will incorporate cutting-edge devices and produce holographic, hypermedia/multimedia "information environments" that can literally synthesize experience (Brand, 1989). The boundary between personal knowledge and propaganda may be totally shattered. Democracy, unless there are alternative means of communication by which true reciprocity can be maintained, will become what the new media say it is.

Is it possible to distinguish predemocratic and democratic interactive information systems from those that are antidemocratic? For that, more must be known through conscious, critical examination about democratic communication and what it entails. There is little to be gained by the scholar or activist who takes as a model the established media and, to a great extent, the "new" media whose only novelty is their appearance, not their ownership or organization. The person seeking knowledge about democracy-supporting information systems must look to the margin, noted Foucault (Kritzman, 1988), where the pressure for change and innovation, for disobeying all the rules, is most intense. A good place to start would be the computer bulletin board in its many manifestations which, for all the sensational treatment it has received in the popular press, has yet to be seriously studied as a social phenomenon or a machinery for potential empowerment. Can action be taken to preempt the antidemocrats' recapture of the public sphere as it pulses on the brink of a new expansion? The growth of interactive information systems to undergird democratic discourse and make possible progressive, concerted political action appears an unavoidable goal.

REFERENCES

Barber, B. (1984). *Strong democracy.* Berkeley, CA: University of California Press.

Brand, S. (1989). Sticking your head in cyberspace. *Whole Earth Review, 63,* 84–86.

Diebold, J. (1983). *Automation.* New York: AMACOM

Englehardt, T. (1989, May 17-23). To boldly go where no ad has gone before. *In These Times,* p. 18.

Epstein, E.J. (1974). *News from nowhere.* New York: Vintage Books.

Ewen, S., & Ewen, E. (1982). *Channels of desire.* New York: McGraw-Hill.

Forbes, J. (1988, July 25). Computer technology takes on role in politics. *PC Week,* p. 12.

Forester, J. (Ed.). (1985). *Critical theory and public life.* Cambridge, MA: MIT Press.

Forester, J. (1989). *Planning in the face of power.* Berkeley, CA: University of California Press.

Forty, A. (1986). *Objects of desire.* New York: Pantheon.

Habermas, J. (1975). *Legitimation crisis.* Boston, MA: Beacon Press.

Hamelink, C. (1988). *The technology gamble.* Norwood, NJ: Ablex.

Kritzman, L.D. (Ed.). (1988). *Politics, philosophy, culture: Interviews and other writings, 1977–84.* London: Routledge, Chapman & Hall.

Mosco, V. (1989). *The pay-per society.* Norwood, NJ: Ablex.

Mumford, L. (1970). *Pyramid of power.* New York: Harcourt, Brace, Jovanovich.

Pool, I. de Sola. (1979). *Technologies of freedom.* Cambridge, MA: MIT Press.

Radical Science Collective. (Eds.). (1985). *Making waves: The politics of communication* (Radical Science No. 16). London: Free Association Books.

Reinecke, I. (1984). *Electronic illusions.* Hammondsworth, England: Penguin.

Rheingold, H. (1986). Virtual Communities. In K. Kelly (Ed.), *Signal.* New York City: Harmony Books.

Rice, R.E. (Ed.). (1984). *The new media: Communication, research, and technology.* Beverly Hills, CA: Sage.

Schiller, H.I. (1972). *The mind managers.* Boston, MA: Beacon Press.

Strauss, L. (1983). *Electronic marketing.* White Plains, NY: Knowledge Industry.

Wicklein, J. (1981). *The electronic nightmare.* Boston, MA: Beacon Press.

Wilson, K. (1988). *Technologies of control.* Madison, WI: University of Wisconsin Press.

Zuboff, S. (1988). *In the age of the smart machine.* New York: Basic Books.

13

Faulty Strategies Or What To Do With Democracy On The Way Into The Media Future

Peter A. Bruck
School of Journalism Carleton University
Ottawa, Canada
and
Institut für Kommunikationswissenschaft
Universität Salzburg
Salzburg, Austria

The recent developments in East-Central Europe have been a stunning success for the international struggle for democracy and human rights. But while the new democratic movements in the hitherto Communist countries chart a new course for their societies, most of their Western sister countries have yet to learn from these experiences. The new political and social formations in East Central Europe are born out of the nonviolent reform-revolutions or, as Ash has termed them, "refolutions."[1]

These transformations are in more than one way historically unique. And they provide a new analytical point of view on what is or is not taking place to the west of East Central Europe. This includes the question of the democratization of communication and media systems. While one will have to wait till after the round of elections in the spring and summer of 1990 to assess what media future might

---

[1] The term *refolution* was invented by Timothy Gorton Ash to name the reform-revolutions which have taken place in East Central Europe in 1989 (Ash, 1989a). For details see the last chapter in Ash (1989b).

come forth from the ruptive evolutions of the last months, one need not delay drawing lessons from the reemergence and vitality of citizens' power.

This is an all the more interesting and necessary task as there is little inclination in the West to do so. More specifically, if one sets the politics of the new citizens' movements in East-Central in relation to the widespread political exhaustion in West-Central Europe—that is, Austria—it is possible to show the challenges facing democratization and communication.

CIVIL SOCIETY, NONVIOLENCE, AND CITIZENSHIP

Many Westerners, politicians, activists, and critics have yet to realize the implications of the democratic transformations in the East for their own political and social life. The springtime of citizens, which stretched from the Hungarian, Polish, and Yugoslavian summer to the East German and Czechoslovak fall and into the Rumanian and Bulgarian winter has changed the face of Europe and the political tectonics of the North.

Conservative critics like to view the popular movements for political and social self-determination and cultural renewal merely in terms of the collapse of communism and the affirmation of the values, institutions, and electoral rituals of liberal democracy (Keane, 1988). Even the most informed observers in the West, like T.G. Ash, consider them as offering "no fundamentally new ideas on the big questions of politics, economics, law or international relations" (Ash, 1990a, p. 22). They might be quite wrong.

It is too facile to say that the transformations of 1989 were a long time coming, but it is quite correct to point to the many diverse and multifaceted activities and struggles in which ordinary people engaged over the last 10 years in developing, maintaining, and defending social relations independent from the totalitarian state (Fedorowicz, 1988).

"Civil Society" was the key term used by these oppositional movements. The term and concept of civil society originates in its modern meaning in the 17th and 18th centuries, and was used to designate the realm of private commodity production and exchange, of private property and individual rights. This realm was defined and secured as a social, political, and legal space by the constitutions won in the American and French revolutions, and the uprisings and revolts of years like 1848. In this sense, the term and concept "civil society" are tied to a bourgeois context of origin (Keane, 1988).

Term and concept were thus developed to name and normatively describe the social space independent of the state apparatus and free from state administration, control, and interference. In the course of the 19th century, the bourgeoisie lost its revolutionary ambition for equality and brotherhood, content with the gains for its own class. And the liberating potential of the market, so effective in the struggles against authoritarian monarchical states and their hierarchical social relations (Williams, 1981; Fedorowicz, 1988; Fedorowicz & Bruck, 1989), proved to be the cause for new social inequalities based on the economics of capitalism. Conceptually and ideologically, bourgeois thought equated the state-civil society distinction with the arrangement of social relations of capitalism. The struggles of the citizens movements in East Central Europe did not only activate the democratic memory related to this concept, they brought back prebourgeois associations with this concept (see also Keane, 1983, p. 33), and they added new dimensions, essential for our common future.

The notion of civil society continued to carry the meaning of a social space created out of the possibility and right to associations that are free from state or state-party control, autonomous, voluntary, and democratic. But the citizens movements added the concept of nonviolence as a form of defence and of political assertion. *Civil* refers then to social conduct, semantically enlarged from the point of bourgeois manners to the renouncing of violence as a means of social struggle and transformation. *Civil* in this sense, connects conceptually outward behavior with a state of mind and mode of desire, creating a continuity between the individual and the social, between the spiritual and the political. This is also meant when oppositionists talk about living in truth or the politics of truth (Havel, 1988; Fedorowicz, 1990). The struggles of civil society arise not only from its conflicts with the state but they also encompass the conflicts which have given rise to the new democratic or social movements in the West (Mouffe, 1988; Habermas, 1981). These conflicts center around the security and improvement of the life-world, questions of environment, self-realization, gender, and equal quality of life.

This leads us to the other dimension added by these struggles to the term of civil society. It is related to the experiences of the denial of and the struggle for human rights. People in the villages, towns, and cities of East-Central Europe have gone long through the trials, temptations, and exclusions brought about by a system that needed not to incarcerate them all, but which poisoned them by monopolizing the distribution of social rewards, stealthily building caste-like structures. The notion of individual rights gains in these contexts a most concrete meaning. It meant being treated equally, and not on the basis of submission to a totalitarian rule, of accommodation and acquiescence, of being gradually sucked into the comforts of the monosystems of privileges. The glaring inequalities of life and the fact that little to no recourse was possible made citizenship a term with an explosive meaning: It called for equal entitlement, dignity, and fairness.[2] Moreover, it claimed participatory rights within all social and political spheres.

The citizens' movements of East Central Europe have just begun to rethink and remake their societies as civil ones. They are building a nonviolent political and social culture where the universal entitlement to equality is realized in citizenship. Nonviolence and civic entitlement offer thus two powerful dimensions to a notion of democratization that is often reduced to the formal aspects of participation in decision making and/or, as is the case in regard to communication, cultural production.[3]

CIVIL AS BOURGEOIS SOCIETY

As Ralph Dahrendorf has recently remarked in reference to Karl Marx's use of the term "buergerliche Gesellschaft," the German language offers its speakers an ambiguity in the use of the terms that can be widely exploited. The term collapses the meaning of civil society and bourgeois society into one (Ash, 1990, p. 21). Some such ambiguity can be found in East Central Europe, but more is to be seen in West Central European countries like Austria.

While civil society to the east of the former Iron Curtain has asserted itself with historically exemplary vigor, the civil society in Austria—and it may be claimed for some other Western countries—has found few means to articulate new strategies for a more democratic life. Rather, neoconservative prescriptions dominate much of the

---

[2] In late May 1989, the sociology department of the Hungarian Academy of Sciences conference organized an international conference entitled "Citizenship in Europe." The conference focused on emergent forms of social organization in East and West, and looked at the entitlements and obligation schemes which constitute people as members of an articulate citizenry.

[3] The report "Many Voices, One World, the International Commission for the Study of Communication Problems," headed by Sean MacBride, advocated more democratic approaches to communication and defined them as processes whereby individuals become more active partners in communication, where the variety of messages would increase, and where the degree and quality of public participation would improve (UNESCO, 1984, p. 132). For further discussion on the question of democratization strategies see Bruck and Raboy (1989).

agenda, and established political forces compete for the bourgeois ideological centre.

Nineteen-hundred eighty-nine has been the year Austria entered into the final vacuum of political-democratic imagination. Such an assertion might be wrong when generalized to all aspects and corners of political life, but it is definitely true for the two established democratic mass parties of the left and right, red and black, that have governed the country since World War II. Emblematic for this downfall from political-democratic vision to the politics of stopgap repair are the troubles of the two party leaders who, called to the helm to clear the deck of corrupt, disgraced, or otherwise compromised lieutenants, found themselves within a few months in the quagmires of having to defend their own personal conduct.

Born out of the horrors of class strife and civil war, the Socialist and Christian conservative political camps formed a historical compromise leading the country to post-World War II prosperity and affluence. The social contract between unions and entrepreneurs institutionalized in the social parity commission chaired by the nonvoting chancellor, that is, head of government, has allowed the two contending political parties over the years to treat the state like their fiefdom and rival each other in carving out spheres of influence and patronage.

The Socialist party, formed between the two World Wars by the powerful social and political visions of Austro-Marxist thinkers like Otto Bauer or Victor Adler, has now a banker as a leader. The Christian democratic party, all along an uneasy coalition between Christian social unionists, industrialists, small businessmen, and farmers is torn by its own internal contradictions.

From the late 1970s on, the political culture was increasingly compromised by a neverending series of scandals of personal enrichment, corruption, law breaking, or public lying which included one chancellor, a finance minister, union leaders, other ministers, provincial politicians, and the lot. At the same time, media and communication policy was being made largely in terms of personnel politics, that is, the scheming and lobbying to guarantee influence through appointments of cronies and confidants in the public broadcasting corporation.

The state has been the tool which the two political parties and camps used to perpetuate themselves and see after their partisans. On the surface of the system, this has meant, for instance, that the party leaders and their representatives, disregarding all possible laws, exercise a large if not final say in the appointment of journalists, department heads, programming directors, and the director-general of the Austrian public broadcasting corporation, ORF.

Structurally, this means for instance that the parties use public funds to finance their educational academies, and raise without shame their budgetary allotment at the same time as they are cutting subsidies to independent publications.[4]

Particularly since WWII, civil society in Austria has been in the hands of the two mass political parties. They formed the decision-making apparatus and reward mechanisms for the two ideological camps running their parallel institutions from kindergarten to seniors' homes. Most spheres of social activity be it amateur sports, hiking, and mountain climbing, automobile associations, or travel agencies and book clubs, they all were divided in a RED and a BLACK organization. When the social system is structured in such a way, the media system cannot be expected to be much different.

For more than a decade, the democratic mass parties have not developed any communication policies (Puerer, 1988; Institut fuer Publizistik und Kommunikationswissenschaft der Universitaet Salzburg, 1986). Media politics was reduced to personnel politics. And nowhere has the problem been more significant than in the area of broadcasting.

BROADCASTING, MONOPOLY, AND CALCIFIED CIVIL ASSOCIATIONS

Broadcasting, which began in Austria in 1924, developed all along in proximity to the state and the governing coalition of interests. The Radio-Verkehrs-AG (RAVAG), founded as a monopoly enterprise, turned into virtually the only mass medium in the years of semicivil war which coincided in Austria with the economic crises of the late 1920s and early 1930s. After the installation of the Austro-Fascist regime in 1934, the RAVAG was used as the chief propaganda instrument of the authoritarian nationalist government. When the Nazis annexed Austria in 1938, they integrated the RAVAG into the "Reichsrundfunkgesellschaft" on the very first day of the "Anschluss" (Fabris, 1988/89).

After the war the Allied forces built up separate radio stations in their zones of occupation, and it was only after their pullout in 1955 that the Austrian broadcasting corporation ORF was created. In keep-

---

[4] A single federal law governs the subsidy for independent periodicals and the political academies of the parties represented in Parliament. Between 1980 and 1985 the budget for periodicals was cut from ATS 7,6 to ATS 6,1 million, while the allotment for the academies was increased from ATS 44 to ATS 55,5 million (Institut fuer Publizistik und Kommunikationswissenschaft der Universitaet Salzburg, 1986, pp. 64–65).

ing with the political arrangements of the day, the administration and management of the new radio and television network was divided into spheres of influence proportional to the political strength of the two mass parties that had governed in a coalition ever since the end of the war.

In the intervening years, three attempts have been made to reform broadcasting, all with the aim to lessen the parties perennial hijacking of the broadcast media. The reform of 1964/66 was initiated by a popular petition signed by 832,000 citizens and spearheaded by independent newspapers. The Broadcasting Acts of 1966, 1974, and 1984 reorganized the internal structure of the ORF, but the de facto grip of the two parties on the medium, its personnel, and programming continued.

On paper some of the reforms seem to be quite impressive. The "Kuratorium" of the ORF, the board of directors, is made up not only of representatives of the political parties in Parliament, but includes members of the nine Austrian federal Laender or provinces and— more significantly—of social and cultural associations. Even the audience has its own body of representation, the "Hoerer und Seher Vertretung," with consultative and recommending powers to the management.

This council of viewers and listeners might have been a model of cooperation and involvement of civil society in broadcasting. It includes delegates from interest organizations like the chambers of commerce and agriculture, the unions, and the churches, as well as representatives from social spheres like the sciences, the arts, sports, tourism, and even consumers.

The spirit of the written law is, however, subverted by the fact that these organizations of civil society lack autonomy and are largely lined up according to the general division of the country into the red and black camps.[5]

They thus do little more than reproduce the ossified system of established power relations. As Fabris and Luger have recently observed, in terms of law and statutes the ORF's structures attempt to approach the ideal of a delicate balance between social responsiveness

---

[5] While a debate on the general outlines of Austria's media future is intermittent at best, the daily papers are never short on stories about the continuous strategizing which is going on in the camps to keep their influence and shore up their voting blocks in the decision-making bodies. For an example, see Hans Werner Scheidl in the leading "quality" paper of the country "Die Presse" "Rote Endzeit im Kuratorium des ORF" (June 16, 1989, p. 3). Board or council members who vote their judgment and not their camp colors are considered traitors and have to fear publicly conducted witch hunts as happened the last two times after the election of a director-general for the ORF.

and political independence, but the ideal is not met (Fabris, Luger, & Signitzer, 1988/89, pp. 3–5). The institutional articulations of civil society are paralyzed by ideological partisanship, bureaucratization, and the narrow consensus parameters of the "social partnership."

In as much as the Austrian mediascape has been kept in stability by the social partnership of the institutional associations of capital, labor, and agricultural producers for most of the last four decades, the absence of public reflection on this situation and of a public debate on democratization and the media future is not surprising.

DEMONOPOLIZATION AND FAULTY STRATEGIES

The reform discourse of the Austrian socialist party, still existing in the 1970s, became largely discredited in the 1980s. Insiders blame technology for the vacuum of ideas. Transborder broadcasting from TV satellites and radio stations in neighboring countries to the west, south, and soon east are blamed for encroaching on the Austrian broadcasting system, leaving little to no room for anything else than swimming with the flood [6]

This conceptual collapse of a social democratic vision has created for the first time since the existence of the second republic a situation where in the public discourse in general and also in regard to broadcasting, the notion of "economy" is categorically set free from the "social." As a consequence, the field has been opened to neoconservative formulations that have developed individual choice as the key category.

Not surprisingly, a campaign sprang up in 1989 that made the abolishment of the ORF broadcasting monopoly the cornerstone for a large-scale media reform in the country. The campaign is organized and financed by the Free Democratic Party, FPOe, which used to be the political reservoir for nationalist, rightist, and some liberal political groupings. But a recent change in leadership and a forceful campaign against the red and black grand coalition of privileges and corruption have given the FPOe a series of stunning electoral victories, including the governmental leadership in the province of Carinthia.

The antimonopoly campaign tries to imitate the petition drive from 1964 which is largely credited, and rightly so, to have given the ORF the limited degree of political independence and journalistic autonomy

---

[6] When recently asked about the existence of a programmatic statement on media and communications policy that takes into account the changing realities, the responsible spokesman for the Socialist Party of Austria, Sepp Rieder, answered that he did not know one (Fabris & Trappel, 1989, p. 112). Rieder is also a member of Parliament.

it has enjoyed. But the current campaign uses key concepts quite different from the ones used 25 years ago. The drive to end the public broadcasting system centers ideologically around notions of freedom and choice, not notions of democracy and independence. Freedom is conceptually detached from the social context of its realization and the social relations of power. "Democracy" has become redefined as the system offering the widest possible consumer choice, and "democratization" does not exist conceptually in this debate on the changes in the media system and communication future.

In most of the Western countries of the North, conservative governments and parties have tended over the last 10 years to formulate quite clear and direct media policies in order to establish broadcasting as a market generating audiences rather than as a sphere of social communication and expressive cultural production. Media policies rode the wider ideological wave of privatization, Thatcherism, and Reagonomics. According to this, public broadcasters should not be protected from competition, at least part of the broadcasting system ought to be privatized, state subsidies must be cut back or eliminated, and incentives for new technologies have to be created. The hope of these policies rests with the market and its ability to create and maintain diversity of products, information, and opinion (see Rowland & Tracey, 1989, p. 475)[7], despite all the evidence to the contrary.

The Austrian campaign for the abolition of the public service monopoly is in some significant ways different from the other neoconservative trends. While politicians of the conservative Christian democratic party talk about the maintenance of the public broadcaster as the leading radio/TV corporation in the country, and argue for increased creativity through competition (see Fabris & Trappel, 1989, pp. 116—118), their calls do not gain much public echo.

Rather, the ideological sentiments that dominate the petition campaign to abolish the ORF monopoly are fuelled by a rebellion against the "Oberigkeitsstaat," the "strong authority state," controlled by the

---

[7] The prospects of the ORF might be quite unclear, but it has not taken the same battering as its West German sister organizations. The public broadcaster ARD, which is in German eyes the largest noncommercial radio and television enterprise on earth, has been increasingly associated with the structures and operations of the now-fallen communist regimes in East Central Europe. A headline from early fall in the leading German newsmagazine *Der Spiegel* read "Die ARD ist wie die DDR" (The ARD is like the GDR) (Schnibben, 1989, p. 114). The quote is from a former department director who switched from the public broadcaster to the private RTL Plus. He added that the GDR might still be better off as the communists there have at least heads made of concrete, while the political maneuvering of the red/black factions in the ARD have left the company without heads altogether (Schnibben, 1989, p. 128).

"old" parties. Public discourse on the topic has been compressed into the simple positions of for or against monopoly, for or against freedom of choice. While communist parties and governments created in East Central Europe a "Baifra of the mind," the grand coalition arrangement in Austria has created what some have termed a Biafra of political and democratic ideas, including ideas regarding the media future (Fruehbauer, 1986, p. 646).

The ensuing one-dimensionality of the public debate has sharply reduced the legitimation efforts required from media entrepreneurs in terms of the necessary public justifications of their projects and demands on the state. In a preemptive move, the ORF has tried with the support of the red/black camps to ride the privatization wave. On the basis of the coalition pact between the two governing parties dating from after the federal elections in 1986/87, the ORF has signed an agreement in principle with the Austrian association of newspaper publishers, Verband der oesterreichischen Zeitungsherausgeber, which provides for the tentative startup of private radio but not TV by the fall of 1990.

According to this arrangement the new radio stations will use ORF transmitters, they will be bound by the programming mandate of the public broadcaster and receive their licences from it. The private stations will be organized on a provincial basis, and their performance will be monitored by the board of directors of the ORF which also can revoke the licence. The new radio will be financed by the sale of a maximum of 60 minutes of commercials per day.[8]

The ORF and the publishers rationalize this arrangement, already termed as "Radio-Print," in their announcement of the deal: The Austrian market would need a rational market order to prevent "financial adventures"; the new radio should not create a competition to the public radio but supplement it; and the electronic media should be exclusively controlled by Austrian citizens. What ORF and publishers did not say publicly is that this arrangement provides essential protection for the advertising revenues of both parties, and that this security of a key income base has been the sole objective shared by the private entrepreneurs and the public corporation.

As a long-term strategy, the deal reproduces the existing power structures and shores up the various interlinked interest positions. In terms of democratization, it excludes outright nonestablishment groups from having any access to the electronic media of communication. Rather, it reinforces the ideological sentiments of the Free Demo-

---

[8] See *Die Presse.* 29/8/1989, p. 1,4,5. *Kurier.* 29/8/89 p. 1,2. *AZ.* 29/8/89 p. 3.

cratic Party and of short-sighted free marketeers who pay no attention to the cultural or social dimension of media production. The arrangement also highlights once more the political clout of the Austrian newspaper publishers. Since the middle of 1987, the daily publishing industry has gone through an unprecedented period of conglomeration and concentration, which has raised serious threats to the democratic process in the country. Within the course of less than six months the newspaper market was turned upside down by a series of mergers and buyouts fueled by foreign capital.

Nearly 55 percent of total Austrian daily newspaper circulation ended up largely controlled by one owner, and—in a country that has had no significant foreign ownership of the daily press since World War II—this owner is a non-Austrian company. The two top circulation papers, *Neue Kronen-Zeitung* and *Kurier,* are co-owned now by the West German WAZ-Gruppe. In the capital of Vienna these papers have a hold on the readership exceeding 80 percent of the adult population.[9] Radio-Print gives the WAZ Gruppe the best access to the electronic media.

The arrangement also indicates how even the heaviest concentration in terms of cross-media ownership has not deterred the two established political mass parties from arranging for a deal that serves their short-term power interests while being quite detrimental for the prospects of a democratic media system.

CONCLUSIONS

Within the course of the next 12 months, Austrian broadcasting will be reconstituted as a market. The then 34-year-old monopoly of the ORF will find an end, and new private radio stations will be licensed. This will take place at a time when media concentration is at an all-time high and when the new distribution technology of cable increasingly erodes the public service monopoly by providing the signals of new foreign TV stations. Cable also shows for the first time significant gains in subscription. Unlike in earlier phases of restructuration, the present changes in the Austrian media system are brought about

---

[9] Since the post war years, Austria has seen a slow but significant attrition of papers in terms of numbers, circulation, and editorial content. The low in terms of total circulation was reached in 1957/58, but it took until 1977/78 to reach the circulation of 1947 (Puerer, 1988). In the last two years one daily newspaper was started, a second one is in planning, and three existing ones have and are making considerable investments to reach new market segments either regionally or demographically. In all but two cases the capital for the investment comes from foreign sources.

largely by economic interests with the interests of civil society being largely traded off. To date, the established interests have used the state directly to cushion technological and economic developments, and minimize the adaptations of the system and its various sectors. Unlike other countries, the Austrian state is directly involved not only in the use of the radio spectrum, but also in the use of print, motion pictures, and sound.

When civil society is to a large degree in the hands of entrenched political groupings, its activist potential is eroded. Austrian civil society has to grow out of the camp divisions that have institutionalized the old class conflict between workers, and bourgeoisie and farmers. The camp division of Austrian political and social life has become a mechanism of hierarchical rule for a class of political administrators who have many interests in common. Moreover, the division has turned into a foil, preventing democratization. It channels all dissent into established institutions, and strengthens the status quo.

The challenges posed by new communication technologies and globalizing media conglomerates will have to be confronted by the Austrian elites. They are ill-prepared to do so. Yet, they control the future of broadcasting and communication policy.[10]

Through the prism of an East-Central European concept of civil society the West-Central situation in Austria does not look encouraging. In terms of political conduct the civil quality is largely missing, in terms of civic entitlement large parts of what used to be free and independent associations have become institutionalized shells for narrow power interests.

The challenge for the citizens' movements in Austria is considerable. They have to regain the continuity between the individual and social, and they have to struggle to realize a widened notion of citizenship. In addition, they have to enlarge the East-Central concept of civil society with the experience of living in a developed capitalist country of the West/North. As media concentration increases and global conglomerates gain more and more control over Austrian media markets, the free and independent interactions of citizens are restricted by the monopolizing powers of big business and big media corporations. The term civil society, then, needs to designate not only the social space free and independent of the legitimation and control needs of the state, but also free and independent of the accumulation needs and commodification dynamics of capital.

---

[10] Although already for three years in Parliament, the Austrian Green Party has not been able to date to develop a media or communication policy. A first discussion paper was drafted by Pius Strobl, the federal secretary of the party, on September 20, 1989.

Democratic critique has, then, not only to recover the notions of civil society and social spaces free from state interference (see Keane, 1988, 1989), but has to understand the cultural and expressive resources of a autonomous citizenry. The conglomeration and vertical integration of various media operations into mammoth media empires run by a single board of directors has its cultural costs, and not only in terms of the concentration of power. Democratization means here also understanding and making understood the implications of the economic transformations for the everyday cultural life of citizens.

REFERENCES

Ash, T.G. (1988, October 13). The opposition. *New York Review of Books,* pp. 3–5.

Ash, T.G. (1989a, June 15). Refolution: The springtime of two nations. *The New York Review of Books,* pp. 3, 4, 6, 8, 10.

Ash, T.G. (1989b). *The uses of adversity.* New York: Random House.

Ash, T.G. (1990, February 15). Eastern Europe: The year of truth. *The New York Review of Books,* pp. 17–22.

Bruck, P.A., & Raboy, M. (1989). The challenge of democratic communication. In M. Raboy & P.A. Bruck (Eds.), *Communication for and against democracy* (pp. 3–16). Montreal: Black Rose Books.

Fabris, H.H., & Luger, K. (1986). Austria. In H.J. Kleinsteuber, D. McQuail, & K. Siune (Eds.), *Electronic media and politics in Western Europe.* Frankfurt-New York: Campus Verlag.

Fabris, H.H., Luger, K., & Signitzer, B. (1988/89). Das rundfunksystem oesterreichs. In *Internationales handbuch fuer rundfunk und fernsehen.* Baden-Baden: Nomos Verlag.

Fabris, H.H., & Trappel, J. (1989). *Die integration der medien. Oesterreich vor der herausforderung durch EG, Europarat und die internationalisierung der medienmaerkte.* Salzburg: Institut fuer Publizistik und Kommunikationsforschung.

Fedorowicz, H.M. (1988, December). The war for information: The Polish response to martial law. *Canadian Journal of Communication, Special Issue,* pp. 13–31.

Fedorowicz, H.M. (1990). Civil society as a communication project: The Polish laboratory for democratization in East Central Europe. In S. Splichal, J. Hochheimer, & K. Jakubowicz (Eds.), *Proceedings of the 3rd International Colloquium on Communication and Culture* (pp. 73–87). Ljubljana, Yugoslavia.

Fedorowicz, H.M., & Bruck, P.A. (1989, Spring). Medien im Widerstand: Polens Zivile Gesellschaft im Informationskampf. *Medien Journal, 13*(1), 23–34.

Fruehbauer, M. (1986). Kommunikationspolitische duerre-oder elektronische medienpolitik auf oesterreichisch. In A. Khol, G. Ofner, & A. Stirnemann (Eds.), *Oesterreichisches jahrbuch fuer politik—1985*. Wien/ Muenchen: Verlag fuer Geschichte und Politik/Oldenbourg Verlag.

Habermas, J. (1981, Fall). New social movements. *Telos, 49,* 33–37.

Havel, V. (1988). *Living in truth*. London: Faber.

Institut fuer Publizistik und Kommunikationswissenschaft der Universitaet Salzburg. (Ed.). (1986). *Massenmedien in Oesterreich-Medienbericht III*. Salzburg/Wien: Internationale Publikationen Gesellschaft.

Keane, J. (1988). *Democracy and civil society*. London: Verso.

Keane, J. (1989, Summer). Liberty of the press in the 1990s. *New Formations, 8,* 35–54.

Mouffe, C. (1988). Hegemony and new political subjects: Toward a new concept of democracy. In C. Nelson & L. Grossberg (Eds.), *Marxism and the interpretation of culture* (pp. 89–104). *Urbana:* University of Illinois Press.

Puerer, H. (1988). *Aktualisierungen. Neue Informationen, Daten und Fakten ueber Presse und Rundfunk in Oesterreich 1988*. Salzburg: Kuratorium fuer Journalistenausbildung.

Rowland, W.D., Jr., & Tracey, M. (1989). Selbstmord aus Angst vor dem Tod? Aktuelle Herausforderungen fuer den oeffentlichen Rundfunk ueberall auf der Welt. *Media Perspektiven, 8,* 469–480.

Scheidl, H.W. (1989, June 16). Rote Eudzeit im Kuratorium des ORF. *Die Presse,* p. 3.

Schnibben, C. (1989). Die ARD ist wie die DDR. *Der Spiegel, 46,* 114–128.

Williams, R. (1981). *Culture*. Glasgow: Fontana Paperbacks.

UNESCO. (1984). *Many voices one world* (Abridged version). Paris: UNESCO.

14

Communication Technology and Democracies of South Asia: The Danger of Curbing Freedom*

Binod C. Agrawal
Social Research Group
Development and Education Communication Unit
ISRO, Space Applications Centre
Ahmedabad, India

Political freedom in the subcontinent of South Asia[1] is a post-Second World War phenomenon. Expansion of mass media coincided with the independence of these countries. The chip revolution along with rapid development in the space technology is just about a quarter century old. So the present mass media scenario in South Asia has a history not more than four to five decades. These obvious historical landmarks are repeated to indicate that one is dealing with very recent technopolitical events in the life of the civilizations which are more than 5,000 years old. Therefore, any discussion and argument related to communication technology and its influence on the political system

---

* Chief Scientist, Social Research Group, Development and Educational Communication Unit, ISRO, Space Applications Centre, Ahmedabad 380 053, India. The opinions expressed in this paper are those of the author and do not necessarily represent the views of the organization to which he belongs.

[1] The term South Asia refers to SAARC (South Asian Association for Regional Cooperation). The countries of South Asia include Bangladesh, Bhutan, India, Maladives, Nepal, Pakistan, and Sri Lanka.

in South Asia must be analyzed within the context of its sociocultural and historical frame.

In this chapter, an attempt is made to examine whether new communication technology like satellite-based broadcasting weakens the democracy. The differing views to this issue can be broadly categorized as "technopositivism," "technoneutralism," and "technonegativism." The "technopositivism" view refers to the opinion of those engineers, scientists, and political leaders who believe that satellite-based broadcasting helps political and emotional integration, thereby strengthening democracy. The "technonegativism" endorses the views of those who think that satellite-based broadcasting in plural civilizations having multiple languages and "world view," imposes the views of a politically dominant minority over the majority. In the process, this kind of broadcasting tends to create emotional dissonance, increases control over information by few, and thereby weakens the democracy. The third view of "technoneutralism" represents views of those who believe that technology by itself does not create any condition for weakening the democracy; rather the aims and goals of the communicators are directly responsible for strengthening or weakening the democracy (for details see Hamelink, 1986). These kinds of philosophical differences expressed by scientists, engineers, political leaders, policy makers, social scientists, and people at large are presented here to argue that "technonegativism" is what seems to be the most visible in the context of India.

PLURALISTIC CIVILIZATIONS OF SOUTH ASIA

South Asia by any stretch of imagination is considered a pluralistic civilization in the classical sense. It is pluralistic because it is inhabited by all major religious and linguistic groups. Above all, it has passed through varied experiences of having governance of different political systems over more than 5,000 years of South Asian history. Throughout its existence, social differentiation based on economic, political, and religious power has been most extreme when a minority ruled over a large majority. These characteristics remained stable and continuous throughout the history in spite of external aggression and internal turbulences. The last abrasion in the long journey of civilization of South Asia was British colonialism which began in the 18th century as a commercial venture and ended up as a conquest of South Asia—a region ravaged by constant war and in-fighting among the local kings and Nawabs.

The 18th-century South Asia, in spite of Britain's best efforts and its colonial hegemony, remained divided into a large number of "small states" in which the territories of the British empire spread like cancer. This was the political situation that influenced the sociocultural life and, more than this, the economic life of the people. The economic life drastically changed due to exploitation of human beings, land, and natural resources. The social life remained in conflict with tradition and new aspirations but continued to be divided between *Raja* (ruler) and *Praja* (ruled). The social structure of South Asia was somewhat tampered with when British introduced "middle class" in the feudal society (Agrawal, 1968).

The local political system in rural South Asia, though varying a great deal from region to region, had some of the characteristics of democracy. Tinker (1967, p. 20) described these characteristics in the following words.

The primacy of panchayat was far from universal even in Mughal times: many villages were under the rule of a landlord or his agent. . . . Although Indian village government has never been "democratic" in Western terms, there was a sense in which the whole body of the villagers took their part in affairs. The old panchayat, whether as a caste tribunal or as a judicial or administrative body, normally conducted its deliberations in the presence of all who cared to attend. . . . The attendant crowd in its respect for authority would confine its observations to an occasional "Shabash" but everyone present considered that he was playing a part in the proceedings. In such ways the inhabitants identified themselves with the life and government of their village.

The information needs were endogenous, hence face-to-face interaction served their purpose. Not many changes have been observed in all these years. Research related to human communication in recent days indicate that most of the communications, especially rural, are interpersonal in the form of exchange of information among friends and relatives or those who know each other. Media effects studies have also found similar pattern of communication in which friends and relatives are considered the most credible sources of information. They are also considered most trustworthy even if the information sought is related to outside the immediate environment and specialized in nature.

THE MASS MEDIA IN SOUTH ASIA

It is in this kind of social-political and economic context that telecommunication was introduced in the mid-19th century by the colonial power. Later, radio was introduced in the third and fourth decades of the 20th century followed by television in the second half of the 20th century. The last to arrive on the scene was satellite which became operational for broadcasting in the 1980s in India. In other countries of South Asia, rented satellites are being used for telecommunication and limited broadcasting.

In the post-second World War period, along with independence from colonial rule, came the expansion phase of mass media, especially the electronic medium of radio. Given the technical limitation of propagation, medium-wave radio stations were set up along with short wave. Other mass media, like film or newspapers, also expanded very quickly in the newly independent countries of South Asia. Expansion of television—which for a very long time was also thought to be luxury for these countries—also followed a similar path. Sudden expansion of television was heralded by the arrival of satellite communication and pressure from the multinationals. The present distribution of mass media in India and, to a large extent, in South Asia are very skewed. Eapen (1986, p. 47) felt that "be it press or broadcasting, the organized media belong to the top 10 per cent of Indian society. Industrial and political power is rooted in this segment." Other estimates show an even smaller percentage of media owners, thereby reflecting an even higher degree of skewness.

SATELLITE-BASED BROADCASTING: THE CASE OF INDIA

India, after almost 15 years of planning and experimentation, introduced satellite-based broadcasting. Important among these experiments were SITE, STEP, and APPLE.[2] The aim of satellite broadcasting was to leapfrog from conventional communication technology to satellite technology which provided (a) distance-neutral broadcasting in which the audience living in remote rural areas and urban areas were not discriminated against, (b) high-speed message dissemination over the entire country and, if required, the whole of South Asia, and (c) instantaneous accurate and reliable information exchange

---

[2] SITE stands for Satellite Instructional Television Experiment conducted in 1975–76. STEP or Satellite Telecommunication Experiment Project was conducted in 1977–79. Ariane Passenger Payload Experiment (APPLE) was an Indian satellite built indigenously and was used for several experiments in early 1980s.

and processing between two or many points in normal and emergency situations.

In 1982, multipurpose Indian National Satellite (INSAT) System became operational with the launching of the INSAT-1 series of satellite. Today radio and television signals are being transmitted to a very large part of the country using INSAT. The television expansion in India is unparalleled in the world communication history. The television expansion march continues today. Except for China, India seems to have the largest satellite-based television transmission system in the world covering over 500 million population. Television ownership has also increased in leaps and bounds from less than four million in 1982 to more than 24 million television sets in 1989.

The future of satellite-based broadcasting is bright as the second generation of Indian National Satellites are being indigenously built and launching capabilities are being developed. Initial designing, fabrication, and testing of this series of satellites are in progress and will be completed in the very near future. The scientists and planners have thought of new applications of satellite-based broadcasting in the areas of education, training, and development. Presently, serious consideration is being given to having a separate "educational satellite." The satellite will be used for formal, nonformal, and open education at primary, secondary, and college levels. Also, it will be used for training and retraining of teachers and a large number of development functionaries. Keeping in view that in a pluralistic and multilingual country like India, where primary education must be imparted in the "mother tongue" (the first language spoken by the child at home), efforts are being made to design such satellites that will cater to such national needs. There are indications that other countries of South Asia may also use this kind of facility for education and development.

Another application of satellite in education relates to the development of information and library network (INFLIBNET). It is proposed that all the universities, national laboratories, and research institutions of India will have INFLIBNET. Such a satellite-based network will provide quick access to all the available library literature within the country and all over the world. Also, this network could be used by the universities of other South Asian countries. Passing references should also be made to business applications of satellite-based telecommunications, as well as administrative applications for national, provincial, and district-level database information networks for the planning and management of development activities. Satellite seems to be opening new vistas of broadcasting: point to point and individual communications. It all amounts to an ever-increasing influence of satellite communications in the socioeconomic, political, and educational lives of the people in India.

THE NONBROADCASTING ELECTRONIC MEDIA

In the nonbroadcasting mode, the audio/videocassette recorders have caught the imagination of both urban and rural music lovers and film viewers. The popularity can be gauged the way videocassette recorders, videocassette players, "walkman," audiocassette recorders, and two-in-one (radio and audiocassette recorder combined) have been imported both individually and in an organized manner. They are also being manufactured with the help of imported kits. There are no authentic estimates of the total number of audio- and videocassette recorders in South Asia. In India alone, it is believed that there are more than four million videocassette recorders as of 1987 (Agrawal, Patel, Rao, Selkhar, Sinha, & Verma, 1989). But the estimated number of both are unknown though they are considered to be very high. The videocassette recorders are largely used for Hindi and English film viewing whereas audiocassette recorders are being used for listening to film songs and some music. There is a small percentage of users who are also using the same for religious and political purposes. The popularity of nonbroadcasting modes of communication is increasing in India and in other countries of South Asia. The content of software is largely drawn from films both from within and outside India.

GOVERNMENT CONTROL

In all the countries of South Asia, governments exercise control through the central authority over radio and television apart from film and print media—one of the legacies of the British colonial rule. At present, for example in India, satellite broadcasting covers the entire country.

In 1989, about 80 to 100 million viewers speaking 15 different languages and several hundred dialects apart from Hindi and English watched television programs transmitted from Delhi—the capital of India. With few exceptions, all these programs were in Hindi or English languages. Television programs in other than Hindi and English languages were subtitled in English. For example, all television programs for higher education are in the English language, though higher education is imparted in a dozen other languages. The majority of the Indian radio and television programs are indigenously produced. Having a very rich film production tradition in the country, television has been dominated by film industry both for content and style.

The national news is broadcast in Hindi and English twice a day in the morning and evening. In addition, the morning telecast is also broadcast for the whole country. In the evening, with the exception of few metropolitan television stations where programs in the language of the province are produced and telecast, the total program telecast from Delhi are meant for the entire country. Exception to this are the primary school television programs; though transmitted from a central point at Delhi, they are produced in the language of each province separately.

The major components of these television programs are (a) news and related information, (b) advertisement-related programs known as sponsored programs, (c) educational and instructional (development) programs, (d) film and film-related programs, and (e) advertisements (commercial and social). Broadly, this pattern has marginally changed over the years. All prime time broadcasting is advertisement related programming.

Exception to this pattern is a district-level television station known as Kheda television run by Indian Space Research Organisation (Department of Space, Government of India) supported by the central television authority. Since 1975, this station has been operational with a short break after satellite-based television broadcasting became operational in Gujarat. At present, it broadcasts an hour program five days a week. It aimes to reach to the poor, small farmers, women, and children in the villages of Kheda district (Gujarat). Communication support for rural development is their goal.

WHO WATCHES TELEVISION?

Who watches these programs? Rough estimates indicate that the majority of the television viewers live in four megapolis of India. Little over one-fourth are from metropolitan cities of the country. The remaining are from cities, towns, and villages—in that order. There are some community television sets installed at government cost both in urban and rural areas. The number of such television sets is very small and their availability for viewing is also questionable. In this respect, satellite-based broadcasting is viewed by a small section of the rich in their homes. This has led to somewhat "privatization" of the "public medium." These are the same viewers among whom some (one out of eight television owners) own a VCR or VCP, who watch video films regularly across the country (for details see Agrawal et al., 1989).

Agrawal et al. (1989, pp. 77–78) concluded that "the profile of the Video-viewers that emerges from the analysis is of urban, educated, professional, businessmen living in a posh/middle class locality earning an assured professed average monthly income of Rs. 2000/—and living in a small family consisting of husband, wife and children. They come from almost all linguistic regions and religious groups thereby signifying observable cultural and linguistic plurality. . . . The most characteristic feature of these viewers is that they are multi-lingual and adaptive to varying environment and the social situation." The social profile of the television viewers would be no different than video viewers who are also television viewers except the total group is relatively less affluent than described earlier.

What happens to those who view or do not view these television programs? There are some tentative but obvious conclusions that can be drawn from the existing studies. First, there is an increase in the information gap between those who view and those who do not view or do not get a chance to view television. In addition, there are some differences between those who only view television as compared to those who view television in conjunction with video. But these differences are of degree and not of a qualitative nature.

Indian television, it seems, caters to the needs of those who own TV. So the sponsored programs are conceived by those who expect television to entertain and inculcate the values of consumerism and ideologies of the "ruling elite." In this respect, television has become an instrument of self-fulfilling prophesy for those who own and run it (Joshi et al., 1985). In no way, then, can the Indian television be characterized as mass medium—rather, it is a "class medium." It sharply divides India between poor and rich; between urban and rural; and between media owners and media nonowners. It has now created conditions in which a majority begin to feel helpless, nonparticipatory, and "information poor." On the other side, few are taking things for granted and expect that the medium is to fulfill their leisure time. Also television must make these viewers feel at par with the rest of Euro-American viewers in terms of their lifestyle, consumer behavior, and values.

These viewers of television, though they feel happy that the language of the television programs is either English or Hindi, complain about language imposition. In reality, they can follow, being multilinguals and having knowledge of Hindi or English apart from their

mother tongue. Language is an extremely delicate issue for the pluralistic civilizations of South Asia. In multilinguistic setting, the language barrier reduces the possibilities of any effective communication
between media owners and nonowners. The classic example on Indian
television are programs meant for higher education that are in the
English language. Cultural plurality in art, music, and theater remains another major hindrance in creating celluloid images that
would be meaningful to a large majority. Television owners, being
multilingual and cosmopolitan, are able to understand, enjoy, and ap-
preciate art forms of other regions. Nonviewers of television, if they
watch these programs, cannot comprehend or enjoy, let alone appre-
ciate the programs. On the contrary, such programs create cognitive
dissonance and apathy.

The centralized television program planning and production—
national political discussions from the capital on provincial and local
issues—are irrelevant for a large majority of the target audience who
do not get a chance to view them. Such a centralized production and
broadcasting loses its meaning by the time it reaches the viewers of
rural areas. It creates a sense of hatred, alienation, and a feeling of
worthlessness.

THE RADIO

In the case of radio, the situation is quite different. Except for a limited amount of centrally produced radio programs—especially news
and current affairs—a large majority of radio programs are produced
at a provincial level in which language and musical forms of a given
linguistic region by and large are presented. However, commercial interests for selling consumer products have been looming large on radio too. Film, music, and song are all-pervasive in the total software
of the Indian radio. The radio transmission covers a very large part
of the country (more than 90 percent in area). Also, there is great deal
of listening to radio in the country (there were more than 50 million
radio sets in the country during 1983). But for "accurate" news, external radio stations are switched on by many listeners especially during
a crisis period. In this respect the credibility of government-owned
radio is low. While listeners of radio cut across the economic classes,
and somewhat across linguistic regions, they remain wedded to their
values and ideologies. Audio cassette recorders have helped to increase the selective listening of film, music, and song apart from Indian classical and western music and song. But, in the process, the

mass participation in radio listening has changed over a period of time. This has been further reduced as a result of increasing influence of television and video.

COMMUNICATION AND DEMOCRACY

Both radio and television have been considered very powerful media by the leaders of South Asian countries. Hence, radio and television have been utilized for political gain. Since 1977 audio/videocassettes have been used for election campaigns, throughout India by all parties in varying quantities. It was considered the second best substitute after mass contact by the political leaders. Political observers and media researchers feel that the use of electronic media in a nontransmission mode is going to be utilized in a big way for mass contact in years to come. They think that to some extent electronic media in a nontransmission mode will help substitute face-to-face campaign and leader-follower direct interaction. Modern techniques of production is helping create bigger-than-life-size images of the political leaders that will mystify the humans into demigods and demigoddesses, thereby pushing them away from a large majority of the people. In order to achieve political goals such a use of mass media would require promotion of a few political leaders or just one political leader. It has already triggered a new political philosophy in which a unitary system is being imposed on a parliamentary democracy.

There is no support from the analysis presented so far for "technoneutralism." The satellite-based broadcasting at the present juncture has created a technological possibility of multiplying radio and television signals from a single point to many points. The technological configuration as it stands has created its own momentum and has emerged after a series of decisions having economic and political considerations and national priorities in view. Hence, it is difficult to argue from technoneutralism of communication. So it is argued that democracy is being influenced by the introduction of satellite-based broadcasting in India and other countries of South Asia.

There is ample evidence to support the view that satellite-based broadcasting has created conditions for social change. The technopositivism view is well supported from the evidence provided in terms of communication expansion and the reach of mass media. Fast expansion of television has helped the electronics industry manifold; centralized broadcasting has provided a new national pastime, and a common point of discussion among those who own and view television. It has also helped create new political consciousness among the television viewers and strengthen one kind of democratic values. It has also induced artificial needs for consumer products, ranging from automobiles to detergents, beauty aids to traditional medicines, electronics to tin food, and many other consumer products. In sum total, a new national climate for a high consumer society has emerged as a result of satellite-based broadcasting in India.

The proponents of technonegativism are arguing somewhat differently. They are pushing the idea that satellite-based broadcasting has helped unite the rich who have high social aspirations for "good living." They ape the lifestyle of the international elite. They desire to acquire lots of material goods. In the process, the satellite-based broadcasting scarcely meets the needs of a large majority. Further, government controlled centralized broadcasting in the pluralistic cultural and linguistic setting have increased the gulf between poor and rich, urban and rural, and media owners and media nonowners. It has added another divide through satellite broadcasting. This division has weakened the democracy in India. One of the touchstones of democracy is peoples participation in the governance of the state—a tradition that is fairly old in South Asia. The satellite broadcasting has reduced the possibility of peoples participation, thereby, weakening the democracy.

As a result of all this, a reverse process has been put into motion. Earlier, it was thought that Indian mass media—like cinema—helped in bringing about an "egalitarianism" in the world of "recreation" and "entertainment" and thereby in political and economic life. It helped "de-class" the highly hierarchical, socially differentiated, and economically divided society. Now, the process of declassing necessary for democracy is not only being halted, but class differences in information and recreation are increasing, thereby curbing individual freedom of the poor who are in the majority. This has jeopardized the process of democratization, negatively affecting the fundamental principles of democracy—equality, justice, and freedom. As the grip on information of the few in power increases, the majority of the receivers are going to be further information-poor and powerless. This is also making them defenseless and they begin to give in without putting up any fight. It is felt that this kind of invisible centralized information power in the democracies of South Asia will lead to the reappearance of a "feudal system" that will be oppressive, ruthless, and dehumanizing beyond recognition. It will bring back the old "Zamindari System" in its worst form, by weakening the democracy and curbing individual freedom.

REFERENCES

Agrawal, B.C. (1968). From commerce to conquest: A historical study of acculturation in India. *The Eastern Anthropologist, 21*(1), 45–58.

Agrawal, B.C., Patel, S., Rao, L., Sekhar, M.C., Sinha, A.C., & Verma, K.K. (1989). *Communication revolution. A study of video penetration in India.* Ahmedabad: DECU, Indian Space Research Organization.

Eapen, E.K. (1986). Transfer of technology: The INSAT experience. In J. Becker, G. Hedebro, & L. Paldan (Eds.), *Communication and domination: Essays to honour Herbert I. Schiller* (pp. 45–52). Norwood, NJ: Ablex.

Hamelink, C.J. (1986). Is information technology neutral? In J. Becker, G. Hedebro, & L. Paldan (Eds.), *Communication and domination: Essays to honour Herbert I. Schiller* (pp. 16–24). Norwood, NJ: Ablex.

Joshi, P.C., et al. (1985). *An Indian personality for television* (Report of the Working Group on Software for Doordarshan). New Delhi: Publications Division, Ministry of Information and Broadcasting.

Tinker, H. (1967). *Foundations of local self-government in India, Pakistan and Burma.* Bombay: Lalvani Publishing House.

15

Interpreting Media in the South Pacific

Peter Gerdes
University of New South Wales
Kensington, New South Wales, Australia

> Each side would assume that the other knew the norms of civilised be-
> haviour and would respect the rules. But this was often a false assump-
> tion: an unconscious trespass could appear a deliberate offence. (Spate,
> 1988, p. 213)

MEDIA AND DEMOCRACY

Media play a vital role in the political structure of every country. In
totalitarian states, media are useful tools for disseminating propaganda that is essential for maintaining power. In democracies, the
media are supposed to reflect the multitude of opinions existing
within society. By providing reliable information and comment media
can help the individual to judge society and form opinions upon which
sound economical and political decisions are based.

Until very recently, all South Pacific nations could at least notion-
ally be regarded as democracies although the constitutional definition
of democracy varied. Unfortunately, the coups in Fiji of 1987 lead by
Colonel Rabuka brought an abrupt end to the widely held belief that
the South Pacific was one of the last regions in the world enjoying
political stability. However, remnants of democracy can still be found
in Fiji.

Democracy means different things to different people. Each democracy has a different understanding as to the extent to which its people

ought to participate directly in the political process. The concept of democracy as "government of the people, by the people, for the people" is highly idealistic and malleable. The Westminister system differs widely from the French or Italian system. The Swiss have referenda and voter-initiated initiatives, the British and Australians have gerrymander. Yet they all call it "democracy" mainly because they can all claim that the citizens elect their representatives after widespread and open election campaigns and in a climate free of fear and pressure.

Media and democracy are indeed strongly linked. In the process of democratization all media have a crucial role to play as mainstays of democracy—the competitive and free flow of news and information is fundamental to the workings of democracy.

SOME DATA

The South Pacific region has become, economically and politically, an important part in global strategic thinking, and this importance will grow further in coming years.[1] Economists, politicians, and journalists in Europe and the United States (but unfortunately also in Australia) are generally little aware of the history of the region which is made up of three more or less well-defined subregions:

- Micronesia, the smallest cultural unit with only approximately 270,000 inhabitants
- Polynesia with approximately 1 million inhabitants
- Melanesia, the largest cultural group which contains 95 percent of the land and 66 percent of the population of the Pacific Islands.

The Pacific Ocean covers approximately 27 percent of the earth's surface and, New Zealand and Papua New Guinea aside, the Pacific islands have a total land area roughly equivalent to that of England. Its myriad of islands are spread over nearly 40 million km2; some are intractably mountainous, others are low-laying coral atolls; some are 600 km from their nearest neighbor. The Marshall Islands, for example, stretches over 1000 km, and consists of 1156 islets, but has a land area of only 180 km2. This made, and makes, travel and trade very

---

[1] When the deputy head of the Soviet Embassy in Canberra, Valery Zenskov, returned to Moscow, he said in an interview that "the fate of the world might be decided in the Pacific region."

difficult. But the islanders are continuously on the move: from the countryside to the townships, from small islands to bigger islands and hence to New Zealand and Australia. There exists a great variety of languages, beliefs, and customs, and the people living in the Pacific value their diversity highly. Twenty-one governments rule 6 million people living in all kinds of political structures, from republic (Nauru, the world's smallest independent nation) to kingdom (Tonga) to department (New Caledonia). Populations are small: Papua New Guinea (PNG) has 3 million inhabitants, Fiji 500,000, 13 of the 22 countries have less than 100,000, some only a few thousand. Most islands are remarkably urbanized whereby the capital exerts a dangerous attraction. The gross national product of most countries is small and hardly provides an economic base for the type of media institutions that Raymond Williams saw as central to the whole social and economic organization of modern capitalist economy. The great variety of languages makes standard access to the media difficult. Although English (and forms of pidgin) in Melanesia and Micronesia and French in Polynesia are the *lingue franche* in the region, there exist thousands of languages—in Polynesia about 40, in Micronesia about 50, and in PNG alone over 700 languages.

TRADITIONAL POLITICS

All island nations have inherited their political systems from their former colonial rulers and more and more of them begin to realize that many of these political structures may have to be changed. Questions about the appropriateness of the present constitution are asked in PNG; in New Caledonia much blood has been shed in the search for a new form of government, and Fiji's political problems are to a great extent baed on outdated political concepts.[2] Traditionally, societies in the South Pacific have always been based on some form of hierarchy. As Spate (1988, p. 40) puts it: "In Melanesia, 'Big-Men' dominated by a Tamany boss's code of generous handouts; in more hierarchical Polynesia there was a code of reciprocity . . . (whereby) the 'goodness' had to do mainly with benefits to the chief." Landrights are still among the most important sociopolitical issues. Land is not

---

[2] Similar questions are raised in the field of law. It seems to become more and more difficult to "reconcile formal court procedures with the story-telling style of much Pacific communication" (O'Callaghan, (1989a). Bernard Narokobi (1983a, 1983b, 1988) has discussed this problem in all of his books, most recently in *Lo Bilong Yumi Yet.*

held by individuals but by groups of kinsmen whereby chiefs often had and have a powerful say in the use of land. The village was and is one of the key political structures. Whoever gets in trouble with the villagers, particularly with elders, can quickly become an outcast. (Today this ultimately means migration to Australia or, more frequently, to New Zealand.) Traditionally, in parts of Melanesia, "political units were very small kin-residence groups," with "no wide political structures . . . and power or rather influences (was) exercised by 'Big-Men' who built up clienteles by displays of calculated generosity." In Polynesia, there were "pyramids of lower and higher chiefs culminating in a paramount who might control a whole island or more" (Spate, 1988, p. 42; Crocombe, 1978, p. 11).[3] Polynesia chiefs wielded enormous power sheltering behind "a network of prohibitions, tapu or tabu . . ." (Spate, 1988, p. 45), but they were responsible for the welfare of their people. South Pacific societies differ greatly in their societal and kinship structure (many have a matrilinear system) but they all show some form of stratification and some form of hierarchy. To quote an example: The Fijian male child is "required to give total obedience, and not to express himself in front of his father. The father is the authority figure . . . the conditioning process, except for persons of high hereditary rank, continues throughout life, teaching everyone to know his place" (Crocombe, 1978, p. 22).

NEW POLITICAL SYSTEMS

Societies in the South Pacific were very developed when they came into contact with explorers, missionaries, traders, and colonists. Chiefs had little to learn from Western powers when it came to running a society. Many of them adapted very quickly to European influences using new means at hand not so much to fight European forces but rather to subjugate other Oceanic societies. The fight against European rule continued but "much of the Islanders' manners and customs survived. They displayed remarkable syncretic powers . . . adopting and adapting new techniques . . . eventually able to take full advantage of the surge of anti-colonialisation in our own times (Spate, 1988, p. 213). All island nations in the South Pacific, some of

---

[3] The "matai" system is still very alive and respected, so much so that the bestowing of "honorary" matai titles on visiting dignitaries has been strongly condemned because "it goes against the oft-expressed desire to preserve the values and ethics embodied in (it)" (*Samoa Observer*, 1989, 1).

which have gained their independence only a few years ago, are firmly rooted in what one can term "Western democratic" thinking. Before independence they were ruled either by the Germany, Great Britain, France, Japan (very briefly), Australia, or the United States. From them they learned about Western political structures. However, after independence, many countries modified their political system somewhat so as to better accommodate its society's true sociopolitical nature. Fiji, for example, attempted to solve its problems of racial division caused by the import of indentured Indian labor and the subsequent Indian immigration. As a result, Fiji had, until its military coups in 1987, one of the most complex electoral systems in the world—and the search for a simple one which could accommodate "democracy" and racial balance at the same time is its major problem at present. In Tonga, the only kingdom in the Pacific, the king still rules supreme, but through a "democratically" elected government. Vanuatu has a uniquely complex background, having had two colonial rulers at the same time, France and England, on top of over 150 language groups that fiercely maintain(ed) their independence. Here, democracy on a local level takes place in the form of extensive discussions in the *nakamal,* the kava bar. However, those elected to parliament may find it sometimes difficult to combine the two roles they play, the local role and the national role. The recent upheaval involving the ex-President of Vanuatu stemmed to some extent from his incapability to combine his chiefly role with the one of President in a Western-style democracy. In PNG, after German and Australian rule, it is still the strong tribal system with its customs that has more influence on the running of the country than the modified Westminster system.

Democracy means different things to different people. Robert Keith-Reid, publisher of the *Islands Business* magazine, described the 1988 election campaign in the Solomon Islands like this: "Solomons' politicians do not usually publicly peddle their wares in the Western style. Since few of them are well-known outside their home districts in the thickly forested archipelago of about 900 islands, they do it the Melanesian way. They concentrate on the forging of quiet deals and understandings, mainly in their home province, that could be a lever into the 38 member parliament" (*Islands Business,* January 1989, p. 24). As a Tongan academic, Konai Thaman, put it: "You have to live in two worlds, some in three worlds. Some in more worlds" (Moala, 1989, p. 33). In the South Pacific, people are living in at least two worlds, and anyone reporting about this region must understand those worlds in order to do them justice.

DEMOCRACY, THE ART OF COMMUNICATION

Democracy depends on communication. The more open the flow of communication between individuals, between individuals and governing institutions, between groups and between groups and governing institutions, the greater are the chances for the creation of a well-functioning democracy. But the quality of the communication is of essence. The Swiss lawyer and political scientist Robert Schnyder von Wartensee is greatly concerned with the state of democracy (Schnyder, 1985, pp. 23–35).[4] According to Schnyder, democracy is based on dialogue that in turn relies on proper communication. Communication works on three levels:

- on a factual level
- on a cultural level
- on a relational level

Proper communication cannot take place if communicators A and B fail to reach understanding on any of those three levels. If, for instance

- A is not interested in B's problem   (factual level)
- A does not understand B's language   (cultural level)
- A fears B   (relational level)

then communication will not be complete and satisfactory.

Thus, on a factual level, citizens often feel either overstretched in their understanding of political issues, or they may feel unconcerned or be unable to relate to the issue. Often a problem concerns them so much that they forget the context within which the problem is based. Thus important components of the problem will be repressed or considered tapu.

Language determines the quality of communication on a cultural level. There is considerable growth of specialist languages (such as the languages spoken in the communications industry, among economists, sociologists, media theorists) but also among adolescents. Generations now talk different languages that, combined with the rapid

---

[4] There is a growing demand in Switzerland for the continuing reevaluation of the concept of "democracy" for fear that after 700 years of democracy, public complacency might lead to its demise.

change of the concept of traditional values, helps to widen the generation gap rapidly.

Most problems arise on a relational level. Many individuals perceive the stratification of society more and more as a simple "them and us" structure in which fear often dictates the quality of communication or even prevents it. Prejudice and thinking in cliches, suspicion, and unproven declarations of guilt prevent free and open communication. Tapus are signs of the fear to face certain problems.

Once communication is in place, dialogue has to be established. Dialogue also functions on three levels:

- a willingness to conduct a dialogue
- an admission and perception of the existence of problems
- the knowledge of judgmental factors used by partners involved in the dialogue.

The willingness to conduct a dialogue presupposes respect of other people's opinions, tolerance, ability to listen, time, and adherence to factuality.

Problems have to be defined so that all participants talk about the same issues. This is becoming more and more difficult because of the growth of the amount of information and the complexity of this information. Consequently, many partners in a dialogue have to resort to simplification, typification, and categorization, using secondary rather than primary information.

Once a problem has been identified and dialogue is entered into, a judgment will have to be made and questions will have to be asked: How serious is the situation? Is action necessary or should the situation be allowed to continue? Elements that may make it difficult to come to an agreement include personal interests, different sets of values, and ideological stances.

Communication and dialogue are the mainstays of democracy. The position of the media is particularly difficult because they have to fill two functions: They are direct partners in the communications process and the dialogue but they also act as mediators between individuals and groups and governing institutions. Media have the duty to gather data that are only possible if the three levels of communication function properly in any direction of society. The different data must then be presented in such a way that the media reflect ongoing dialogues in society. At the same time they are themselves part of this ongoing dialogue. Thus much of the proper functioning of a democracy will depend on the media.

A DIFFERENT UNDERSTANDING OF DEMOCRACY

In all Pacific countries (with the exception of those still effectively under colonial rule, such as New Caledonia, Tahiti, Wallis and Futuna, and postcoup Fiji) exists the belief that the present political structures are firmly based on the principle of democracy, that the people have their say, can speak and write and vote freely (Crocombe, 1978, pp. 58, 70). What does not seem well understood outside the region is the fact that this sense of democracy does not necessarily correspond with general Western ideas. Societies with tribal or clan systems are based on structures of authority that give everybody the freedom of expression but put the ultimate decision in the chief's hands; however, not before matters have been thoroughly debated by all, which explains why political processes—even in the wake of a military coup—take such a long time in the Pacific. In traditional society—and in many respects these island states are still traditionally run—a person or a group knows who the source of information is and how trustworthy that source is. Moreover, this information can be "tested against personal experience . . . Lying and misrepresentation were (are) not respected by anonimity or mobility, and a sense of collective identity dictated against violating community norms" (Real, 1989, p. 22). The individual's place in society is clearly defined and cannot be defied for fear of becoming isolated. For the outsider it looks as if the "factual" and "cultural" levels of communication were intact, but that the "relational" level is not functioning. It would seem that the six criteria established by Schnyder cannot be applied to all societies that claim to be democracies. In the Pacific, more dialogue seems to exist than in many Western societies but the judgmental criteria seem to be considerably different. If on a Micronesian island the burning down of a chief's house is not reported although the motives for the fire could have strong political implications, it may be that the reporter is a commoner who is, by custom, not allowed to talk publicly about his chief. (This "dependence" situation is not considered "exploitative." It is the norm, which may be the reason why communism finds it hard to really gain a foothold in the Pacific. Concepts of socialism are easier to introduce since many Pacific societies traditionally practice "socialist" behavior.) To the outsider, the local journalist may seem to be slack or cowardly—in fact, he may be one of the best in the country.

WHOSE STANDARDS?

Not understanding the different concepts of "freedom" and "democracy" and the basis upon which they are built has as a consequence the misinterpretation of actions and attitudes. Communication on the cultural level does not take place and judgmental factors are different. Thus reports by overseas journalists often confuse and insult the indigenous leaders and mislead local and overseas readers. The media, particularly overseas media, rather than being a means of support of democracy become a means of disinformation and obstruction. In one of the first articles raising this issue and quoting Western Samoa as an example, Murray Masterton (1985), an Australian journalist teaching journalism at the University of the South Pacific, said that a Samoan chief, or Matai, cannot be asked questions in a straightforward manner "and it will likely not be done until there is a radical change in either Samoa's politicians or Samoa's journalists, or both."[5] Robert Keith-Reid (1978, p. 6), a journalist working from Suva, similarly observed: "Pacific Island leaders are easily hurt or made angry by what by metropolitan standards are the most innocuous stories."[6] Masterton accepts that there exist cultural differences that make even the mildest form of investigative journalism impossible; for instance, under circumstances where only the Matai have the vote, few if any journalists earn enough to pay taxes, and the broadcasting system is government-owned. And yet Masterton seems in two minds about the situation. As an Australian journalist he cannot accept it but finds it hard to condemn the situation outright: "Society will have to change in Western Samoa before its inhabitants can experience journalism as

---

[5] Journalists like Masterton would willingly throw out any traditional values for the sake of being able to introduce "modern" journalism into a country. The fact alone that some local papers, most recently *The Samoa Times,* carry editorials defending "Tradition and Democracy" (1989) only means that local journalists have not lost the appreciation of tradition and its political implications.

[6] A Samoan Member of Parliament has recently stated that "criticism leveled at the Speaker or the Prime Minister inside parliament should not be allowed to spread to the "four corners of the world" through radio and newspaper coverage" (*Samoa Observer,* 1989). This suggestion was strongly rebuffed in the editorial of the same day. The same paper does not hold back with criticism of the Samoan government of which it said, e.g., that it is "in a lethargic state of activity refusing to move a muscle" (*Samoa Observer,* 1989).

we know it . . . By our measures Samoa's press is prejudiced, irresponsible and self-serving and its radio news without initiative or courage to the point of being government-censored. Yet to all appearances the society is placidly healthy" (Masterton, 1989, p. 115).[7] What Masterton seems to forget is that the structure of society in Samoa up till now may have had enough internal controls and supports to make a critical press superfluous. If financial irregularities occur within the government, they are well known outside—the size of the community and the oral tradition make this possible. The so-called "grapevine" works very efficiently in nations of that size. Hence the Western type of journalism may be inappropriate, at least in some of the smaller nations. Media have to be adjusted to the political and cultural concepts that form the basis of the society within which they function. At the same time they have to be adapted to the ongoing modernization of these societies.

THE REGIONAL MEDIA

More and more government officials in the Pacific region criticize overseas (particularly Australian) media. PNG's Michael Somare, Fiji's Colonel Rabuka (for obvious reasons) and Vanuatu's Father Walter Lini have been the most outspoken. The Solomon Islands' Prime Minister, Solomon Mamaloni, however, has stated recently that "the value of the press is that they dig up things and reveal things. I think that is right" (*Islands Business,* June 1989, p. 28).[8] They complain about misinformation which may strongly undermine the democratic processes in their countries particularly because only few of those countries have their own, in the Western sense, "independent" media (Obundo, 1985; Molnar, 1988). Telecommunications in the re-

---

[7] Masterton's recent survey on the perceived quality of the media in the region not surprisingly shows that most respondents thought that reporting of the region by local journalists is substandard. Most of those surveyed would have been at least partly educated overseas and heavily exposed to overseas media. For them, the local media are as backward as transportation by mule would be for an American (though that form of transportation does have many positive values). Masterton's findings are not corroborated by the most recent study on PACNEWS and its dissemination and effect (Sullivan & Valbuena, 1989).

[8] Similarly, the Catholic Bishop of Tonga and editor of the church's hard-hitting newspaper *Taumu's Lelei* has called for more openness towards overseas journalists. "We must accept their point of view. We created the trouble, not them. We cannot just take their aid problems" (*Pacific Islands Monthly,* 1989, p. 46).

gion are, in general, very good when one takes into account the area that has to be covered. The Pacific Islands News Association (PINA) is very active. The PACJOURN project caters for the training needs of print media journalists, PACBROAD for those in broadcasting. PACBROAD and the regional news exchange agency, PACNEWS,[9] are now under the umbrella of the Pacific Islands Broadcasting Association. The South Pacific Commission Media Centre trains personnel from various government departments in the use of media. All island nations have a radio system, often government-controlled (and carrying advertisements) and there exist several commercial radio stations, in Fiji, New Caledonia, and particularly in Micronesia. But all radio stations tend to keep their political comments to a minimum. Radio is the primary news source and is indispensable. About the effects of radio on the cultural life in the region little is known.[10]

The literacy rate in the South Pacific is, in parts, still very low; in Vanuatu, for example, it is 19 percent. Thus, small markets and problems with distribution provide little encouragement to the print media which do exist in all nations, either in the form of privately owned newspapers or government-run publications. Local newspapers are generally timid although freedom of speech is guaranteed in all nations. Direct censorship does not exist, but in Fiji Colonel Rabuka managed to shut down both major newspapers for some time, one of which, the *Fiji Sun,* refused to succumb to the pressure of self-censorship and closed down completely. The major newspapers are the Papua New Guinea *Post-Courier, Niugini News, The Fiji Times,* and the *Pacific Daily News* on Guam. Only one of the island states, PNG, has a local television station. Many, however, are discussing the introduction of television. In Fiji, the arguments between the government and the Australian Bond Media group have gone on for years. In PNG, the issue of television has been strongly linked to cultural values: Licences were granted, revoked (for fear of erosion of local culture), and granted again. In Micronesia, commercial TV programs are either imported on tapes and rebroadcast or beamed directly irre-

---

[9] For the first study on the background and the effectiveness of PACNEWS see Sullivan and Valbuena (1989).

[10] Borofsky (1982) maintains that "radio does not seem to have a direct effect on the acquisition of traditional knowledge. Rather its effect is indirect through the context of other Westernizing influences—such as political and economic changes—which reduce the effectiveness of traditional learning styles . . ." (Media Release 1989), but also stresses that "it seems that people who are open to Westernizing influences are also open to traditional knowledge" (Moala, 1989, p. 33).

spective of the fact that most of the goods advertised are not available in the country.[11] The Cook Islands have just decided to establish a satellite and video hookup with TV New Zealand which should bring television to Rarotonga by Christmas. Nieu has had such a link since October 1988. The most prominent medium, however, is video. On all islands, the consumption of video has grown exponentially over the last few years. This has given rise to fears, particularly among the older generation, that video would erode family traditions and values in general even faster than TV. However, there are also positive sides to video: UNESCO is at present sponsoring a training program in video production and direction for educational purposes specifically aimed at the South Pacific.

Political discussion based on media information is therefore greatly limited. Fiji and PNG are the only South Pacific nations with a press comparable to Europe's or Australia's. In all other countries, the media have a tendency to promote the government view, and provide entertainment and some form of education. Local media really exist on the basis of negotiation. We may call this "censorship," locals may call it "cultural pressure." But political discussion does exist in these countries. Oral tradition is still strong and ongoing. There are few places in the Pacific where the media as we know them would be seen as essential in the process of democratization. A balance has to be struck between what is economically viable (for small nations, newsprint and ink or electronic equipment is simply too expensive) and what is, in a modern and developing society, essential for the exchange of information and an intelligent political debate.

OVERSEAS MEDIA

Overseas media make their appearances in the South Pacific in several forms. Newspapers are distributed but with great delays and at exorbitant prices and are thus available mainly to expatriates and a financial and political elite. Satellite television footprints cover parts of the region (Fell, 1986, 1988; Richstad, 1988).[12] In parts of PNG some Australian commercial broadcasts can be received. The most

---

[11] The absurdity of this form of television is well illustrated in two documentaries: *Yap . . . How did you know we'd like TV?* directed by Dennis O'Rourke, 1986, and a Special Broadcasting Service (SBS Television) "Dateline" program entitled *Manna from Heaven,* broadcast in Sydney in 1986.

[12] A useful television news flow analysis covering both Australian public networks (Australian Broadcasting Corporation (ABC) and Special Broadcasting Service (SBS) has been published by Derek Overton (1989).

powerful foreign media are the shortwave radio services. Radio Australia plays a major role in keeping the region informed about regional and international events. Following the renewed discovery of the region, and particularly after the coups in Fiji, Voice of America, the BBC, and—most recently—Radio New Zealand have decided to massively boost their output to the region. (The improved RNZ shortwave service will, typically, be run jointly by "RNZ and the Ministry of External Relations and Trade" (Media Release, 1989).) Many local radio stations rebroadcast at present Radio Australia's news and presumably will rebroadcast other news services as soon as the reception improves. The information received on the islands about the state of the outside world is thus almost exclusively shaped by overseas media and through limited sources (Richstad, 1984, 1988). Murdoch's News Ltd owns the principal newspapers and magazine in the South Pacific; PNG's commercial TV company is owned by the Australian Bond Media group who is also waiting for a broadcasting licence in Fiji.

Leaders in the South Pacific are rightly concerned not only about the way their countries are reported overseas but also with the ease with which in a few years foreign media transmissions, mainly TV, will be received by their own people.[13] The issue was raised at the 1989 South Pacific Forum meeting. PNG's Foreign Minister, Michael Somare, wants to establish a "code of conduct" for foreign journalists working in the region, an issue that will also be discussed by the Pacific Islands News Association (PINA) in October (*Islands Business,* 1989).[14] The carelessness with which overseas media report events in the South Pacific is as astounding as are the devastating effects such

---

[13] According to market researchers AGB McNair Anderson, television in PNG is dangerously popular. It is estimated that 40 percent of PNG's 3.8 million people have access to television. The director of sales of PNG's EM TV is quoted as saying "we were taken aback by the amount of TV watched here . . . They are switching us on when we come on at 3 pm and switching us off when we finish at 11.30 pm" (O'Callaghan, 1989b).

[14] The issue was also raised in a very critical article in the *Samoa Observer* of July 26, 1987 entitled "The Annual Forum Event once again" in which examples of superficial reporting by overseas journalists were given. During the 1989 South Pacific Forum held in Kiribati, the Deputy Prime Minister of PNG, Akoka Doi, has proposed that a seminar be held for media representatives in order to improve their understanding of the region. He was backed by Vanuatu, Fiji, the Cook Islands, and Niue. Doi has been quoted as saying "the problem is very serious and damaging to the image of the country and also the industry investment opportunity for Papua New Guinea and the Forum country members." The Australian Prime Minister, Bob Hawke, however, has praised the Australian media for their reporting and their understanding of the region (*Sydney Morning Herald,* July 12, 1989). Further comments can be found in *Pacific Islands Monthly,* August 1989, 15, and *Pacific Islands Business,* August 1989, 5 and 20–21 where the publisher of the magazine defends a number of regular correspondents in the South Pacific.

reports can have on political perceptions and particularly the economy. Somare had a major case when he was presented on Bond's Australian Channel 9 (which can be received in Port Moresby) as Vanuatu's Prime Minister Father Walter Lini with whom he does not see
eye to eye. And Lini's government was not impressed when Australian
television presented footage apparently showing the aftermath of a
"riot" in Port Vila, in fact showing the aftermath of cyclone Uma
which had devastated the town two years before. On the other hand,
none of the journalists writing about the riots by parts of the PNG
army in February 1989 picked up the real meaning for local people of
the damage done to Parliament House. In Melanesian culture, destroying property is one of the biggest insults and injury anyone can
inflict. Parliament House by definition belongs to all people in PNG.
The Army openly defied customary law not to touch other people's
property and damaged the building. By doing so the Army showed
that it would be willing to break all rules.

OVERSEAS JOURNALISTS

The problem with overseas journalists seems to be that few have any
idea of cultural concepts. "Western" training is mostly based on reporting "facts" but very little attempt is made to train journalists for
the encounter with other cultures where "facts" may not be what they
seem.[15] To define culture is a task in itself but Jan Servaes (1989, p.
47) has provided a definition that is very useful in this context: "Culture can be defined as a social setting in which a certain reference
framework has taken concrete form—or has been 'institutionalized'—
and which orients and structures the interaction and communication
of people within this historical context." Things *are* done differently
in the Pacific. In Tonga, there *is* no "tradition of public accountability
and the sort of public sensitivity and political subtlety that go with
accountability" ("Fumbling at the Forum," 1988), and the tribal culture in PNG *does* resist Western type of administration. In a nation
like the Cook Islands with a population of 18,000 and an electorate
less than half this number, the parochial style of politics inevitably
becomes the dominating feature of political life. In *Tales of the Tikongs,* Fijian academic and writer Epeli Hau'ofa has one of the locals
giving advice to an overseas adviser: "Forget the Law and forget the

---

[15] Derek Freeman's criticism, most recently supported by Samoan women, of Margaret Mead's findings about growing up in Samoa indicates how difficult it can be for
outsiders to get to the truth.

Constitution. It's the will of his Excellency and the Great Chiefs that makes things move in Tiko . . . forget about truth. Truth is foreign thinking, and this is Tiko . . . Democracy and Tiko don't dance" (Hau'ofa, 1983, p. 44). Another academic—and lawyer—PNG's Minister of Justice, Bernard Narakobi, has published several books on the issue of cultural differences. He has coined the term "the Melanesian way" which for him is a philosophy, "a notion of the Melanesians as people with a coherent and systematic identity and culture, a total cosmic view of life complete with perceptions of land, family, death, marriage, property, law and politics" (Twyford, 1989, p. 72). Although Narakobi may give the impression that he resists modernization, careful reading of his works does indicate that all he wants is (a) more respect and understanding for tradition as a socially cohesive force, and (b) a slowing of progress, including "progressive" forms of media.

One of the harshest critics of the activities of overseas media in the region is a senior government official, Grace Molisa, private secretary to the Prime Minister of Vanautu. She accuses journalists of seriously misunderstanding and maligning her country, of "ram(ming) freedom of the press down our throats" and "writ(ing) preconceived stories" (*Pacific Islands Monthly*, 1989, p. 45). In doing so, journalists not only misrepresent, they actively encourage certain factions in society in their thoughts and actions. Thus, these factors eventually will be more governed by the attitudes and opinions of overseas media than by those of the local community. Only journalists who understand traditions, customs, and cultural difference will be able to bring about a positive form of modernization. In political terms this means that only by taking into account the past can the media adequately explain, nurture, and support the ideas of a modern democracy.

Perhaps it is too much to expect an overseas journalist to learn that in Melanesia parallel cousins (children of two brothers) are regarded like brother and sister whereas cross-cousins (children of brother and sister) are regarded like husband and wife (Crocombe, 1978, p. 12). Repercussions from actions taken by cousins can only be properly evaluated when the kinship system is known. This may be an extreme example but when reporting Vanuatu's political problems involving ex-President Sokomanu and Barak Sope, none of the Australian journalists made reference to the kinship relationship that links the two politicians and may explain many of their actions. One may well doubt Colonel Rabuka's assumption that the Indonesian reporting about his coups was "factual. Because they have a culture which is similar to ours . . ." (Taga & de Bruce, 1988, p. 7). But he is right when he points out that Australian reporters at the time did not understand that a meeting of the Great Council of Chiefs would not come to a conclusion within a few hours but could take weeks, even months—that time has a different function within this culture. Exceptions among journalists do exist, and there is hope that the stationing of journalists in the region over a long period of time might actually bring them in contact with current cultural values, with rituals, and with vested interests—and might hence help to improve the presentation of facts as they have to be perceived in the region.[16]

LOCAL JOURNALISTS

So, hopes could be pinned on developing indigenous media and training local journalists. There is no shortage of such training programs (Molnar, 1988; Yu, 1983). But all those programs are based on either American, European, or Australian principles and values, and are mostly taught by overseas specialists who see the journalist as someone taking on an adversarial role, a concept that is not acceptable in Pacific societies. It is therefore not surprising that Richard Phinney, having studied the profiles of PNG journalists, comes to the conclusion that they are very much like the typical Australian "journo" except that they believe that the Pacific region is badly served by the imbalance in the flow of news and that "journalists have a responsibility to help governments develop a country," the meaning of which Phinney has not further explored (Phinney, 1985, p. 46). Media imperialism begins with the training of local journalists who will have to become part of the "streamlining" or "modernisation" process that helps to undermine tradition, a tradition which is very much alive and a guarantor for stability.

Muhlhausler has shown how the eradication of languages can be related to problems of independence and communications (Mulhausler, 1986, p. 34; Crocombe, 1978, p. 87). One could build an argument along the lines that language and custom form the basis of Pacific societies, and that the introduction of a *lingua franca* brought about a great loss of detail in the communication process. The media that use the *lingua franca* as a basis are therefore prone to misunderstandings. (It is easy to forget that on the islands there exists a cosy

---

[16] The lack of understanding of cultural concepts may be bad among journalists but it is worse among politicians—and the consequences of their actions have much more far-reaching effects. The way in which the Australian government (headed by Labor Prime Minister Bob Hawke and advised by his Minister for Defence, Kim Beazley) has handled the coups in Fiji and political unrest in Vanuatu clearly shows that the lack of understanding of events that to a great extent are culturally driven can lead to overreaction and panic.

form of elitism: Leaders and journalists have enjoyed (Western-type) education and are well informed. They can easily understand each other. The leaders' refusal to (Western) treatment from local or overseas journalists may well have its roots in the knowledge that they are still part of a different society. As politicians they have to claim to be part of the traditional society in order to be elected on the local level.)

Similarly, democracy is a concept imposed on custom bringing with it the loss of traditional (and proven) problem-solving mechanisms. If the media as we know them promote democracy, they promote an inappropriate system and foreign mechanisms in an inappropriate language—thus they are rather promoting frustration than understanding (Narokobi, 1983a, p. 83).

No training manual makes an attempt at solving the problems that face local journalists confronted with an inner conflict as the result of pressures put on them by the medium for which they are reporting and the culturally imposed restrictions that may prevent them from approaching certain groups of people who might know the facts. Tapus are alive and well in the South Pacific. Problems are built-in into the modern education system: "There is a tendency to ignore things to do with spirituality, with morals . . . We are doing our darndest to get people to de-emphasise the moral aspects of education which is a very big part of our traditional education system" (Moala, 1989, p. 37). For journalists, the situation is worse:

> The biggest problem facing budding island journalists is their lack of preparation for the pressures placed of (sic) them solely because they are members of an island community with built-in relationships and allegiances. They are not prepared for the immense pressures that come from relatives, traditional leaders and political factions and, as a result, often become mouthpieces for those factions. If they fight this tendency, they often become discouraged and quit when they are ostracised" (Iyechad, 1981, p. 17).[17]

William Haomae (1981, p. 19) held out a lot of hope when he said that

> in coming years, journalists, without being subservient, will have to learn a style of operation that sees all news . . . get into print, yet making some allowances for island sensibilities. They will have to learn to

---

[17] For lawyers the situation is similar: "A local magistrate is under enormous pressure. Honiara town is quite small: you almost know everybody . . . If I sentence a man to jail, within six months I am bound to see him about or bump into him at the market" (O'Callaghan (1989a).

get island leaders to accept criticism coolly with the realisation that a free press most often needs to be cruel to be kind.

The question is: How does a local journalist overturn thousands of years of cultural training?

THE SOUTH PACIFIC, MEDIA, AND DEMOCRACY

Schnyder (1985) claims that democracy can only function properly if the communication between individuals and groups functions properly and leads to dialogue. It is my argument that the media are senders and receivers of communication and participants in dialogue, just like any other group. However, they also have an intermediary role to play in that their presentation of facts and opinions must help improve communication and dialogue between individuals, groups, and governing institutions. South Pacific countries not only have their special internal forms of communication and dialogue, they also have to live with two very different types of media, the local and the overseas media of which the latter not only reflects inward but also outward. The island countries have little control over their presentation abroad and yet it is this presentation that influences their economy, internal political attitudes, and—progressively—their social life. In order to show how well Schnyder's criteria apply, it might be useful to summarize the findings in a diagram (Figure 15.1).

Figure 15.1. How Well Do Communication and Dialogue Work in the South Pacific?

South Pacific Society			
	Internally Between Indiv/Indiv Group/Group	With Local Media	With Overseas Media
COMMUNICATION Factual level Cultural level Relational level	Well Well Limited	Well Well Limited	Limited Limited Limited
DIALOGUE Willingness Admission of problems Judgmental factors	Well Limited Limited	Limited Limited Limited	Limited Limited Limited

It would seem that within the South Pacific society itself, the admission and perception of problems is limited because of growing social differences. Whereas certain groups may be totally unaware of problems, others, usually the better educated groups, realize those problems. But even for them it is becoming more and more difficult to cope with the complexity of modern society that often leads to attempts to solve single problems without regard to the overall set of problems. The criteria by which to judge problems and issues are now less clear than before, not least because of value changes within the society and the acceptance of ideologies imported from overseas. The problems on a relational level are the result of the hierarchical structure and the existence of tapus. However, as was shown above, these elements have been well-integrated in the democratic thinking of South Pacific societies.

The local media face several problems. On a relational level the traditional social structure, hierarchies, and tapus may still prevent proper communication. On the level of dialogue, local journalists are caught between their training along "Western" lines and the perceived local demand for information. Which problem to highlight, in which form, and for whom are difficult questions to answer in small and educationally strongly stratified societies. Moreover, the journalist's day-to-day existence, limited resources, and the very limited space and airtime make it difficult to present thoroughly reflected judgments.

The latter problems apply to many overseas journalists as well. However, the overseas media when covering the region are faced with numerous problems that would indicate that their role in strengthening democracy in the region is very limited indeed if not downright nonexistent.

On a factual level, overseas media are almost exclusively interested in negative aspects only. They do not speak the same "language" (literally and in a cultural sense), they know little about value concepts, and on a relational level they prefer to deal with cliches, prejudice, and suspicions. Their one advantage is that they can deal with tapus but this in turn may upset the local society. Occasional visits only and lack of time do not allow them to establish facts and participate in a dialogue. Opinions are formed on the basis of superficial impressions. There is no time nor a real interest to investigate the complexity and importance of a real or perceived problem.

Whereas the South Pacific societies have all the elements necessary to maintain and continue their basic democratic structure, the local media have yet to overcome several obstacles—many of which are of a traditional nature and many of which are imposed by governmental institutions trying to protect their privileges—before they can be seen as contributing strongly to the maintenance of democracy. Overseas media at present act more as a destructive element in the ongoing process of democratization of the region. Lack of background knowledge, negativity, superficiality, and prejudice inevitably create a misleading picture of the political and social situation in the region.

To maintain peace and harmony in the South Pacific region, the classical Western concept of "democracy" may not be absolutely essential. To achieve "consensus," however, another element of democracy has long been a traditional approach in order to maintain stability and independence in the region. Outsiders have to understand that what matters is the maintenance of a societal structure that, over centuries and in spite of massive outside interference, has survived remarkably well and is well suited to carry those nations into the 21st century. The island nations will not be able to withstand completely the onslaught of the media. Should the media play a part in maintaining "democracy" as it is understood locally, a new form of journalism has to be found, one which grows from within the local society but also uses the best standards of traditional Western journalistic procedures. Outsiders, for their part, will have to develop more understanding of the Pacific way of thinking. Both sides want and have to know more about each other but both sides have yet to learn a lot in order to establish communication and dialogue. If this does not happen, more and more friction between island governments and overseas media (and, to a considerable extent, governments) will develop and thus undermine those traditional, reasonably stable democracies. Westerm media have yet to learn to respect democracies that are different.

REFERENCES

Abundo, R.B. (1985). *Print and broadcast media in the South Pacific.* Singapore: AMIC.

Australian International Development Assistance Bureau. (1989). *Australian Media's Treatment of the Developing World. How does it rate?* Canberra: CGPS.

Borofsky, R. (1982). Telecommunications and traditional knowledge. *Pacific Islands Communication Journal, 12* (1).

Crocombe, R.G. (1978). *The New South Pacific.* Wellington.

Elkin, A.P. (1963). *Social anthropology in Melanesia.* London.

Fell, L. (1986). *International communication: Australia and the South Pacific.* Unpublished paper, Canberra.

Fell, L. (1988, May). The communications revolution. into the 21st century. *Pacific Islands Monthly*.

Freeman, D. (1983). *Margaret Mead and Samoa: The making and unmaking of an anthropological myth*. Canberra.

Goonasekera, A. (1987). The influence of television on cultural values—with special Reference to third world countries. *Media Asia, 14*(1).

Haomae, W. (1981, Winter). Training should foster awareness. *Pacific Islands Communications Journal*.

Hau'ofa, E. (1983). *Tales of the Tikongs*. Auckland.

Iyechad, G.L. (1981, Winter). Coping with community pressures. *Pacific Islands Communication Journal*.

Keith-Reid, R. (1978, April). Freedom of the press·in Pacific (sic). *Pacific Islands Communication Newsletter, 8*(1).

Keith-Reid, R. (1989, July). *Islands Business*.

Lent, J.A. (1986). *Four conundrums reconsidered: Assessing communications problems in the Third World, 1974–86*. Unpublished paper, Canberra

Lent, J.A. (1989). Mass Communication in Asia and the Pacific. *Media Asia, 16*(1).

Masterton, M. (1985). Samoa, where questioning is taboo. *Australian Journalism Review, 7*(1,2).

Masterton, M. (1989, May). "Mass" media in the South Pacific. *Media Information Australia, 52*.

May, R.J., & Nelson, H. (1982). *Melanesia: Beyond diversity* (Vols. 1 & 2). Canberra.

Mead, M. (1943). *Coming of age in Samoa*. Harmondsworth: Penguin.

Moala, J. (1989, January). Koani Thaman's changing times. *Islands Business*.

Molisa, G. (1989). *Pacific Islands Monthly*.

Molnar, H. (1989). *Media development and training requirements in the South Pacific*. Melbourne.

Moorehead, A. (1966). *The fatal impact*.

Morgan, F. (1986). *New visions: Old echoes. Radio and television training in South East Asia and the Pacific*. Unpublished paper, Canberra.

Mühlhäusler, P. (1986). *International communication and small languages in Australia and the Pacific*. Unpublished paper, Canberra.

Narokobi, B. (1983a). *The Melanesian Way*. Suva.

Narokobi, B. (1983b). *Life and leadership in Melanesia*. Suva.

Narokobi, B. (1988). *Lo Bilong Yumi Yet*. Suva.

New Zealand Minister of Foreign Affairs. (1989, May 24). Media Release.

O'Callaghan, M.L. (1989a, March 23). Tradition renders courts impotent. *Sydney Morning Herald*.

O'Callaghan, M.L. (1989b, June 26). PNG turns on to television. *Sydney Morning Herald*.

Overton, D. (1989). Two worlds: International coverage on the ABC and SBS TV Evening News. *Media Information Australia, 52*.

Phinney, R. (1985). A profile of journalists in Papua New Guinea. *Australian Journalism Review, 7*(1,2).

Real, M.R. (1989). *Super media. A cultural studies approach.* London.

Richstad, J. (1984). News flow in the Pacific Islands Press. *Pacific Islands Communication Journal, 13*(1).

Richstad, J. (1988). Flow of news and information in Asia and the Pacific. *Media Asia, 5*(2).

Rivers, W.H.R. (1924). *Social organization.* London.

Rivers, W.H.R. (1968a). *The history of Melanesian society.* Oosterhout.

Rivers, W.H.R. (1968b). *Kinship and social organization.* London.

Schnyder von Wartensee, R. (1985). Rede mitenand. *Der Dialog in der Demokratie.* Aarau. NHG.

Servaes, J. (1989). Towards a more "cultural" interpretation of normative press theories. *Media Asia, 16*(1).

Spate, O.H.K. (1988). *Paradise found and lost.* Rushcutters Bay.

Taga, L., & de Bruce, L. (1988, December). In Fiji, they call them "the Aussie Paparazzi." *New Journalist.*

Twyford, P. (1989, January). Man of Justice. *Islands Business.*

Walcot, K. (1984). Perspectives on Publishing, Literacy, and Development. *Pacific Island Communication Journal, 13*(1).

Yu, F.T.C. (1983). Training of Pacific Islands Journalists: Some Questions. *Pacific Islands Communication Journal, 12*(2).

16

Democratization of the Malaysian Mass Media: Political and Social Implications*

Mohd Hamdan Adnan
School of Mass Communication
Institut Teknologi Mara
Selangor, Malaysia

Democratization of Malaysia's mass media do have various political and social implications. Malaysia under the government of Dr. Mahathir Mohammed is seen to enhance the democratization of mass media in Malaysia in numerous ways.

Democratization of the mass media in Malaysia can be defined as the level of media freedom in the country with regard to its content and its capacity to grow and multiply.

A number of criteria can be used to gauge the level of mass media democratization. In Malaysia the following are some of the means that mass media democratization can be evaluated.

One, the freedom of the Malaysian media to report and comment on happenings and issues in the country. In Malaysia the level of media freedom to report bravely and accurately does have room for improvement. This is especially so with regard to reporting political issues and happenings or certain governmental affairs. However, with regard to reporting weaknesses in the working of government agen-

* Acknowledgment is made to Sankar'an Ramanathan, senior lecturer, School of Mass Communication, Institut Teknologi Mara, Malaysia.

cies or implementation of government projects the Malaysian government has been seen as being rather liberal. In fact, a number of programs in the electronic media and special pages in the print media dealt a lot on the weaknesses of government agencies and occassionally on policies.

With regard to freedom of expression, John Lent (1987) commented that it seems some improvements have occurred in Malaysia over the past 15 years. First, it appears that criticism is more tolerated; books of a critical nature are on shelves now, not locked away in banned book rooms as before; letters to the editor express public concerns, and most importantly, satire is on an upswing. A decade ago, the political cartoons and the satirical magazines were not here.

Two, mass media democratization in Malaysia can be judged by the number and type of laws affecting communication in the country. In Malaysia, laws affecting communication can be considered numerous if not comprehensive. Communication, whether interpersonal or through the mass media, is regulated by Article 10 of the Federal Constitution of Malaysia and more than 45 laws (see Appendix) with a wide range of penalties including detention without trial (Mohd Hamdan, 1987). Some of the newer laws pertaining to mass media or harsher amendments to communication legislations have been enacted under Dr. Mahathir's government. However, it must be pointed out that it was the British Colonial Government that left Malaysia with a legacy of controlled media.

Three, democratization of the mass media in Malaysia can also be calculated through the number of publications allowed to be published in the country. In recent years the number of new publications in Malaysia have mushroomed. Nevertheless, what should be assessed also is the quality of the publications and how free they are in expressing their views.

Four, democratization of the mass media in Malaysia can also be measured by the number of foreign publications allowed to enter the country. In this respect the Malaysian government has banned all communist publications and obsence materials. This is because the Malaysian government since the Second World War has been facing communist insurgency and because the national religion is Islam. Nevertheless, other magazines are free to enter the country. Once in a while foreign publications that offend the government or the citizens' sensitivities are barred from entering Malaysia. For example, the latest book to be banned by the Malaysian government is Salman Rushdie's hugely controversial book, *The Satanic Verses*. This action was taken out of respect for Muslims who comprise more than half of the population as well as the fact that Islam is Malaysia's national religion.

Five, democratization of the mass media in Malaysia can also be rated by the amount of new communication technologies being introduced into the country. According to John Lent (1987) Malaysia has been a trendsetter in this area, having had its news agency (BERNAMA) and at least four dailies computerized, and having introduced early on satellite stations, teletext, and so on. On this matter, there is strong debate as to whether rapid importation and usage of the latest communication technologies would enhance the democratization process in the country and the mass media, or would bring the reverse effects. Questions as to the impact of the new information technologies on Malaysian society in the areas of privacy and the right to know, labor and employment, creativity, use of leisure time and brain power, democratic principles or the gap between the haves and have-nots still need to be answered.

As such, technology—broadly speaking—does not *only* produce positive effects, but can produce negative consequences as well. Schiller (1976) noted that the dominant class controls the industrial state (and thus its technological progress), and employs mass media as the way to resist the task of social reorganization, which is necessary to assume any fundamental technological innovation. Therefore, one must also ask who are the owners and the users of new information technology and whose interest do they present.

Also, one might want to study how to conciliate in any country the control of technology with a democratization process. According to Maicas (1982), if we bound our analysis to the issue of the new technologies, we check that either the hardware or the software are submitted to the private capital, which does not only obtain economic benefits, but also gets cultural and political influence for its own interest.

Six, democratization of the mass media in Malaysia has been assumed by the privatization of the electronic media. Some local communication scholars (accused of being functionalists) have equated the willingness of the government to allow for the establishment of a private (not government-owned) television company as proof of the democratization of the mass media in Malaysia. This notion is further strengthened by the privatization of the telecommunication industry. On the other hand, trade unionists in Malaysia have labeled the government privatization of the electronic media as the commercialization of the media, saying it has nothing to do with the country's democratization. This is congruent with the democratic system in Malaysia inherited from the West which is linked to capitalism.

Seventh, the pattern of ownership of the mass media can also be an indicator of the level of democratization in this particular industry. Not much democratization can be said to occur if the media industry is controlled by a few people even though it is privately owned.

In Malaysia, analyzing the ownerships of the privatized communication industries clearly shows that the main shareholders are usually personalities very close to the ruling government. Hence, Malaysia's mass media are controlled by a small minority that has the political and economic power. These minority managed the mass media where they have interests in such a way to enable them to protect their ideology and interests. Not withstanding, for Malaysia, Lent (1987) commented: "encouraging is the fact that the number of media have remained although a number are owned by common groups. But, at least in Malaysia, the media have not been merged and otherwise sodified into one voice as has happened elsewhere." This means in Malaysia the various print media compete strongly with each other for readers. The competition among the numerous dailies and weeklies and the political parties' newspapers have somehow added to the democratization of the mass media in Malaysia. It has improved the quality of coverage and content as well as the production of the media concerned. As will be discussed this trend can be observed in both the print and the electronic media.

Nevertheless, with the private TV company, it quickly becomes apparent that advertising exerts a role extremely vital to its functioning and even it existence. As such, programming is geared towards capturing as many kinds of audiences as well as wide of an audience as possible so as to convince advertisers the profitability of advertising in it. Consequently, inadequate thinking is given to the consequence of such programing on Malaysian society.

Unfortunately, the government electronic media, in its effort to maintain or win back its audiences from the private station, began to imitate the private station which has found success by aping American programming and importing popular programs that could injure indigenous values that are positive.

However, as a consolation, with the stiff competition between the government television stations and the private station the quality of local television productions have improved technically and content-wise. Television producers are given more room to comment or to cover issues that are traditionally considered to be sensitive. They are now more willing to test the waters, so to speak. On this basis, it can be said that privatization of the television station has contributed to the democratization of the electronic media.

The government, to ensure that the television stations do not go overboard with its democratization tendencies, has enacted the Broadcasting Act, 1987, giving the Minister of Information almost limitless power to control the broadcast media. This include the right to check program contents and advertisements that can offend public sensitivities.

Eight, other than the system of government reflecting the level of democratization in the nation's mass media, the attitude of the current leadership toward the industry can also be an index. Malaysia's Prime Minister, Mahathir Mohamad, in his address to the World Press Convention in Kuala Lumpur on September 18, 1985, said that the media have an important role to play and must be allowed leeway to play that role including the criticism of authority.

According to Mahathir,

> By and large, the role of the Press in ensuring good democratic practices and hence sustaining democracy itself is not only right but also truly indispensable. It is indeed a means of communication between a democratic government and the people. Through it not only will the people be kept informed of all that the government and its leaders are doing, but the leaders too will learn of the attitudes, needs and problems of the people. A responsible democratic government must accordingly regard a free press as an asset which facilitates good government.

However, Mahathir qualified the above statement by saying that freedom given to the mass media must be exercised with responsibility. He stressed,

> It must be given the freedom to express opinion freely, even the right to be wrong; but it must do so without prejudice and without malice. Just as in a democratic society no person or institution has the right to destroy society or to destroy democracy, the media has no such right. An irresponsible press is a negation of the right of the people in a democratic society. So long as the press is conscious of itself being a potential threat to democracy and conscientiously limits the exercise of its rights, it should be allowed to function without government interferences. But when the press obviously abuses its rights, then democratic governments have a duty to put it right.

Mahathir further elaborated,

> In representing the inevitably selected views of various groups of people and in pressing its own views, in pursuit of its perception of the public good, on those occasions when it is involved in the pursuit of the public good, the media must act with the humility that it demands of those in

power. Just as it is right in saying that a government has no monopoly on constructiveness and wisdom, the media must recognise that it too has no monopoly on constructiveness and wisdom. Just as the public servant must be prepared to accept criticism, so too must the media be prepared to accept criticism. Just as the government is not above the law, the media too is not above the law. It simply will not do if a public servant is subject to the laws on state secrets but in the name of freedom others are not. Just as the media is not to be made subservient to the executive, the legislature and the judiciary, in the same way and to the same extent the executive, the legislature and the judiciary are not to be made subservient to the media. Just as the government cannot be allowed to have the freedom to do exactly as it pleases in society, so too the media cannot be allowed to do exactly as it please in society.

Dr. Mahathir further adds, "The media must be allowed to compete in the economic marketplace and curry the favour of its target customers, but it must do so within the bounds of decency and responsibility. Contrary to what is thought in many of even the best journalistic institutions, the deadline is not sacred. The public good is sacred . . . and always sacred."

However, it is generally known that Mahathir has not much respect for the mass media or journalists. He has often struck out at the press which, in his opinion, is too free, irresponsible, only reports news that distorts public opinion, overemphasizes sensational news, and is very dangerous because it can affect the position of national leaders (Zaharom & Ramli, 1989).

As for the journalists, Mahathir in 1981 wrote, "Their righteousness is usually a gimmick they employ for the sake of their jobs—not for democracy." In 1985, Mahathir said: "The ability of the journalist to influence the course of events is out of proportion to his individual rights as a citizen of a democratic society. He is neither especially chosen for his moral superiority nor elected to his post. A free Press is as prone to corruption as other institutions of democracy."

Mahathir's attitude toward the media and journalists can be reflected by the number of laws ensuring that the mass media remain "responsible" that have been enacted or strengthened under the blanket excuse of national security and national unity during his prime ministership. However, it must be noted again here that a number of the restrictive laws pertaining to the mass media are a carryover of the British colonial days and that the other Malaysian prime ministers before Mahathir have also made use of the relevant laws to silence the media in the name of national security.

However, under him, printing permits of four newspapers—*Sin Chew Jit Poh* (a Chinese daily), the *Star* (an English daily), the *Sun-*

day Star (an English weekly belonging to the Star Group), and *Watan* (a Malay biweekly) were revoked. The four newspapers' publishing licences were revoked because their coverage was alleged to have contributed to the tense situation in the country.

However, each paper is now back in business and slowly becoming its normal self, although each did start off rather cautiously.

To test the democratization of the mass media, it is also important to know the people's view of journalists. In Malaysia, complaints against media representatives are seldom heard. Certain politicians and community leaders, though, do ocassionally allege that journalists misquoted them, allegations which more often than not failed to get public sympathy.

A preliminary study by Hamdan (1987) on how Malaysians view journalists discovered that generally the public has a positive image of journalists. They felt that journalists are a courageous breed and have contributed greatly to national development. Ninety-three percent of the respondents taken from the capital city of Malaysia believed journalists play a vital role in the economic, social, and political development of a country. The main reason for their belief is the assumption that the mass media is a government tool to create an awareness about development among the people. Because of this, respondents felt journalists could do a good job in creating public awareness on issues affecting the society, economy, and politics. Some also felt that journalists could be regarded as the people's representatives or spokesmen. Any dissatisfaction expressed by the people could be channeled through journalists for appropriate action by the authorities.

The respondents view of journalists could mirror the people's thinking regarding the role of mass media in democratization for Malaysia. As such they believed that the media can play a vital role as an agent of democracy for the people. Also, their view implied that they believe the mass media in Malaysia is undergoing democratization and that the government does tolerate some investigative reporting by journalists in the name of public interest as long as it does not unduly injure the government position.

MALAYSIA: GOVERNMENT

To understand the development of the democratization of the Malaysian mass media, it would be more meaningful to understand the government and the people of the country, than to be familiar with the history and development of the country's mass media and its role in Malaysia.

Malaysia as a nation came to being on September 16, 1963 through the Federation of the then-independent Federation of Malaya, Singapore, North Borneo (renamed Sabah), and Sarawak. On August 9, 1965, Singapore separated to become a fully independent republic within the Commonwealth. This leaves Malaysia a federation of 13 states comprising of former British protectorates. Like other developing nations, it has strived to shrug off its colonial legacies.

Malaysia has a constitutional monarchical parliamentary form of government. Its supreme head of State is the "Yang Di Pertuan Agong," a Sultan elected every five years among the 11 Malay Sultans of the Malay states in Malaysia. He has to act in accordance with Government advice. The Sultans in the 11 Malay states retain their preindependence position except that generally they can no longer act contrary to the advice of the Executive Council (the state cabinet). The other states are each headed by a governor federally appointed for four years who also acts on the advice of the state Cabinet.

At the federal level Malaysia has a bicameral legislature comprising of a Senate of 69 members and a House of Representatives consisting of 177 elected members. Out of the 69 senators, 26 are elected by the various State Legislatures and 43 appointed by the Agong. Members of the Lower Houses are elected. Malaysia's Houses of Parliament are modeled after the Houses of Parliament, United Kingdom.

At the state level, each state has a unicameral legislature.

A general election on the basis of universal adult suffrage, with each constituency returning one member, is required by law at the end of every five years at both the federal and state level. Malaysia is among the very few developing nations that has conducted elections regularly since the first election in 1955.

In Malaysia only the constitution is supreme. It is a written constitution that is rather rigid. However, it provides for the enactment of laws to further define the parameters within which freedom of speech and the mass media is allowed, to ensure that they will act responsibly and not abuse their position. Since independence, a number of new acts have been enacted as well as existing laws being amended to meet various situations and events that had occurred from time to time to further define or refine the various restrictions already imposed to regulate a healthy environment for national development and national progress. The various pieces of legislation provide for penal consequences for any breach of their provisions.

Despite the various restrictions imposed, a Chief Justice of Malaya, Abdul Hamid Omar, argued,

In this country, the press enjoys a very substantial degree of freedom nevertheless subject to certain restrictions and restraints by way of legislative imposition" (Speech at the Malaysian Press Institute seminar—"The Press, the Law and the Courts", March 1987). However, he conceded that "excessive encroachments or interventions would significantly undermine this fundamental principle and render it meaningless. We all live in a society of parliamentary democracy and are subject to the laws of the land. We acknowledge that there will have to be legal restraints on the freedom of an individual by means of legislative impositions which are constitutionally permissible, and which are imposed primarily in the interest of security and public order. Nontheless, these restraints being ipso facto exceptions should be subordinate to and not prevail over the fundamental principle.

MALAYSIA: THE PEOPLE

Malaysia, with a land size of 127,581 miles, has a population of 17.15 million (1988 Census). The people are broadly divided into three main racial groups—Bumiputra (indegeneous people, 61.2% or 10.50 million), Chinese (29.9% or 5.14 million), and the Indians (8.2% or 1.4 million). Each groups has its own religion, culture, language, and practices.

The national religion of Malaysia is Islam. About 60 percent of the people are Muslims. However, religious freedom is protected under the Malaysian Constitution.

Any materials that offend the sensitivities of the major religious groups in the country will inevitably be banned. Hence, any religious issues in Malaysia are sensitive issues and the mass media are well advised to report these issues in a way that does not injure the feelings of any religious groups. A discussion with several editors (Syed Arabi and Latiffah Pawanteh, 1989) revealed the dilemma they constantly face in reporting sensitive issues. One said that if an incident is expected to be sensitive, he would rather not use the story at all, especially if it pertains to religion.

It must also be noted here that the diversity of its people make democratization of the mass media a very sensitive issue for the government. In fact, it is a consistent excuse of the government for not fully democratizing the Malaysian mass media.

As a pluralistic society, Malaysia's economic and political stability depends on the level of unity achieved among people from diverse racial, religious, and cultural backgrounds. According to Vasil (1971), "What distinguishes Malaysia from other developing countries is the extremely precarious balance of her multi-ethnic population, which some observers describe as 'a plural society par excellence'." This plurality (Syed Arabi and Latifah Hamzah, 1989) by its very nature makes the society prone to incessant ethnic and religious animosities and, consequently, political instability.

As a matter of fact, Malaysia from 1945 to 1969 has endured 22 racial disturbances with the May 13, 1969 incident as the most serious. In this May 13 incident hundreds were killed, Parliament was suspended, and the country was temporarily put under control of a National Operations Council. In the aftermath, plans were made for the restructuring of society to eliminate economic disparities and ethnic identification by class or race. The procedures are spelled out in a series of five-year plans called the New Economic Policy (NEP). The NEP is scheduled to end by 1990. Currently the Malaysian govenment has formed The National Economy Consultative Council (NECC) comprised of 150 individuals representing political parties within the government and oppositions, all ethnic groups, social movements and distinguished individuals to assist in formulating the National Economic Policy for post-1990.

Also, as a result of the May 13 incident, the Malaysian government has spelled out a national ideology that is called the "Rukunegara." The Rukunegara sets out five goals for the country (national unity, a democratic way of life, a just society, a liberal approach to cultural traditions, and a technologically progressive society) based on five principles (belief in God, loyalty to the King, upholding the Constitution, rule of law, and good behavior and morality).

This restructuring provides wide-ranging implications to the Malaysian mass media. The emphasis on the national language—that is, Bahasa Malaysia (Malay)—has resulted in broader use, increased circulation, and a higher quality in the publications employing it. Media are expected to cooperate with government policy and assist in development (Elliott S. Parker, 1984).

MALAYSIA'S MASS MEDIA

In Malaysia, the existing communication system includes electronic media, print media, telecommunications, film, video, traditional media, and interpersonal communication.

Mass media in Malaysia is a mixture of government-owned and private enterprises. The print media is basicly private while the electronic media, specifically television, is either government-owned or private. Currently, radio is totally government-owned. Efforts are being made to privatize radio. In fact, the government is thinking of making its broadcasting department into a corporation. The telecommunication services are increasingly being privatized.

Malaysia has also established a national news agency named BERNAMA. On May 1, 1984, BERNAMA took over local distribution of all foreign wire services. This means all foreign news entering the country through foreign news agencies must be via BERNAMA, making it the sole distributor of news from all foreign news agencies. The government reason for this action is that it wanted to save money because a lot of foreign exchange is spent by the various newspaper companies to buy news from the various foreign news agencies. The big media companies feel it is one of the government's strategy to control the press. Despite the initial protest by editors from the major newspapers on the ruling, it now seems to be accepted by them. Inadvertently, the smaller newspapers are also becoming more competitive because they also now have more accessibility to foreign news as compared to before the ruling when the major newspapers monopolized the foreign news. In this way the BERNAMA ruling on foreign news has added to the democratization of the mass media in Malaysia by making the smaller newspapers more competitive.

In August 1984, BERNAMA became one of the first national news agency in the world to be computerized and later to be the first fully computerized national news agency. With computerization, BERNAMA is able to bring out new possibilities like packaging and tailoring of news and information to be transmitted to suit the needs of different institutions, be they newspapers, banks, hotels, or commercial firms.

MALAYSIA PRINT MEDIA

According to Parker (1984), like the population, newspapers in Malaysia were essentially started by immigrant groups and the colonial master. The first English newspaper, the *Prince of Wales Island Gazettte* (1805–1827), began in Penang in 1805 to serve British interest, particularly the colonial community.

The first Chinese newspaper in Malaysia was the *Chinese Monthly Magazine*. It was published in Malacca by William Milne, a missionary who worked for the London Missionary Society. The paper's ultimate objective was to propagate its religious activities and proselytize for converts in mainland China. Other Chinese newspapers emerged. Their contents were related more closely to their ethnic constituency and contained great amounts of news from the homeland. The same characteristics can be said of the Indian newspapers that first appeared in 1897 with the publication of *Tangai Sinegan*. Similarly, the Malay-language newspapers, which also first appeared in 1987 with the publication of *Jawi Peranakan*, had an orientation to the overseas Arab community, reflecting the Malays' need—in terms of Islam being their religion and hence providing lots of news about Islam and Muslim nations. Thus, according to Syed Arabi and Latifah Pawanteh (1989) the ethnic clientele of such newspapers created a demand for, and consequently encouraged reportage of, features and news items of ethnic interests. Thus the economics of publication itself propagated a structure of coverage heavily biased toward ethnic needs and concerns.

In the early years of the 20th century, newspapers began developing a stronger identification with their own local ethnic communities in Malaya. However, they were still mainly oriented toward their homeland.

At the beginning of World War II, when Japan invaded the country, some newspapers—mainly Chinese—went underground. The rest were either closed or became the Japanese propaganda organs.

Currently, Malaysians are served by over 76 newspapers. About 35 are in Mandarin, 18 in English, 4 in the national language of Malay, seven in Tamil, and the rest in the minority or ethnic languages or a combination of two or three languages.

Generally, newspapers in Peninsular Malaysia are national in nature. That is, they are distributed throughout the nation. However, in East Malaysia, generally the newspapers are contained in the states concerned. Also, a few of the newspapers, particularly the Chinese, are published and sold only in the area of its publication.

It must be noted that the Education Policy of Malaysia, which makes use of the national language as the medium of instruction mandatory in schools, has led to a rapid increase in the circulation of the Bahasa Malaysia newspapers. However, it must also be noted that the other language newspapers such as Mandarin and English are not too badly affected by it. Most of the elites and the English-educated continue to read the English newspapers. Hence, their circulation has not dropped drastically. As with the Mandarin and Tamil newspapers their circulation has more or less stabilized. However, with the emphasis on the national language in the education system and English as the second language, most of the new-generation readers would be more at home reading the Bahasa Malaysia newspapers and, probably for those who can afford it, the English Language newspapers will continue to be an important source of information especially regarding business news.

Other forms of the print media that have become very popular is magazines. Despite the fact that Malaysians have long been exposed to international magazines, the number of local magazines have proliferated. This trend can also be attributed to the success of the national policy.

Also, there is a trend in Malaysia for magazines to concentrate on more specific subjects and on becoming specialized. Further, more interest and pressure groups are allowed to publish their own publications in magazine format to be sold to the general public.

Political parties' publications, especially the opposition, have also become popular in Malaysia and have a substantial following. The sales of these publications usually go up when there are some controversial issues and the belief that the regular dailies are not giving adequate coverage or that the news is biased for the ruling parties.

Nevertheless, there is a case where an interest group journal is banned by the government and another group is refused a permit to publish its journal in the national language even though it is given a permit to publish a monthly magazine in English. As for the banned journal, the reason given by the government was that the journal had touched on a foreign policy of a neighboring nation in a very negative manner and the offended country had complained while the publisher had not given any good reasons as to why its publishing permit should not be withdrawn. In Malaysia, each publishing permit must conform to the type of content and interest that it had stated when applying for it. Any publisher violating its stated scope can have its permit revoked temporarily or even permanent and there may also be a fine or even imprisonment.

For the social reform group that is not given a permit to publish a magazine in Bahasa Malaysia, no clear reason is given by the government. However, it is widely speculated that the government does not grant the permit because it does not want the Malays, especially those in rural areas, to be filled with the notion of social justice and reforms. The involved group had challenged the government in court for rejecting the publishing permit but failed because the government had earlier legislated a law giving the Home Minister full power to reject any request for a publication permit even though he has no valid reason.

PRINT MEDIA CONTENT

With such laws, one can expect the print media to play safe with its content. Elliot Parker (1984) observed: "News content and immediacy are not always the most important considerations. Newspapers carry a high proportion of undated, timeless material about development and government activities. Sixty percent of the news in Malaysian papers originates from government. Reporting tends to be bland and uncritical. Opinions and editorials are usually about international local subjects." In 1989, Parker's observation generally remained true.

Nevertheless, Parker admitted: "There are exceptions. The first Prime Minister of independent Malaysia writes a coloumn, 'As I See It,' for the Penang-based *Star* newspaper that is often critical, and the small weekly tabloid *Watan* has been critical of some government policies. The pseudonymous columnist Sri Delima, in her column 'As I Was Passing' and cartoonist 'Lat' offer perceptive scenes of Malaysian society." Surprisingly, these exceptions are increasing in Malaysia. This was noted by Lent (1987). The biweeklies, weeklies, and newspapers of political parties have been rather liberal in their reporting and somehow the government is seen as tolerating such contents.

However, the established dailies are more conservative in their reporting and are more prone to be progovernment. This tendency is reflective of its ownerships. The major established newspapers are known to generally belong to the political parties in power. It is also widely suspected that the chief editors of these newspapers are political appointees. Hence, their reluctance to touch on issues that would make their political masters upset or angry for they might get themselves replaced, as did happen to certain chief editors who are suddenly replaced or transferred to other positions. As such, one can suspect instances of self-censorship in the print media.

Nevertheless, with the less established newspapers getting bolder and more popular, the major newspapers have to do better in order to not lose its readers. On the other hand, by being rather conservative in its reporting and thus leaving the readers unfulfilled, the established newspapers have somehow motivated its readers to look for alternatives. Hence, the proliferation of new publications to satisfy readers' needs. In this instance, it must be noted that the Malaysian government has been rather liberal with the number of permits it has issued to start new publications. As such the government has also encouraged the growth of the publishing industry in Malaysia by its "democratization policy."

RADIO

Radio broadcast in Malaysia began in the 1930s by a group of enthusiastic amateurs. The foundation for an organized radio service in the country was laid by the formation of the British Malaya Broadcasting in 1935. It was controlled by the British colonial administration whose actions were less dictated by the ethnic preferences of the market. In 1946 the Department of Broadcasting was formed. Hence, radio did not develop a comparable diversity of ethnic content as in the print media.

Radio in Malaysia is still fully government-owned. Currently, there are four domestic radio networks: National Network (National Language), Blue Network (English), Green Network (Mandarin), and Red Network (Tamil). Supplementing these networks are regional radio stations. Today, Malaysia has 18 radio stations.

Radio transmissions in Malaysia cover 90 percent of the Peninsular (West Malaysia), 95 percent of Sabah, and 55 percent of Sarawak (East Malaysia). For 1988 it was estimated that about 7 million Malaysians are radio listeners.

Nearly all radio programs are produced locally. Foreign programs are also aired due to strong interest. For example, the Blue Network plays the American Top Forties pandering to the taste of youth and young at heart.

For the regional stations, "talk-back programs" are becoming very popular. In these programs, broadcasters invite listeners to participate in their programs by telephoning their queries or comments regarding subjects that are being discussed. Government officers are often invited to give their responses to queries or views given by listeners who phone in. Most of these programs are aired live. Participations by listeners to these talk back programs are very encouraging.

There are assumptions that these calls are usually from people who can afford telephones in their homes and therefore of the middle class. Discussions with producers of the radio talk back programs show that about a third of the calls came from offices or public telephones. Also, some of the complaints received are from squatters regarding conditions in their areas and wanting the relevant authorities to do something about it.

Producers of these programs usually screen calls from listeners before passing them to the broadcasters. However, this does not seem to discourage listeners from calling in to give their views or questions, which might range from dissatisfaction of government services to defective products. In fact, it can be said that the radio talk back programs in its own way have made radio a democratic channel despite it being a government media. Hence, it has contributed toward the democratization of the Malaysian mass media while giving Malaysians a medium to air their opinions and seek answers to questions with regard to government activities and even policies.

TELEVISION

Television made its debut in Malaysia in black and white on December 29, 1963, the same year the nation was born. Fifteen years later it went color. In 1972, educational TV was started.

A private television station came into being in 1984 as a result of Malaysia's Incorporation move. The private station, called TV3, quickly gives a strong competition to the two existing government television channels. As mentioned, this somehow affected the content and quality of television programming for the better. This helped to arrest the phenomenal growth of home video that has caused a large number of Malaysians (mainly Chinese) to be addicted and thus become inaccessible to government messages through the electronic media. It was reported that video rental outlets that were thriving in numbers and customers began feeling the pinch when TV Malaysia and TV3 started broadcasting new exciting programs to win back their audiences that had switched to video.

In February 1988, TV3 opened itself for public subscription. Newspaper reports in mid-March claimed that TV3 shares was 50 times oversubscribed. Nevertheless, it is known that the main shareholder of TV3 is Fleet Group Sdn. Bhd., the investment arm of UMNO, the chief partner of the ruling coalition which initially had been given the licence to operate the station.

Nevertheless, TV3 is providing more avenues of employment for communication graduates. It further injected capital and manpower investment which are necessary prerequisites for the success of mass media privatization and expansion, if not democratization when seen from the capitalistic democratic tradition of Malaysia.

In term of content, television in Malaysia has the highest foreign content compared to the other media, including radio. An analysis of the government television showed that about 45 percent of its program is entertainment, feature films, and dramas. About 22 percent are educational/informative and religious programs. The rest include sports, children programs, and advertisements. Of this, approximately 30 percent are local and 70 percent imported. A basic objective of government-owned television is to transmit 70 percent local programs. For now more than 40 percent of Malaysia's television programs are locally produced.

As for TV3, about 70 percent of its contents are imported and the rest are local productions. The operating licence for TV3 called for 30 percent local content. Efforts are intensified to increase TV3's local content. Further, it is also known that the government has set conditions to ensure that TV3 is operated on the principles of the national ideology (Rukunegara), of Islam being the official religion, and of national security. Also, TV3 must reflect the national aspirations. To this effect, Malaysians saw the emergence of the Broadcasting Act, 1987. Despite the various regulations, audiences for TV3 are increasing and more than two-thirds of Malaysians are viewing it. The same goes for the government television.

TELECOMMUNICATIONS

The telecommunication system in Malaysia provides basic services such as for telephone, telex, and telegraph. It also provides a communication infrastructure for the broadcasting, civil aviation, police, and fishery department.

January 1, 1987 saw the Malaysian telecommunication system take the first step in the privatization of telecommunication services through the formation of Syarikat Telekom Malaysia Berhad (STMB), replacing the Telecommunications Department, a full government agency. In replacing the department, STMB is expected to play a central role in the development of communication in Malaysia. It will have the sole responsibility for providing and operating telecommunication services in the country. This means STMB enjoys a monopoly in the provision of basic telecommunication services in Malaysia. The monopolistic condition is deemed necessary because the size of telecommunications network in Malaysia is thought to be inadequate to justify the possibility for more than one body responsible for basic telecommunication services like telephone, telex, telegraph, and so on. Another reason given as to why STMB shall remain a monopoly despite opposition from certain quarters is that telecommunication is capital-intensive and it is necessary to have sufficient volume to justify more than one organization providing telecommunication services in Malaysia.

According to Malaysia's Minister for Energy, Telecommunications and Posts, the country still lags in the provision of a modern and efficient telecommunications network, which means it lacks one of the vital catalysts for economic advancement (*Business Times*, 1/3/88). The ratio for the number of telephones to every 100 people in Malaysia, for example, is relatively small. With a total of 1.1 million telephone users, it has only seven telephones in every 100 of its population compared with Sweden (82), U.S.A. (80), UK (51), Italy (36), Singapore (34), and Taiwan (29).

As more people increasingly needing information speedily accelerates the growth of the telecommunication industry, the future of

STMB looks rosy indeed. In Malaysia, privatization and liberalization of telecommunications began with the transfer of shares to *bumiputras,* a move aimed at safeguarding *bumiputra* interests. The "political necessity" of raising the *bumiputra's* stake in this section—it has been assumed—will slow both the growth and the competition, and businesses will "need to understand that success will be measured only in the long run and short-term gains will be difficult to realise. This means foreign investments will have to be conducted under proxies allied in joint ventures. It also means, in place of state-controlled entities in telecommunications, a new breed of organizations will emerge.

As such, there are people in Malaysia who view telecommunications development as a two-edged sword: On the one hand, there is a need to improve this sector, and on the other, telecommunications opens up the country to international economic, political, economic, and cultural influences—resulting in the gradual erosion of positive traditional culture.

After privatization of telecommunications in Malaysia it can be clearly observed that more villages—including those rather isolated, plus squatter areas—are enjoying public telephone facilities. These public telephones are well maintained. One observable result are that people in these areas are also participating in radio talk back programs.

POLITICAL AND SOCIAL IMPLICATIONS

Generally, the democratization of the mass media in Malaysia has brought about positive political and social implications. As said, the process has contributed to the growth and maturity of the Malaysian mass media. This can be seen from the number of new publications emerging and new programs in the electronic media that seems to serve the people's interests. Also, this can be seen from the improved quality of coverage and production motivated by the healthy competitions among mass media which are proliferating. Consequently, more Malaysians are attracted to expose themselves to the mass media.

In order to attract more readers or audiences, the mass media have provided more space or air time for the people to voice their grievances whether against the authority, the bureaucracy, and officialdom, provide organizations, or the commercial sector.

As such, the mass media themselves are increasingly championing the plight of the ordinary people and ensuring that the relevant authorities take notice of the grievances and resolving it. For example, according to Rejal Arbee (1988), BERNAMA ex-chief editor, Malaysia's national news agency assigned its reporters periodically to depressed areas in various parts of the country—including the remote areas—to report on actual conditions faced by people living in those parts. Areas covered include living conditions, amenities, health and education, and their livelihood.

Currently, the mass media are also actively cooperating with various government agencies and public interest groups in order to improve services to the people as well as to safeguard them from being exploited. As such, the mass media are working closely with local authorities to enhance their services for the people. Also, a number of the mass media groups—including the government television and radio—are working closely with various consumer organizations to report on exploitation of consumers by trade people and others.

Hence, the mass media in Malaysia—with democratization—are increasingly coming to the forefront to not only ensure that the people really get the protection afforded to them but to explain to them their rights as provided for in the laws of the nation. However, it must be noted that advocacy is not new to Malaysian mass media. It has been used to propogate and maintain colonialism, spread Christianity, spread and modernize Islam, promote Malay literature, and further the struggle for independence (Parker, 1984). But it is only now that the mass media in Malaysia is more involved with the daily welfare of the common people and providing them with the channels to improve their life.

Democratization of the mass media have also enhanced their credibility, particularly for television. A study on political issues by the School of Mass Communication, Institut Teknologi Mara (1987) on 2,000 respondents from a basically rural area found that 70 percent of them felt that television is more credible than the other mass media. Somehow they felt that it is easier to believe what can be heard and seen rather than just read or listened to alone. However, these people admitted that the mass media are becoming an important source of information regarding political issues and that the reports are generally truthful. Hence, only 4.3 percent of the respondents blamed the media for a political party debacle. In this case, political party allegations that the media greatly contributed to their fiasco and that the media are the "devil's mouthpiece" do not hold water.

However, in a 1989 by-election a number of the established newspapers showed a photograph of a political party candidate (belonging to the party that had accused the media of being the "devil's mouthpiece") of not wanting to shake hands with his opponent from the government party. In this case, another established newspaper had shown that the particular candidate had actually shaken hands with his opponent. This opposition party used the misrepresentation to their advantage by showing both photographs to the voters and consequently they won the by-election. Hence, the papers that carried the wrong photographs were discredited and lost some of their credibility and their readers.

Whatever, because of the number of alternatives in the print media, it managed to retain itself as being a valuable source for political news. However, the various newspapers begin to portray distinct images of themselves, such as being progovernment, antigovernment or neutral/objective. Readers in Malaysia usually buy newspapers that mirror their own political preference. As said, the major newspapers in Malaysia are generally owned by parties of the ruling coalition or personalities close to the government. Nevertheless, for the nonpolitical content, all the print media in Malaysia tries to show its objectivity.

CONCLUSION

For Malaysia, democratization of the mass media has in many ways benefitted the people, the government, and the country. It has contributed to the rapid development of the communication industry in Malaysia. More Malaysians are reached.

However, a pervasive communication effect may also bring negative influences if not properly monitored or regulated. With communication technology's rapid advancement, communication can be very personalized. Also, it can intrude into people's privacy. It can also be used as an instrument to control the people or only certain people may benefit from it.

There is an urgent need for the government to review the many laws pertaining to control of communication to ensure a healthy development of the mass media in Malaysia so that it can be freer and more dynamic. This would ensure that the mass media will serve public interest rather than its own interest or government interest.

In order that the mass media in Malaysia serve the needs and aspirations of the people effectively, a comprehensive and dynamic communication policy would be appropriate. However, whatever policy is formulated must be subjected to continuous evaluation with regard to its appropriateness, taking into account the rapid technological development in the communication industry. Also, the opinion of the people ought to be consulted when preparing any communication policy or when amending it.

Further, efforts must be made to ensure that Malaysians can fully benefit from the democratization of the mass media—also to ensure that they can cope with the rapid changes brought about by the new communication technologies and to ensure as well that everybody benefits from those changes.

Finally, studies must be conducted to avoid any ill effects of citizens being overly exposed to the world as brought about by the latest communication technologies or by unsuitable television programs, imported or local. As a developing nation, Malaysia cannot afford to ignore any adverse effect from too free or too controlled a mass media system in the country. What is important is that the people have access as well as choice with regard to the mass media and that it is appropriate to the needs of the people and the nation. The mass media, on the other hand—with more freedom—must be totally responsible so as not to give the government excuses to legislate laws to restrict its development and independence.

REFERENCES

Ahmad R.A. (1988, May). *Communication development and human rights—Malaysia.* Paper presented at the Seminar on Communication Development and Human Rights, India.

George, T.J.S. (1985, November). *The importance of plurality and diversity of sources and outlets for the communication process in Asian Societies.* Paper presented at the BERNAMA-AMIC Seminar "Communication Challenges in Asia, Malaysia.

Government of Malaysia. (1988). *Towards preserving national security.* Paper presented at the Malaysian Parliament.

Karthigesu, R. (1987, December). Commercial competition to government monopoly in television implications of the Malaysian experience. *Kajian Malaysia, V (2).*

Lent, J. (1987). Impact and development of the communication industry. *Sasaran Issue 9, 14,* 33.

Mahathir, M. (1981, July 9). Freedom of the Press—Fact and fallacy. *New Straits Times,* pp. 14 and 19.

Mahathir, M. (1985). *Keynote address at the World Press Convention.* Kuala Lumpur, Malaysia.

Maicas, M.P.I. (1982, September). *Mass communication and democracy (the crux of democratization).* Paper presented at the International Association For Mass Communication Research 1982 Conference, Spain.

Majid, T. (1984, January). *Electronic democracy: Global and national contexts.* Paper presented at the 6th. Pacific Telecommunications Conference, Hawaii.

Mohd, H.A. (1985, January). *Media Development and Trends in Malaysia.* Paper presented at AMIC country representative Meeting, Singapore.

Mohd, H.A. (1987). Malaysian View of journalists. *Sasaran Issue, 9,* 24–25.

Mohd, H.A. (1988). *Communication and the Law in Malaysia.* Paper presented at the Workshop on Law for Journalists, Malaysia.

Parker, S.E. (1984). Malaysia. *World Press Encyclopedia,* pp. 614–627.

Parker, S.E. (1987). Future of the information revolution in Malaysia. *Forum Komunikasi, No. 1,* 29–35.

Ramanathan, S. (1988). *Objectivity of the mass media vis-a-vis the needs and desires of Malaysian society.* Paper presented at a Seminar on the Role of Mass Media in Promoting National Integrity.

Ramanathan, S., & Mohd, H.A. (1988). *Malaysia's 1986 General Election— The urban-rural dichotomy.* Singapore: Institute of Southeast Asian Studies.

Schiller, H.J. (1976). *Communication and cultural domination.* New York: International Arts and Science Press.

Syed Arabi Idid and Latifah Pawanteh. (1989). Media, ethnicity and national unity: A Malaysian report. *Media Asia, Vol. 16, No. 2, 1989,* 78–85.

Vasil, R.K. (1971). *Politics in a Plural Society: A Study of Non-Communal Political Parties in West Malaysia.* Kuala Lumpur: Oxford.

Zaharom, N., & Ramli, M. (1989). *Paluan Ke Atas Media Di Malaysia.* Paper presented at Seminar Sains Politik, USM.

APPENDIX A:
LAWS REGULATING MASS MEDIA IN MALAYSIA*

Act

1. Censorship of Films and Public Entertainments Sarawak Cap 136
2. Cinematograph Films (Censorship) Act (Rev. 1971) (Am. Act A 242, A490)
   Act 35 1952
3. Cinematograph Film Hire Duty Act (Am. Act. A 148)
   Act 45/1965
4. Printing Presses And Publications Act
   Act 301 1984
5. Copyright Act 1969 (Revised 1982)
   Act 10
6. Courts of Judicature Act (Rev. 1972) (Am. Act A279, A328, A530, A556, A600, A606
   Act 91 1964
7. Defamation Act (Rev. 1982)
   Act 286 1957
8. Elections Act (Rev. 1970) (Am. Act A 95)
   Act 19 1958
9. Local Government Elections F.M. Am. Act 19/1961 49/1961 13/1963 1965 55/1966 60/1966 A55
   Act 11/1960
10.
11. Election Commission-Rv. 1970 Act
    Act 31
12. Election Offences (Revised 1969 Rep 1971 (Am Act A245)
    Act 5
13. Houses of Parliament (Privileges and Powers) F.M.
    Ord. 15/1952
14. Indecent Advertisements-F.M. (Am. F.L.N 332/58)
    Ord. 16/1953
15. Internal Security Act Rev. 1972. (Am. P.U. (B) 336/75)
    Act 82
16. Judicial Proceedings (Regulation of Reports) Act.
    Act 114
17. National Library Act
    Act 80
18. Local Newspapers (Reprint 1965) Sarawak
    Cap 139
19. Lotteries F.M. (Am L.N 332/1958 Act 65, A133)
    Ord. 86/1952
20. Medicines (Advertisement and Sale) (Am. 332/1958 Act A84 A333)
    Ord. 10/1958
21. National Archives (Am.-Act 85)
    Act 44/1966
22. Official Secrets
    Act 88
23. Patents Sarawak (Re. 1968)
    Cap 61

24. Patent Rights of Government
    Act 53/1967
25. Pertubuhan Berita Nasional Malaysia (Bernama News Agency)
    Act 119/1967
26. Post Office Act (Rev. 1978)
    Act 211
27. Preservation of Books
    Act 35/1966
28. Registration of U.K. Patents (Rev. 1978)
    Act 215
29. Registration of United Kingdom Patents Sabah Ord 1/1956
    Cap 124
30. Securities Industry Act
    Act 280/1983
31. Sedition (Rev. 1969) Am. P.U. (A) 282/1970
    Act 15/1948
32. Telecommunications (Rev. 1970) (Am. Act 115, A373)
    Act 0/1950
33. Theatres and Places of Public Amusement (Federal Territory)
    Act 182/1977
34. Trade Descriptions Act
    Act 187/1977
35. Trade Marks Act 1976
    Act 175
38. United Kingdom Design (Protection) Rev. 1978
    Act 214
39. U.K. Design Protection-Sabah
    Cap 152
40. U.K. Design Protection-Sarawak
    Cap 59
41. Public Order (Preservation)(Revised 1983)
    Act 296/1958
42. Patents Act Act 291
    1983

*Source–School of Administration & Law, Institut Teknologi MARA

Author Index

Subject Index